D0469614

LIVING ABROAD IN
THAILAND

SUZANNE NAM

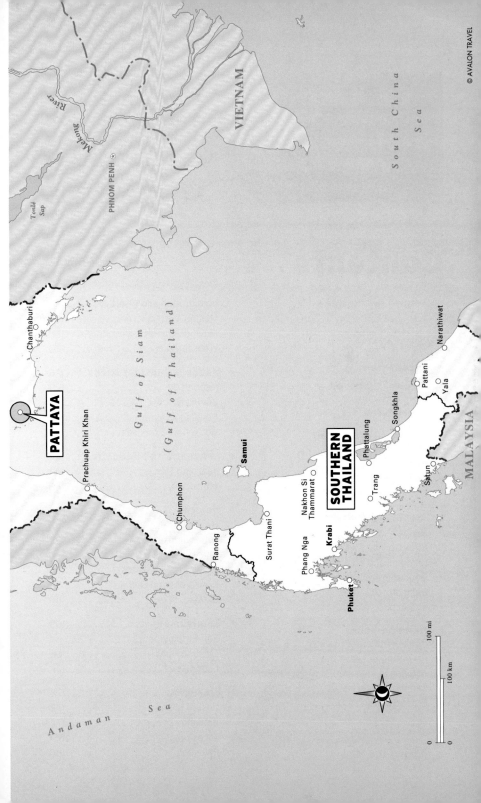

PATTAYA

SOUTHERN THAILAND

VIETNAM

MALAYSIA

South China Sea

Andaman Sea

Gulf of Siam
(Gulf of Thailand)

Tonlé Sap

Mekong River

PHNOM PENH

Chanthaburi

Prachuap Khiri Khan

Chumphon

Ranong

Surat Thani

Samui

Phang Nga

Nakhon Si Thammarat

Krabi

Phuket

Trang

Phattalung

Songkhla

Satun

Pattani

Yala

Narathiwat

100 mi

100 km

© AVALON TRAVEL

Contents

At Home in Thailand

When I arrived in Thailand I wasn't sure what to expect, but five years into my adventure I'm happy to say that living here has exceeded my wildest dreams. And I'm not the only one – many expats try to extend their time here once they arrive. The combination of vibrant cities, a fast-growing economy, friendly people, a higher standard of living, and a beautiful landscape make Thailand a paradise.

Visitors are always surprised at how convenient and comfortable the country is. Thailand boasts good roads, running water, electricity, and high-speed Internet service in all but its most remote corners. And because Bangkok is such an international city, anything anyone could possibly want – from maple syrup to fresh feta – is available if you know where to find it.

Despite the economic growth, life in Thailand still has a community feeling to it, even in the biggest cities. Every side street functions like a little village, where neighbors bow or wave when they cross paths, local vendors sell fruits and vegetables, and everyone knows everyone else's business.

Walk a couple of blocks in any city and you're bound to find street food vendors selling fried chicken, papaya salad, or iced coffee, hole-in-the-wall noodle shops, 24-hour mini marts, and other signs that much of life in Thailand takes place in public. In Bangkok, you'll also find fancy coffee shops, cosmopolitan restaurants, high-end shopping malls, and efficient public transportation. Although there are some bureaucratic obstacles you'll need to plow through to work, live, or retire here, they are seldom insurmountable. Tens of thousands of Americans and Western

Europeans are already here, so there are ample services available, whether you're renting an apartment, need someone to shepherd you through the visa process, or are looking for a nanny. Add to this some world-class beaches and close proximity to the rest of Asia and you can see why Thailand is considered the perfect place for expatriates.

However, despite its being a tropical country with plenty of gorgeous beaches and islands, living in Thailand isn't a permanent vacation. The biggest challenge for foreigners is learning to understand Thailand's culture and people. Though Thais are generally welcoming to foreigners, the combination of typical Western forthrightness with typical Thai politeness can have frustrating consequences. It's easy to withdraw into the pampered life of drivers and international supermarkets and expat friends and barely interact with normal, everyday Thai people. Most native-English speakers find Thai a very difficult language to learn, and many give up entirely. As a result, they feel even more alienated from the people around them and more confused by the culture. And witnessing poverty, child labor, and extreme wealth disparity day after day can also take its toll.

Still, if you're planning a move to Thailand, consider yourself lucky. Life in Thailand is going to be quite different from life back home, but for the most part it will be more interesting, more convenient, and a lot more fun. Come in with a positive attitude and an open mind and you'll enjoy your time here, learn a lot about an exotic and interesting culture, and perhaps have the adventure of your life.

▶ WHAT I LOVE ABOUT THAILAND

- Cheap, fresh, and delicious street food available from early morning to late at night
- Never feeling cold
- Taxi drivers routinely quizzing me about my life, then telling me I speak Thai well even when I stumble over words and can't understand them
- Shopping for cute shoes and dresses at the markets, and usually paying about $5 for each
- Thai fried chicken
- Having neighbors and street vendors wave hello and smile when I'm out walking my dog
- Wet markets filled with fresh fruits, vegetables, meats, and fish
- Thai massage
- Getting my hair washed, straightened, and styled for less than $10
- Hopping on the back of a motorcycle taxi when I'm in a rush
- Gorgeous beaches and warm, clear water
- Cheap flights to almost anywhere in the country
- Orchids of every color imaginable

WELCOME TO THAILAND

© SUZANNE NAM

INTRODUCTION

Is Thailand right for you? Despite the gorgeous beaches and its reputation as a vacation getaway spot, chances are your life in Thailand won't be a constant party. You'll be working, butting up against a whole new set of rules and social customs, and trying to navigate bureaucracy in a foreign language. Thais and Westerners share a lot of common ground, but many things are different, including predominant religions, views on government, and even the fruits and vegetables that are available. Deciding whether to move to Thailand is not a decision that should be taken lightly.

Although moving here means some dramatic and sometimes difficult lifestyle changes, keep in mind that most foreigners who come here to live or work for a few years leave only grudgingly, and many who come for a year or two end up staying for five or 10. Why? Despite the challenges you'll face if you relocate to Thailand, many aspects of everyday life will be easier. Thailand is an amazingly pleasant place for expatriates to live. Smaller than the state of Texas, Thailand is filled with exotic Buddhist temples, amazing beaches and

© SUZANNE NAM

islands, and friendly welcoming people. It is a country on the move, with a fast-growing economy and a young population emerging from the shadows of the Third World into the ranks of middle-income countries.

Thailand is home to a world-class city, Bangkok, where the vast majority of expatriates are based. Like most major cities in developing countries, Bangkok is a study in contrasts. People live in slums alongside million-dollar condominiums, old ladies hawk homemade sweets around the corner from gleaming high-rise office buildings, colorful public buses crammed full of commuters belch exhaust at red lights next to the latest-model Mercedes. It's not a clichéd paradox—this is life in developing Asia.

These contrasts create a fortuitous situation for expatriates: Almost anything you could possibly want from home, be it excellent pizza or the latest best-selling novel, is available in Bangkok, but so are many other wonderful things unique to Thailand that you'd never be able to get anywhere else. It is the best of both worlds.

You can find anything you want in Bangkok, but outside of the capital city, life will be very different. For those who base themselves in popular tourist areas, including Chiang Mai, Phuket, or Pattaya, there will be plenty of services catering to foreigners, plenty of people who speak English, and plenty of uniquely Thai experiences to be had, not to mention great beaches or mountains just a few minutes away, but it may take extra effort to craft a normal life and feel at home.

Those who choose to live in the countryside or in smaller cities will find life in Thailand a little more challenging. Things will move more slowly, fewer people will speak English, and creature comforts are less likely to be available. But expatriates who move to less internationalized parts of the country are rewarded with more opportunities to connect to Thailand and its people.

The Lay of the Land

COUNTRY DIVISIONS

Thailand is divided into 75 provinces, called *changwat,* and one special administrative area that is home to Bangkok and surrounding areas. Although the country is officially divided into six different regions—northern Thailand, northeast Thailand, central Thailand, western Thailand, eastern Thailand, and southern Thailand—many break it down into just four, combining western and eastern Thailand with central Thailand. Each province is further divided into districts, called *amphoe,* of which there are a little over 900 if you count Greater Bangkok's different districts (which are confusingly referred to as *khet*). Within each *amphoe* are subdistricts called *tambon,* and within a *tambon* are *moobaan,* or villages.

Each of the country's provinces is named after the province's capital district, so, for example, while Chiang Mai is a province, it's also a capital district. How can you tell whether someone is referring to the province or the district? The former is referred to as *changwat* Chiang Mai and the latter *amphoe muang* Chiang Mai.

GEOGRAPHY

Located in the center of the Southeast Asian Peninsula, Thailand's irregular shape defies any easy analog in nature, but it has loosely been compared to the shape of an elephant's head, with the northern part of the country the animal's face and ears and the thinner southern part in the Malay Peninsula its trunk. The country is bordered by Burma on much of its western side, with the lower western region bound by the Indian Ocean; by Burma and Laos in the north; and by Laos and Cambodia in the east. The Gulf of Siam cuts a horseshoe shape into the lower central part of the country, and the far southern border is shared with Malaysia.

Thailand covers 512,000 square kilometers (198,000 square miles) of land over four geographical regions. The central region, home to the country's capital, is the southern part of the river basin of the Chao Phraya River. The northernmost region is mountainous and forested, with four major rivers flowing north to south. The northeast region is mostly flat plateau lands, and the southern region is the Malay Peninsula, with coastline on both sides and hundreds of small islands flanking the landmass.

The North

Mountains cover much of the northern part of the country with ranges that continue from neighboring Burma and Laos into Thailand. The highest point in Thailand is at Doi Inthanon, at 2,565 meters (8,415 feet), in Chiang Mai. The four major rivers—the Nan, the Yom, the Wang, and the Ping—run from north to south and flow into the Central Basin on roughly parallel routes in four major river valleys, where most of the population of this region lives.

The Central Basin

The Chao Phraya River Basin, fed by the four rivers that begin in the north and three other major rivers, is conspicuously lacking any significant elevation, something you'll notice in Bangkok and the surrounding areas. This area is

plains in central Thailand

characterized by flat green expanses as far as the eye can see. It is the country's most fertile land and is particularly well suited for growing the region's staple grain, hence the nickname the "Rice Bowl" of Thailand. South of this region is the Gulf of Siam.

The Northeast

The Khorat Plateau covers most of the country's northeast region, called Isan, and makes up one-third of Thailand's land mass. The plateau, bordered to the north and northeast by the Mekhong River, has an average elevation of 183 meters (600 feet), but it slopes downward from the highest point in the northern part of the region, where it borders Laos, to the lowest point in the south, where it borders Cambodia. With surrounding lands dropping off around it and less ability to retain water, the Isan Plateau contains the country's least fertile lands, although the population in this part of Thailand is mostly agricultural.

Southern Region and the Islands

Thailand's peninsula stretches from the bottom of the central basin around Phitsanulok Province all the way to the Malay Peninsula. At its thinnest point, the narrow strip of land between the Gulf of Siam and the Indian Ocean is known as the Isthmus of Kra. Home to smaller mountain ranges that cut down the center of the peninsula and dramatic karst landscapes, the region is among the most beautiful in the country. It is here, primarily on the west coast, that you'll see many mangrove forests with trees that flourish in the brackish muddy water at the coast.

CLIMATE

With the exception of the southern region, Thailand has three seasons—cool, rainy, and hot. To someone used to a temperate climate, it may be difficult to notice any difference between them, as regardless of the time of year or part of the country, most days are as hot or hotter than a typical North American summer day. The cool season, from November to February, is generally mild, with temperatures in the 20s and 30s Celsius (70s to 90s Fahrenheit). Although there may be occasional showers, this time of year usually sees little rainfall and less humidity. In the north and in the mountains, weather patterns are similar, although temperatures can drop into the low teens Celsius (high 50s Fahrenheit) at night. At the highest elevations these lows can be even colder.

The hot season spans March to May, and it's during this time of year that temperatures in Bangkok will soar into the mid-30s Celsius (high 90s Fahrenheit) during the day, sometimes breaking 38°C (100°F). Chiang Mai won't feel much better; in fact, temperatures there can climb slightly higher there than in the capital. Although it is not the rainy season, rain begins to pick up in April, and May is sometimes one of the wettest months of the year. The rainy season spans June to October, generally peaking in September across the country, when average rainfall in Bangkok is 330 millimeters (13 inches). This is a season of frequent flooding, even in major cities.

Monsoon downpours affect every region in the country.

© SUZANNE NAM

The southern part of the country is essentially a tropical rain forest climate, with average temperatures around 30°C (85°F) throughout the year. Rainfall follows a similar pattern as in the rest of the country, although on a slightly different schedule. December through May are the region's driest months, with little or no rainfall. Beginning in April, rainfall picks up, and the wet weather continues through November.

Flora and Fauna

Because Thailand is a tropical country stretching nearly 1,900 kilometers (1,200 miles) from north to south, it has an incredibly diverse range of flora and fauna in varied habitats. The country's terrain starts from the high mountains in the northwestern hill tracts along the Tanasserim Range to the hill plateau of the northeastern region, moving down through the central plain into the eastern corner adjacent to Cambodia and into the peninsular region south of the Isthmus of Kra to the Malaysian border.

Sadly, Thailand has a less diverse range of vegetation and animal life than it once did due to the impact of humans, such as poaching and deforestation, although the government has taken steps in recent years to prevent further destruction of the natural environment. There are now over 100 protected national parks in Thailand that provide opportunities for visitors to get an up-close look at the country's natural beauty. The largest of these is Khao Yai, a 2,000-square-kilometer (770-square-mile) sanctuary that contains more than 70 species of mammals, including tigers and elephants, as well as 320 varieties of birds, not to mention hundreds of types of vegetation.

FLORA
Trees
It is estimated that about 25 percent of Thailand's landmass is covered with forest, with the UN's *World Development Report* ranking the country 44th in the world in terms of natural forest cover. Thailand's forests can be classified into two main types—evergreen and deciduous—with two basic types of tropical forest: monsoon forest (with a dry season of three months or more) and rain forest (where rain falls at least nine months of the year). The mixed deciduous forest in the northern region is considered the most commercially valuable forest of Thailand.

Northern, eastern, and central Thailand mainly consists of monsoon forests,

THAILAND'S NATIONAL PARKS

Whatever part of Thailand you choose to live in, you won't be far from a national park, as there are more than 100 scattered throughout the country's four geographical regions, plus two dozen marine parks encompassing open water and islands. Most parks have at least basic facilities, and many have campgrounds with showers. Some even rent out bungalows and cabins. Here's a list of the largest parks by region:

Region	Park
Central	Kaeng Krachan
	Khuean Sri Nakarin
Northeast	Khao Yai
	Phu Kradung
North	Doi Phu Kha
	Si Lanna
South	Khao Panom Benja
	Sirinat
Marine	Mu Ko Chang
	Tarutao

while southern Thailand is predominantly a rain forest zone. Many of these forests overlap, with some zones featuring a mix of monsoon forest and rain forest vegetation. Meanwhile, a quarter of the country's forests consist of freshwater swamps in the delta regions, forested crags (found everywhere), and pine forests at higher altitudes in the north.

There are hundreds of tree species native to Thailand, with some of the most well-known including an array of fruit-producing varieties, such as the widely popular rambutan and durian. There are also rubber trees (*Hevea brasiliensis*), the lovely floral frangipani (*Plumeria rubra*), the durable rattan—a climbing palm found deep in Thai jungles used in furniture—and the much-utilized bamboo (*Bambusa vulgaris*). In fact, Thailand is believed to have more species of bamboo than any country outside China, and its wood has been used for centuries in everything from buildings and tools to weapons and cooking utensils. You might even find yourself cruising down the river on a bamboo raft if you're touring in the north. Two other highly sought-after trees are the rosewood (*Dalbergia cochinchinensis*) and teak (*Tectona grandis*), popular for use in fine furniture due to their durability and beauty, much to the detriment of the forests. In the past, Thailand was a center of teak logging; today it is banned in all but controlled plantations in response to severely depleted resources. The government now has a policy to protect 15 percent of Thailand's land area as forest.

Other Vegetation

Flowers have long played an important role in Thai society, used as offerings at temples or spirit houses, in festivals such as the annual Loy Kratong celebration, or even as food in certain dishes. It's not surprising, then, that the country has over 25,000 species of flowers. The best-known is the orchid, Thailand's national floral symbol. Botanists have found there are 17,500 species of orchid around the world, and 1,150 of those species originated in Thailand's forests. Today there are a number of orchid farms around the country dedicated to the breeding and exporting this highly coveted flower.

Given the diversity of Thai cuisine, it's only natural that the country is also home to a wide range of herbs and food plants. Among the most common are several varieties of basil, Kaffir lime, mint, pepper, chili, cumin, garlic, lemongrass, and ginger, many of which grow wild throughout the country, particularly in the mountainous north.

FAUNA
Mammals

Thailand is home to approximately 300 species of indigenous mammals, mostly found in the country's national parks or wildlife sanctuaries because poaching and development has drastically depleted their numbers in many areas of the country. These include tigers, leopards, elephants, bears, gaur (Indian bison), banteng (wild cattle), serow (an Asiatic goat-antelope), deer, pangolins, gibbons, macaques, tapirs, dolphins, and dugongs (sea cows). Forty of Thailand's 300 mammal species, including the clouded leopard, Malayan tapir, tiger, Irrawaddy dolphin, goral, jungle cat, dusky langur, and pileated gibbon, are on a number of international endangered species lists.

© SUZANNE NAM

macaques

Although once highly revered, elephants today are treated with far less respect in Thailand. Few travelers will escape a trip to the country without witnessing an elephant walking down a city street, mahout (trainer) perched atop ready to accept a few baht from those who would like to feed the exhausted animal. Many domesticated Asian elephants have been born and raised in captivity and put to work in the logging industry in rural villages. Using elephants for jobs like this is now illegal in Thailand, so their owners have found work in the many tourist camps that offer rides to foreign visitors. A small number of wild elephants do remain, however—mostly in national parks, as their native habitat is dwindling. Ironically, for centuries elephants were highly valued creatures in Thailand, used in battle to fight the Burmese on many occasions. A white elephant even features on the flag of the Royal Thai Navy, and the Order of the White Elephant is one of the country's highest honors, bestowed by the king. Contrary to popular belief, white elephants are very rarely completely white, although the skin has to be very pale in certain areas for it to qualify as a genuine "white elephant" and thus a prized commodity.

Chances are that visitors will also encounter more than a few primates in Thailand, as there is no shortage of the crafty little fellows, whether they are hanging from telephone lines in Lopburi, looking for handouts at temples, or stealing cameras from bewildered tourists. Species include white-handed *lar* and pileated gibbons, as well as different varieties of long- and short-tailed macaques and langurs.

On the other hand, traditional hunting and poaching for medicine has left Thailand's wild cat populations decimated. The tiger is the largest and most well-known of Thailand's wild cats, and populations are kept and bred in captivity by private collectors. The country's Western Forest Complex, which features 17,870 square kilometers (6,900 square miles) of protected jungle habitat, is currently home to 720 tigers, according to a study released in late 2007 by Thailand's Department of National Parks, Wildlife, and Plant Conservation. But Thailand's parks and wildlife reserves could hold up to 2,000 wild tigers, about three times their current numbers, if the government steps up efforts to control poaching. Using survey data from camera traps in the Huai Kha Khaeng Wildlife Sanctuary in 2004, researchers determined that the density of tigers in the rugged hilly reserve about 300 kilometers (186 miles) west of Bangkok were three times lower than in comparable but better-protected tiger reserves in India. Many say the problem is that Thai law is too soft on tiger traffickers, imposing small fines rather than jail time on offenders. Tigers are mostly under threat due to habitat loss and poachers who sell their skins and body parts to medicinal and souvenir markets, mostly in China.

Bears in Thailand don't fare much better. There are two species found in the country, the Asiatic black bear and the Malayan sun bear. The black bear is bigger, recognizable by the white V on its neck and found all over the country. The sun bear is smaller and more aggressive, and is commonly found in Thailand's southern region. Although it is prohibited by law, bear cubs are often taken from the wild to be pets, while older bears are known to have been poached for their gall bladders and paws to be used in traditional Asian medicines.

© SUZANNE NAM

one of hundreds of amphibian species in Thailand

Reptiles and Amphibians

Thailand features about 313 reptile and 107 amphibian species, a population that includes 163 species of snakes, 85 of which are venomous. Among these are the common cobra (of which there are six subspecies), king cobra (hamadryad), banded krait (three species), Malayan viper, green viper, and Russell's pit viper. Thailand's largest snake is the reticulated python, which can grow up to 15 meters (45 feet) long and is found in the jungles of northern Thailand. There are also many lizard species throughout the country, including geckos and black jungle monitors.

Birds

Birdwatchers will be kept busy in Thailand, as the country is home to over 1,000 recorded resident and migrating species. Distribution varies according to the geography and climate. Among the more predominant species are various types of partridge, quail, pheasant, fireback, duck, goose, woodpecker, barbet, hornbill, trogon, kingfisher, bee-eater, cuckoo, *malkoha,* parrot, parakeet, swiftlet, needle-tail, owl, frogmouth, dove, nightjar, pigeon, crane, crank, sandpiper, jacana, plover, gull, tern, kite, eagle, vulture, falcon, cormorant, broadbill, oriole, flycatcher, fantail, robin, fork-tail, starling, bulbul, warbler, babbler, laughing thrush, sunbird, and spider hunter, to name a few. One of the best ways to go birding is by heading to one of Thailand's national parks.

Hornbills and kingfishers are two of the most popular species due to their unique features. Thailand has 15 species of kingfishers, and most of them have bright plumage. Kingfishers typically perch in trees in an upright exposed posture, plunging into the water for food. Some species, such as the white-throated kingfisher, inhabit inland areas. They're commonly seen around rice fields looking for lizards, frogs, and insects, and they will amaze even the most jaded of nature lovers, providing an absolutely stunning sight when the sunlight hits their shiny blue feathers. Hornbills, meanwhile, make their nests in holes in trees and are easily recognizable by their hooked beaks. Of the 54 species of hornbill worldwide, Thailand is home to 13 varieties. Hornbills are primarily frugivorous (fruit eaters), though they will eat small reptiles, insects, and even other smaller birds when they are molting or rearing young.

Loss of habitat due to human development is the greatest threat to Thailand's birds. For instance, shrimp farms along the coast are robbing waterfowl of their intertidal diets, while the popularity of bird's nest soup has led to the overharvesting of swiftlet nests in the south. About 30 of the country's bird species are listed as being critically endangered, which means they face possible extinction within 50 years.

Serious birders will want to check with the Bird Conservation Society of Thailand (www.bcst.or.th), an excellent source of information on the latest sightings, tours, and data.

Social Climate

Relaxed, friendly, and *warm* are the adjectives typically associated with Thai people, and despite being stereotypical, they are accurate. *Mai pen rai,* loosely meaning "no worries," must be uttered in the country millions of times a day, and a *sabai* (relaxed and comfortable) attitude permeates almost everything and everyone, unless you're dealing with government bureaucracy or the police or are involved in any kind of financial transaction.

There are plenty of type-A personalities in Thailand (the kind of economic development the country has enjoyed in such a short time couldn't have happened without some amount of driven industriousness), and most people, especially manual laborers, work hard, but almost without exception people like to have fun. Another word you'll hear frequently is *sanook,* meaning "fun" or "pleasure." As you begin to pick up some Thai and chat with friends, colleagues, and neighbors, you'll quickly notice that everyone asks you *"sanook mai,"* meaning "Was it fun?" or "Are you having fun?" *Sanook* extends to everything from slapstick television comedies to boisterous groups of workers drinking beer on a Friday night.

THAILAND AND FOREIGNERS

Thanks to Thailand's history, the country's large tourism industry, and the open curiosity of Thai people, Thailand is a comfortable country for foreigners to visit and to live in. If you're relocating to Bangkok, Chiang Mai, the islands, or any other area popular with the millions of foreign tourists that visit every year, no one is going to stop and stare at you on the street because you look different. Thais are used to guests, and they are generally extremely good hosts. The downside is that some Thais, especially those who earn a living from the tourist industry, can view foreigners as business opportunities and nothing more. Most people aren't this way at all, though, and once you get to know people more than superficially, you'll find the majority of Thai people to be generous, genuinely curious about you, and very helpful.

Thais are accepting of the way other people do things but also hold fast to their concepts of the "Thai way" of doing things, which sometimes means that you, as a foreigner, can do things your way but can't expect them to do things that way. This holds true in personal as well as business interactions. A great example is topless sunbathing: It's technically illegal in Thailand, although some Western women go topless on Thai beaches. If you ask most Thai people how they feel about it, they'll admit that it makes them uncomfortable and that they would never do it, but for foreigners, "if it's OK in their culture, it's not a problem here."

HISTORY, GOVERNMENT, AND ECONOMY

Thailand is the unity of Thai blood and body
The whole country belongs to the Thai people
Maintaining thus far for the Thai
All Thais intend to unite together
Thais love peace but do not fear to fight
They will never let anyone threaten their independence
They will sacrifice every drop of their blood to contribute to
  the nation
Will serve their country with pride and prestige full of victory.

– Thai national anthem, written in 1939

History

When Thai people today sing their national anthem they sing to the glory of their country's history. Modern-day Thailand is almost unique in the world as a country that has never been fully occupied or colonized by a foreign power, and this is is a major source of pride for the Thai people.

The country we now know as Thailand has changed considerably since the establishment of early settlements by indigenous peoples, through integration of migrants from other lands, and the presence of small independent kingdoms as recently as a few hundred years ago. Known as Siam for most of its history, the power of the nation has risen and fallen often, and its boundaries have moved backwards and forwards across most of Southeast Asia (arguments continue over some borders even today). It has survived through the times of great empire-building by the powerful and often ruthless Europeans, and still been able to maintain a national identity, while allowing that identity to be shaped and influenced by allies and enemies alike. Recent times have seen an end to the rule of a powerful and much revered monarchy with a move towards constitutional democracy, which at times has resulted in a bewildering frequency of coups, unelected military governments, elections, counter-coups, internal unrest, protests, and blood on the streets.

At 8 A.M. and 6 P.M. daily, flags are raised and lowered in towns and villages all over Thailand as the national anthem is played over loudspeakers; many people do stop what they're doing and stand still, or occasionally sing quietly, a constant reminder of the Thai identity.

PRE-HISTORY

In the late 1990s, archaeologists in Lampang in northern Thailand uncovered fossilized remains of skulls from *Homo erectus,* an ancient ancestor of *Homo sapiens* who would have been alive more than 500,000 years ago. This discovery led to a new theory, supported by the unearthing of stone tools also dating back to these times, that there had been an indigenous group of people within Thailand and that the area of north Thailand was one of the cradles of early Asian civilization. Evidence of later civilizations has been found in many places in Thailand, including the oldest known burial site, from 37,000 B.C., which was found in a huge cavern at Lang Rong Rien in Krabi, and remains found at Sakai Cave in Trang dating back to 10,000 B.C. Despite these finds, much about very early life in Thailand remains open to speculation.

Later settlers of north Thailand were *Homo sapiens* from the Neolithic period who moved away from the hunter-gatherer lifestyle in the 4th millennium B.C.

and settled in areas with an abundance of natural wild food and game. They supplemented their diet by cultivating crops such as rice, which had been cultivated in south China for a few thousand years and would grow easily in the swamp lands, such as those around the site of Ban Chiang in northeast Thailand.

Investigation of Ban Chiang shows a settlement initially occupied from around 3600 B.C. by people who produced rice husk–tempered pottery and used stone tools in their daily lives. As agriculture became further developed the water buffalo was domesticated, being used for rice farming and to haul carts. Over future centuries hand tools became more sophisticated in the earliest usage of bronze in Thailand. Occupation of Ban Chiang continued almost continuously for the next 4,000 years, with metal-working skills developing further as evidenced by the iron tools, spearheads, and jewelry found in graves dating from around 1000 B.C.

These dates put the development of settlements such as Ban Chiang roughly in line with other emerging civilizations in Europe and the Middle East. But few weapons of war were found, and none of the excavated skeletons appeared to have died in a warlike manner, even though some were clearly important leaders. Technological skills were most likely acquired through contact with other burgeoning areas of civilization such as south China, but it appears that the inhabitants of this area were relatively at peace with their neighbors, and had little need to be involved in, or provoke, aggressive behavior.

THE ORIGINS OF THE PEOPLE:
A.D. 1 TO A.D. 600

There are a number of theories on how the population of Thailand initially expanded; two are generally agreed to be the most plausible. Evidence from linguistics gives rise to the popular theory that speakers of the T'ai language migrated from south China down the Mekong River around the turn of the millennium. They would have established new settlements, or joined with existing ones, and so pockets of inhabitation gradually developed from Lamphun in the north to Pattani in south Thailand. Another theory allows for the T'ai speakers to move south in the same way, and for the indigenous inhabitants of the Malay Peninsula to move north, occupying the empty lands or integrating into existing settlements as they did so.

What is certain is that larger communities soon developed and, as coastal settlements started to receive visitors from foreign lands, trade quickly became established. India became an early contributor to the ethnic mix of Thailand as Indian traders reached the Andaman coast around the 1st century A.D., continued around the Malay Peninsula and Indonesia, and then proceeded northwards through the Gulf of Thailand and into northeast Thailand. They brought with them the religions of Hinduism and Theravada Buddhism, both of which became part of the developing culture of the time.

Around this time a vaguely defined part of Southeast Asia was referred to as Suvarnabhumi in Sri Lankan texts. The name refers to a "golden peninsula" or "land of gold" situated in a fertile region where people came from the mountains, the plains, and the seas to join together, sometimes cooperating, sometimes fighting each other for dominance. Other later references are made to "Sien" by the Chinese, to "Syam" by the Khmers of Cambodia, and to "Sem" by the Mon people of Burma. All of these can be taken to have developed from "Sayam," a word from the Pali language of ancient India that can mean "gold color" and could be considered an alternative way of referring to Suvarnabhumi. The people of this region retained no historical records of their early history, however, so it's impossible to know if they considered themselves to be Siamese or whether this term was adopted in later years.

MON DVARAVATI PERIOD: A.D. 600 TO A.D. 1100

The Mon people of modern-day Burma were among the first to dominate this area of Southeast Asia. The Mon migrated from China around 1000 B.C. and settled to the west of Thailand, but in time they cast their influence over much of central and western Thailand. This area was administrated from the capital of Nakhon Pathom (the largest town in Thailand at the time), though many other large towns existed under their control throughout Ratchaburi and Lopburi Provinces, and as far as Prachinburi Province further to the east. Very little is known about how the Mon Empire functioned. No real records exist, and the physical remains do not say much about their social or political structures, though general agreement is that it consisted of a conglomerate of relatively autonomous states that shared a common culture, rather than being a tightly controlled regime.

Certainly, the Mon people also encouraged Theravada Buddhism, and allowed the Indian Hindu style to influence their Buddha images and sculptures that, along with bas-reliefs and architectural remains, are all that this period leaves behind. The Mon Empire declined under the approaching Khmers and withdrew to south Burma along the borders with west Thailand where the Mon people still remain today, fighting for independence against the incumbent Burmese government.

KHMER EMPIRE:
A.D. 1100 TO A.D. 1200

Coming to the area of modern-day Cambodia at the same as the Mon, the Khmer people began a significant phase of expansion around A.D. 800, and within 200 years their empire had extended west into Thailand to encompass Lopburi, and south as far as the Isthmus of Kra at the head of the Malay Peninsula. They built trade routes around Thailand, as well as Laos and Vietnam, and profited hugely from the agricultural produce of their occupied lands, pouring their acquired capital into massive building projects in central Cambodia.

With them they brought their language, based around a form of Sanskrit, their style of art and architecture, and their religions of Hinduism and Mahayana Buddhism. As they propagated their empire they absorbed the local cultures of conquered people, so many traditional aspects of life, such as the practice of animism and the belief in spirits, continued to play a part in people's lives. This was a relatively authoritarian society run centrally from the area of Angkor in central Cambodia, though the capital was formally relocated to the glorious city of Angkor Thom when construction was completed in A.D. 1200. This city, along with Angkor Wat, provided a superb example of the Khmer's skills in extravagant stone architecture.

They built many huge stone monuments around their empire during its 600-year dominance, such as the temples standing at Phimai and Phanom Rung in northeast Thailand, now restored to their former glory. As well as these stone edifices to the might of the Khmers, they produced many stone and bronze artworks of Hindu gods and Buddha images, with intricately carved stone lintels showcasing the distinctive Khmer style. Sadly, many of the Buddha images were destroyed in the 13th century after the Khmer king completely rejected Buddhism and turned entirely to Hinduism.

In time the Khmers ceased their expansionist policies, and the strength of their rule and ability to control their empire weakened as the fervor and capability of their kings waned. In the 14th century A.D. they started to experience troubles at their borders from rebellious states in Vietnam and Thailand, and from the Mongol Empire, which was gaining power to the north. The capital was moved from Angkor Thom to Phnom Penh in 1432, after it had been subjected to a series of successful attacks by foreign powers, and only the cultural influence of the fading empire remained in the formerly occupied lands.

SUKHOTHAI:
A.D. 1238 TO A.D. 1378

Situated north of the central plains and in the outer reaches of the Khmer Empire, this town was under the control of two Khmer-appointed governors named Kun Bang Klang Thao and Kun Pha Muang. Previously princes of an independent kingdom, they were unhappy at remaining under the rule of the Khmer Empire and in 1238 announced a rebellion, renamed the town Sukhothai, meaning "dawn of happiness," and declared the town and its people to be independent from the Khmer.

Using the common religion of Theravada Buddhism they forged allegiances with the ruling families of other independent states, and encouraged Thais in occupied towns to throw off the oppression of the Khmer Empire and join with them in establishing a new nation for all Thai people. The kingdom needed to be under the reign of one king and, as Kun Pha Muang was married with a Khmer and therefore deemed to be less trustworthy, Kun Bang Klao Thao became King Sri Inthradit of Sukhothai, and the first king of Siam. A nation had been born.

A golden age began, with more material prosperity than ever before since they did not have to pay tithes or taxes to any ruling foreign powers. The celebration of the newly founded nation expressed itself in works of artistic and architectural greatness, all tempered by the memory of being for so long under the yoke of others, carried with the inherent piety of earnest followers of Buddhism. A liberal policy of governance was adopted with no taxes and no slaves, which encouraged other independent states and recently liberated towns to join the kingdom; consequently there was a rapid expansion of borders from Lampang in the north, to Vientiene in Laos, and south to Nakhon Si Thammarat on the Malay Peninsula.

The kingdom grew quickly in size, and also in numbers. In the mid-13th century many Chinese Yunnan in south China fled from the rampage of the Mongol Empire, settling in the Sukhothai kingdom. The Chinese and people from other states that became part of the kingdom brought new influences that were readily assimilated into a culture that had been highly Khmer in nature. Also, in taking advantage of the withdrawal of the Khmers from trade in the area, Sukhothai renewed and further developed trade with China, India, and Japan. Sukhothai's population, power, and reputation had grown substantially in a very short period of time.

After King Sri Inthradit died, his son Ban Muang ruled for a short period before being succeeded in 1279 by his younger brother, who came to the throne as King Ramkhamhaeng. He influenced the way Thailand would develop in future years, and he would be the first king of Thailand to be accorded an official title that reflected his contribution: "King Ramkhamhaeng the Great." He developed a strong alliance with the Yuan dynasty of China, and with their assistance Sukhothai became a center renowned for the production of glazed ceramics known as Sangkhalok-ware. He also continued the expansion of the kingdom to include east Burma and much of Laos, and contributed to the demise of the once mighty Srivijaya Empire of Sumatra by taking much of the Malay Peninsula for Sukhothai.

His contribution to the culture and care of his people is as extensive as his contribution to the growth of his kingdom. He organized a system of writing that led directly to the development of the Thai alphabet still in use today, and which was used in 1283 to produce the Ramkhamhaeng Stele, a stone tablet extolling the virtues of the king and his realm, now on display at the National Museum in Bangkok. It tells of a land with no taxes on merchandise, inheritance, or roads, where the leader was so available that anyone with a grievance could ring a bell outside his palace and the king "goes and questions the man, examines the case, and decides it justly for him." He provided for his subjects' spiritual needs by inviting Ceylonese monks who had previously settled in Nakhon Si Thammarat to bless Buddhism in his country as a recognized descendant of their Theravada school, and in doing so they introduced a new influence to the architecture of Sukhothai temples. The economy was still relatively small scale with high dependency on agricultural self-sufficiency, but this did not appear to be a problem—the stele recounts that "There are fish in the water and rice in the fields," and "So the king was praised by the people."

However, the great strength of Ramkhamhaeng at this time ultimately contributed to the downfall of the Sukhothai kingdom; after Ramkhamhaeng's death in 1317, the integrity of the kingdom started to falter. Some southern states developed politically and economically, acquiring sufficient power to challenge that of Sukhothai and declare themselves independent. The kingdom subsequently fell apart and in 1378 Sukhothai became a tributary state to the emerging power, Ayutthaya.

LANNATHAI:
A.D. 1259 TO A.D. 1578

This was a thriving, independent kingdom in north Thailand sited on fertile plains next to the Mekong River; though only one of a number of similar self-ruling kingdoms, it has a longer history and a larger influence on modern Thailand than many others. The first leader was King Mengrai, who founded a capital at Chiang Rai then later moved it to Chiang Mai, leading to both becoming important cities in the north of the country throughout the history of Thailand. He forged an agreement with King Ramkhamhaeng of Sukhothai and King Ngarm Muang of Phayao for peace between the three kingdoms; this lasted for many decades and allowed each to develop a level of prosperity. But the king did not extend this peace to all sides and sought to extend his kingdom eagerly, pushing the borders into present-day Laos, north Burma, and south China.

Due to its location and the acquired influences from these neighboring states, Lanna developed a culture decidedly different from the Thai kingdoms of the central plains. Not only did they have their own dialect and system of writing, but their diet was more centered on the sticky white rice that grew abundantly in the area, their dress reflected the cooler climate of the region, and their attitude has been said to be more laid-back and in keeping with their slower pace of life. Nevertheless, the kingdom was said to have flourished over the next 200 years, allowing culture and arts to develop. The middle of the 15th century under King Tilokoraj is seen as an important time for Lanna art and literature, and therefore important for Thai history.

The people of Lanna courageously repelled many attacks from both the Burmese and their erstwhile allies of Sukhothai over the years, and their attempts to expand kept them at war with the people of Laos almost continuously. But this relatively small kingdom did not have the resources to sustain these efforts and to withstand their more powerful aggressors indefinitely, and after King Phraya Kaeo's death in 1526, the kingdom was internally weak and struggling for survival. Lanna was first annexed by the Burmese and eventually retaken by the Thais when it was absorbed into the greater kingdom of Siam.

AYUTTHAYA:
A.D. 1350 TO A.D. 1767

One significant state that established independence around that time was based around the ancient community of Lavo just to the south of Sukhothai; the state was ruled by Prince U Thong. During an outbreak of cholera U Thong relocated his court further south to an island formed by the confluence of the Chao Phraya, Pasak, and Lopburi Rivers. Over time, the city became a significant power in the region and in 1350, U Thong declared himself King Ramathibodi, and the new city of Ayutthaya to be the capital of his kingdom.

The new location was much better than the former. The rivers flooded seasonally and the surrounding areas were highly fertile, ideal for rice terraces. The rivers provided easy transport and access to the sea, which was to be invaluable in the development of trade; boats soon became a common means of transport, and a network of canals was constructed that criss-crossed the city itself. The oft-flooded plains and the rivers also provided a natural defense, improving the new city's resilience against future attacks.

The surrounding land was apportioned into groups of villages according to the hands available to work it; land was also granted to high-ranking officials depending on the labor they could muster and afford. The vitality of the fertile basin, and this system that ensured it was well tended, quickly led to a surplus of rice—Ayutthaya's first exportable commodity.

The kingdom expanded quickly under King Ramathibodi and his successors, acquiring Sukhothai and its realm to the north and lands to the east reaching all the way to Angkor. Many areas remained self-governing principalities or tributary states, allowing Ayutthaya to increase its power and population without the need for direct rule, but the states were required to adopt new laws passed at Ayutthaya and pledge an unwavering allegiance to the king. Some states were less eager to join with Ayutthaya, and minor battles and skirmishes were common as the new power met with old resistances in its desire to expand.

In the middle of the 14th century, the Cambodian king attacked two towns in the east in an attempt to reclaim them as part of Cambodia, and Ayutthaya responded with a full invasion of Angkor Thom, taking the capital completely for the first time. For many years the two countries had fought almost constantly over the balance of power, taking a terrible toll on their people. While tactical sophistication had its place in some battles, sheer force of numbers was the preferred approach at the time. As a result, towns and villages were stripped of any men—and often many women—who were of fighting age, and they were expected to carry out the duty owed to their king in these fearsome clashes. Both sides always suffered heavy losses and, as an expected spoil of war, prisoners were taken back to the victor's homelands as slaves, though often they were eventually absorbed into society, adding more variety to the ethnicity of the region.

By the middle of the 15th century, Ayutthaya had extended its reign to cover most of central and northern Thailand, though Lanna still successfully defended its independence and fighting continued in other states where Ayutthaya was still trying to gain the upper hand or drive out separatists. Angkor Thom had been taken once again, though not for long, as the Cambodians were able to regain control in one of their pushes westwards. Trouble was also brewing with the Islamist trading state of Malacca in the far south of the Malay Peninsula as they tried to extend their influence northwards into Ayutthaya's territory, but at the time Ayutthaya had the strength and resources to persevere with these far-flung campaigns.

At the heart of the kingdom, the city of Ayutthaya flourished, in just 100 years transforming from a sparsely populated island into a major city filled with majestic temples and an extensive network of waterways. This level of growth needed a more rigorous style of governance than the benevolent kingship of Sukhothai, as well as an administration system, and thus a class system was duly developed, with absolute power always remaining completely with the king. The influences of the Hindu religion had provided the title of devaraja, or god king, and the monarchs of Ayutthaya used this title and the divine right that it provided to support their autocracy. Minor members of the monarchy, or those holding important positions or titles of nobility, were the next ruling class, and with this power came all too common abuses—corruption, exploitation, and oppression. Commoners and servants were seen as the lowest class and often struggled in serfdom to generate wealth for the ruling classes, though it was both possible and common for peasants to avoid this by ordaining as Buddhist monks, allowing them to exist outside of the class system.

The 16th century brought some changes that would alter the face of Thailand forever. A Portuguese diplomatic mission to Siam in 1511 was allowed to establish an embassy in Ayutthaya, the first step in the forthcoming European influence. Soon afterwards, in 1516, the Portuguese signed a treaty to supply arms and munitions in large numbers, giving Ayutthaya significant advantages in its ongoing wars, but also the first sign of any dependence on foreign powers. There was also an increase in immigration by the Chinese, who controlled much of Ayutthaya's internal trade by the start of the 16th century, and also influenced state matters through positions of power in the civil administration and in the military.

Throughout the 16th century, the kingship of Ayutthaya changed hands frequently, usually as a result of an assassination on the orders of a jealous sibling—often the victim was a child heir to the throne who was easily dispatched.

Nevertheless, a system of administration supported by a closed class system and protected by corruption, greed, and modern firepower led to Ayutthaya furthering its interest in matters of trade, becoming one of the primary marketplaces for commodities from Malaya, Indonesia, India, and Persia. Ayutthaya's own exports included hardwoods and sap from the plentiful forests, hides from the prolific wild game, the much sought-after elephant ivory and rhinoceros horn, tin from huge natural deposits in Phuket and Nakhon Si Thammarat, and dried fish and rice from the rivers and plains. Relations were established with the Ming and Manchu dynasties in China, who bestowed political sanction and recognition on the kingdom. Trade with the Chinese brought in fine luxury goods such as silk and cotton, drawing more merchants from further afield.

In the middle of the 16th century these merchants would have arrived to a city bigger than Paris or London, containing 375 Buddhist temples adorned in gold foil and precious stones, and enjoying an ever increasing inflow of money from trade and homage from its many tributary and vassal states. In 1569 they would have seen the Burmese, aided by rebellious Siamese royal families, successfully sacking and plundering the city, stripping the city of treasure, and decimating the population, taking many Siamese men and women back to Burma as prisoners.

Thailand regained control before the end of the century at the leadership of Prince Sanpet II, who was held hostage in Burma from an early age to ensure the loyalty of his father, who then reigned over Ayutthaya as a Burmese vassal state. Released from the Burmese in exchange for his sister, he remained loyal to his captors until he heard of an assassination plot against him. With the support of his army and local townsmen he declared Ayutthaya and its realm independent from Burma and successfully liberated the city and its people.

Prince Sanpet II became King Naresuan in 1590 upon the death of his father. Astute in internal political matters, he appointed court officials to govern each state in the kingdom under his direct control. This reduced the possibility of treason and loss of the kingdom, allowing King Naresuan to concentrate on repelling the continued attacks of the Burmese. In 1592 these two forces came together in a decisive battle at Nong Sarai, where King Naresuan set an ambush for the Burmese, then charged them on elephant-back, armed with lances. Cutting into the Burmese army, he singled out the Crown Prince, who was an old childhood enemy from the Burmese palace, and killed him with a thrust of his lance. This defeat of the Burmese left them subdued for a long time, and was the culmination of a series of achievements for which this king is remembered as "King Naresuan the Great."

The arrival of the 17th century brought significant trade interest from the Dutch, the British, and the French. King Narai (1656–1688) resisted Dutch efforts to dominate and control trade, resulting in an unsettled relationship between the two nations. More amicable agreements were made with the French, and in general the foreign presence increased in the royal court. Fear of foreign rule led to a coup d'état while King Narai was gravely ill, and one of the king's close counselors declared himself King Phra Petraja (1688–1702). One of his first acts was to eliminate all foreign influence, in order to recover political control and to regain the support of the Siamese people. Naturally this caused a strain in foreign relations and it was some time before foreign diplomats were welcome in what the French themselves had called "the most beautiful city in the East."

Ayutthaya was under pressure from many directions—Lanna in the north was still fighting to maintain independence, the Khmer were pushing in from the east again, and the armies were committed to invasions of Malacca's territory in the south. In addition Burma, under a strong administration, was looking for revenge against their old adversaries. They made massive headway during the 1760s and inflicted severe defeats on the Siamese as they moved onwards to Ayutthaya. In April 1767, after a 15-month siege of the city, Ayutthaya was lost to the Burmese and razed to the ground. Art, treasures, and religious sculptures were removed, temples destroyed, and all official paperwork and records were lost. Many Siamese lost their lives, and many more were taken back to Burma as prisoners.

THONBURI: 1767 TO 1782

The Siamese way of life had been torn apart by the Burmese. Trade had almost completely ceased, land had been lost to the Burmese occupiers, thousands of lives had been lost, and many of the royal family and other important civil leaders had been killed or imprisoned by the Burmese. A Siamese general called Phraya Taksin escaped the sacking of the city, regrouped to the east, then returned to Ayutthaya to chase off the Burmese defenders, and finally declared himself as King Taksin (1767–1782) in December 1767. By now the kingdom consisted of five mostly independent areas, with the king's influence being much diminished compared with the power of the rulers of Ayutthaya.

King Taksin based his capital at Thonburi, across the Chao Phraya River from present-day Bangkok, seeing this as a place with natural defenses and an important position for trade. The king re-established diplomatic relations with China, who recognized him as the rightful ruler of Siam, and after successfully uniting the independent areas of the country in wars to drive the Cambodians further to the west, he also achieved the reunification of Siam itself and in doing so was accepted throughout the country as being worthy of the title "King of Siam."

Economic losses caused by the fall of Ayutthaya were slowly recovered as King Taksin forged diplomatic ties with surrounding countries, with the purchase of arms to ensure a successful defense of the fledgling capital being an important priority. As strength and cohesion returned to the nation, lands that had been lost during the uncertainty after Ayutthaya's loss were reclaimed and the southern boundary was successfully pushed south to Penang, and much of Laos was claimed to the east.

In his final days King Taksin dismissed ministers in his cabinet who felt he had gone mad (because he was so absorbed in his Buddhist faith that he declared himself to be a divine figure); in turn they staged a coup and had the king executed.

RATTANAKOSIN: 1782 TO 1932

After King Taksin was executed, General Chao Phraya Chakri was declared as King Buddha Yodfa Chulalok (Rama I, 1782–1809), the first king of the Chakri Dynasty that continues to this day. He relocated the capital from Thonburi to the commercial area known as Bangkok across the Chao Phraya River in order to place the natural obstacle between the capital and the Burmese border. He commissioned master architects from Ayutthaya to build the Grand Palace as a place for him to reside and as a new administration center for Siam. In 1785 the new capital was inaugurated under a new, majestically long name, but was referred to as Krung Thep by the people, and remained known as Bangkok to all foreigners.

Intent on ensuring Buddhism had a strong foundation after the demise of the temples in Ayutthaya, the king reestablished the monkhood and ordered a grand council to revise the Tripitaka, the Buddhist Canon that had become fragmented after the fall of Ayutthaya. Over 250 monks worked daily for five months before the final version was complete: 45 volumes of more than 500 pages each, all handwritten in the ancient Pali language. This was a defining step for Thai Buddhism.

The king sought to reconstruct the successful Ayutthaya governance model to a degree, but without completely imitating it. He oversaw the codifying of the laws of the land in a similar way to the Tripitaka; the volumes became known as the Three Seals Law—some say the name derives from the seals of the ministers of north, south, and central Thailand that adorned the covers, but others feel the Three Seals are a symbol of the threefold duties inherent in the texts: the king's duty to his subjects, the subjects' duty as citizens, and the overarching aspect of their duty as Buddhists.

King Rama I extended the borders of the country to possibly their greatest extent: The Burmese had been pushed back deep into Burma, the eastern borders extended to Luang Phrabang in Laos, Cambodia was occupied almost entirely up to the Vietnamese border, all but the very southern tip of the Malaya Peninsula had been taken, and Chiang Mai had finally been fully incorporated into the kingdom. As the country's stability returned, the king made it known that merchants and traders were welcome to return to the country following their much reduced presence since the loss of Ayutthaya.

In just 27 years he had reconsolidated the people of Siam and put the country very firmly back on the map. He had revitalized its society, political system, and religion. He even rewrote the Hindu classic the Ramayana to produce the Thai version known as the Ramakien as another contribution to the culture of his people. He founded the city of Bangkok, re-established trade, and established the long line of the much revered Chakri Dynasty. His contribution to his people was recognized in 1982 when henceforth he became known as "King Rama the Great."

His successor, King Phuttaloetla Nabhalai (Rama II, 1809–1824), continued his work capably, though much less aggressively. He also made a huge contribution to the arts and cultural aspects of life, with his reign being seen as a second golden age of Thai literature and a time when the whole country enjoyed a respite after the upheaval of the previous decades. He himself was an accomplished poet, inspiring many works of the time, but also an artisan who assisted in the carving of the door panels of the wiharn at Wat Suthat, which are considered to be a supreme masterpiece of woodcarving. He also commissioned the renovation of Wat Makok on the west bank of the Chao Phraya River, renaming it as Wat Arunrachataram and designing the main Buddha image himself. Nowadays this temple is known worldwide as the famous Bangkok landmark of Wat Arun.

As Rama II had a less warlike approach than his father, the borders of Siam did recede slightly during his reign. Concessions were made with Britain during the Anglo-Burmese war that essentially give Burma its modern-day borders, and vassal states on the Malay Peninsula had been lost. Wars had mostly been averted in the east and the kingdom still held huge tracts of land across Cambodia and Laos, along with parts of north Burma and south China at the west and north borders.

On the death of King Rama II, the next in line, Prince Mongkut, was considered too inexperienced to rule, so he entered the monkhood while his half-brother was appointed to rule as King Nang Khlao (Rama III, 1824–1851).

King Nang Khlao was considered to have ruled well, using his experience to reopen relations with China and the West, though he only agreed to conservative treaties that ultimately protected Siamese interest in matters of trade. But the economy boomed, and the king used part of this wealth to build the famous Wat Pho and to renovate many other temples as a sign of his dedication to the Buddhist faith.

Prince Mongkut, meanwhile, had spent his years studying languages, Western scientific method, and European culture, as well as becoming an expert on Buddhism and developing wisdom through his experience as a monk. When he did finally accede to the throne as King Mongkut (Rama IV, 1851–1868), these virtues helped him enormously when dealing with Wwestern powers. His fluency in languages facilitated the establishment of diplomatic relations. With the help of the foreign expertise he started to modernize Siam, undertaking road- and canal-building projects to improve the infrastructure, overseeing a thorough reorganization of the Thai army and civil administration, and even introducing other Western ways such as ordering the nobility to wear shirts whilst in his court.

Throughout all of his dealings, he was careful to protect the identity and interests of Siam at a time when much of Southeast Asia was being swallowed up as colonies by the Western powers. He charmed the British representative who arrived expecting to be rebuffed as the British had been by the last king, and carefully agreed concessions with other European powers where necessary. Throughout all he maintained his touch with the common people and personally listened to petitions from his subjects once each week.

He employed an English teacher called Anna Leonowens to tutor his many children; her subsequent books about her experiences inspired the films *The King and I* and *Anna and the King*. Both of these films have been perceived to be unrepresentative of King Mongkut's greatness by Thai powers that be, and both the films and the books are banned in Thailand for their inaccurate portrayals of him as well as the over-dramatic and historically inaccurate course of events put forth as Thai history. However it should be noted that Leonowen's books were considered to be fiction when they were first published, and are often felt to better represent her Victorian imperialistic views colored by flights of fancy rather than any real contribution she may have made to the modernization of Siam.

King Mongkut's death was brought about as a result of one of his final achievements. In 1868 he hosted a group of French and British astronomers in observing a total solar eclipse that he had predicted using Western astronomical techniques. They observed the eclipse from a marshy area infested with mosquitoes, and both the king and his son contracted malaria. His son survived, but the king died several days later. His legacy of modernization long survives him, and he is now remembered as Thailand's father of modern science and technology.

He was succeeded by his son, who became King Chulalongkorn (Rama V, 1868–1910) at just 17 years old. The Chief Minister became Regent and ruled the country whilst the young king continued with his studies and visited other countries for the next four years. He was the first king to travel out of the country to any great extent, and on visiting the Dutch- and British-occupied Burma, India, Malaya, and Indonesia, he became eager to adopt more of the Western ideas without having to bend to their rule, and made an effort to engage constructively with the Western powers rather than to try to fight against them or take the other extreme of closing the country to the outside world.

Once fully in power, he initiated a series of changes to end slavery in Siam, and made internal changes such as updating the dress code in the royal house, and started to fill the royal court with like-minded young men, often immediate relatives, who wanted to be part of the modernization of Thailand, though it wouldn't be easy. In time he developed a public welfare system and reformed the government and administration in the Western style with a cabinet and ministries, and himself acting as a prime minister above them.

The development of roads and canals continued, and a large-scale railway project was conceived with the assistance of engineers from Britain and France. Post and telegraph services were introduced and with better communication and means of access, more control and authority was brought to bear over remote, less lawful provinces. The introduction of the baht as the standard currency along with an auditing system and the central allocation of budgets ensured that the country's finances also came under greater scrutiny than ever before.

Rama V utilized the temple schools system to offer a level of education to children in every village; able students were encouraged to further their studies and those with greater financial means (usually the royalty) often studied at the best overseas schools where they would experience Western methods first hand and associate with the children of the elite from other countries.

The king traveled widely within the country, eager to see his subjects face to face and to learn of their lives, and to enable them to see their king in action. Sometimes he preferred to travel almost in disguise, with no entourage except some family or close friends, and with no special ceremony, attending village celebrations or weddings as he passed through. His travels also took him overseas and he traveled twice to Europe, where he was warmly received throughout, being seen as a royal equal by all and affecting people through his "inherent likability" and graciousness.

In his vision to make Siam a free and progressive country, he had been obliged to make some concessions. In the 1893 Franco-Siamese treaty, Siam agreed to relinquish its hold on the west of Cambodia, preferring to cede this land to the French and avoid the possibility of escalating action rather than risk an attack by the formidable colonialist through an act of defiance. In 1896 an Anglo-French accord guaranteed the independence of Siam, with both sides seeing it as an important buffer between their colonies.

But the heartland of Siam had remained secure, and the king had skillfully negotiated and ruled through a vital time in Thailand's history by avoiding rule by any foreign power. His modern and progressive reforms had touched almost every part of Siamese life whilst cultural and religious values had flourished. Modern Thailand is very much a result of his work and King Rama V the Great is still one of Thailand's most loved and revered kings, with him also being honored by UNESCO as an outstanding world leader due to his many contributions to his country.

His son came to the throne after him as King Vajiravudh (Rama VI, 1910–1925) and brought with him a very Western education, having spent many years studying in England. Despite this he was a staunch nationalist, and though he wanted to continue with his father's policies of modernization, he believed that the national identity was strengthened by keeping some of the old ways and traditions alive.

Rama VI took the first steps towards providing compulsory education for all, and opened medical clinics throughout the country that offered free vaccines. Other modernizations he adopted included the abolition of polygamy (for all except the monarchy), that all of his subjects must take surnames (which had never previously been used), and changing the national flag to the tricolor red, white, and blue still used today.

Siam initially chose to remain neutral during World War I, but in 1917 they formally declared war on Germany and Austria-Hungary, and a small force of 1,284 volunteers was sent to France for flight training along with a unit of medical nurses. After the war Siam's international political reputation was greatly enhanced, and after much lobbying, extraterritorial rights were ceded by the United States in 1920, and by France and Britain in 1925. Siam had also become a founding member of the League of Nations in 1920 and was now on an equal political footing with some of the most powerful countries in the world.

Despite his successes, Rama VI died at a time when the country was starting to suffer badly from economic problems as fluctuations in rice prices and massive state expenditure had caused a huge trade deficit and large amounts of foreign debt. He had survived an earlier military coup attempt in 1912 by those who were increasingly unhappy at the state of the economy, and by the end of his reign the reputation of the monarchy was not what it had once been. After the death of Rama VI, his brother came to power as King Prajadhipok (Rama VII, 1925–1935). Having developed very liberal views during his schooling in England, he sought to influence the government accordingly, being especially aware of the welfare of his subjects and the growing pressure from a small group of foreign-educated young men who sought greater participation in the government of the country. As the whole world fell into the grip of the Great Depression, difficult and unpopular financial measures had to be taken that caused further unrest.

The monarchy was now in danger of falling completely, but the king felt that the Siamese people were, on the whole, not ready for true democracy. He convened a special meeting with his officials to negotiate a solution.

Those who wanted a change in power included, on one side, a group of radical young intellectuals called the People's Party, led by a young French-educated lawyer called Pridi Banomyong who saw the corruption and abuse of power by the ruling elite as the cause of his countrymen's sorrow. On the other side was the military faction headed by Phibun Songkhram, a young military officer who felt a government should provide strong authoritarian rule, and Phraya Phahon, an older and more moderate military leader who could garner the support of the armed forces to support their combined cause with force, if they should need it.

The king agreed to allow a non-violent coup d'état to take place on June 24, 1932. The inevitable course of events expected by the monarchy for so long had finally come to pass and the 700 years of absolute rule by the Chakri Dynasty effectively came to an end.

CONSTITUTIONAL MONARCHY: 1932 TO PRESENT

On December 10, 1932, King Prajadhipok signed Siam's first constitution, transforming the country from an absolute monarchy to a constitutional monarchy. He would continue to reign, but not to rule, and democratic elections would be held every four years, with everybody being entitled to a vote to establish a representative government. A new chapter in Thailand's history had begun.

The first election took place on April 1, 1933, and the people of Siam voted that Phraya Manopakorn Nititada, who had been acting as prime minister since the coup, should become the first official prime minister of Siam. But after only 80 days Phibun Song-khram, who had installed Phraya Manopakorn Nititada originally, led another bloodless coup, and on June 21, 1933, there was an announcement that Phraya Phahon, a moderate military officer, was now in power. Two of the leaders of the 1932 revolution that intended to bring democracy to the country had effectively ignored the democratic wishes of the people and now had rule over the country.

For the next few years, the country struggled to find its feet with its newfound political freedom. The balance of power swayed between the left-leaning People's Party and

King Rama IV's statue in Bangkok

the right-wing military contingent as elections, coups, and counter-coups took place, and in 1935 the king could no longer support the way the country was being governed. He abdicated without even announcing a successor.

The government selected the 10-year-old nephew of King Prajadhipok, who would take the throne as King Ananda Mahidol (Rama VIII, 1935–1946). He had been born in Germany and, apart from a brief trip to Siam when he was 13, he continued his life and studies abroad and so had very little effect on what was occurring within in the country. This left the People's Party in government, but with the military holding the true power behind the scenes.

In 1938 Phibun Songkhram became prime minister and his government encouraged nationalist feeling almost to the point of fascism, utilizing the popular media to promote their views and encourage support for their cause much in the same way as Hitler and Mussolini had done in Europe. The Chinese business community, who now controlled nearly 85 percent of the merchant trade in Siam, was targeted with policies such as increases in taxes for Chinese businesses in an attempt to economically disable them so their share of the market would move to the Siamese, and Chinese schools and media were even closed down in an effort to drive people away.

The regime even viewed the name of the country as one that had been inherited through usage by other countries and so changed it from Siam to prathet tai in the Thai language. This uses the ancient word for the T'ai people, which is also interpreted as "free," and so translates as "country of the free," or Thailand. The regime also adopted a new nationwide slogan of "Thailand for the Thais," which reflected its nationalist views and left non-Thais quite sure of exactly where they stood.

At the outbreak of World War II, Thailand declared neutrality, but before long they recognized the might of the Japanese and eventually allowed them to use Thailand as a key staging point for their operations in the region.

Phibun Songkhram formally announced an alliance with the Japanese in 1942, and a declaration of war was made against both the United Kingdom and the United States, but the Thai ambassador in Washington refused to deliver the declaration to the American officials. He stated that Phibun's government and its actions were illegal and started the Seri Thai movement to overthrow Phibun. Thailand remained host to the Japanese, so Bangkok and other major cities were bombed heavily by the Allies, causing damage, deaths, and economic losses.

The regime of Phibun was increasingly failing the Thai people, and signs started to show that Japan would lose the war. This led to support for the Seri Thai movement, which had managed to infiltrate the government, and Phibun was finally ousted as prime minister. His replacement was a liberal who withdrew from the occupied territories in Burma and Malaya, and after the war the new government did everything they could to aid the British in disarming the Japanese and repatriating their prisoners of war. They repudiated the declarations of war issued by the previous government and reverted to the usage of "Siam" as a rejection of the nationalist regime's introduction of "Thailand," but they still faced the wrath of the British, who considered the country to be a defeated enemy. Nevertheless, the Americans recognized the steps taken by the new government and used their influence to encourage lenience, so that Siam received little punishment for the role it had taken during the war.

In 1945 the young king returned to Siam and received a joyous welcome from the people. He appeared in public and partook in royal activities, but foreign observers considered that he did not appear comfortable in his role as king and maybe was not really ready for the responsibility that this carried. Three days before he was due to return to Switzerland to conclude his studies, he was found dead in his bedchamber from a single gunshot wound. An inquiry and a series of trials eventually convicted the king's secretary and two pages on charges of conspiracy to kill the king; all three were executed. However, the actual course of events surrounding the king's death was never fully explained to the people of Thailand and it remains something of a mystery.

The throne and the title passed to the 19-year-old younger brother of the deceased king, though King Bhumibol Adulyadej (Rama IX, 1946–present) was not coronated for another four years. The king not only needed to complete his studies in Switzerland, but also to change the focus of those studies to subjects that would be valuable in his new position, choosing to take law and political science. His uncle, the Prince of Chainit, was appointed to act as regent, and once again Siam had an absent king.

Democratic elections had taken place, but the elected prime minister, Khuang Abhaiwongse, had stood down after only two months to make way for Pridi Banomyong, one of the instigators of the 1932 coup. He had taken power in March 1946 but then resigned under pressure just a few months later following questions about his involvement with the death of the former king. The country was without effective leadership once again, and in November 1947 the military stepped in, leading to Phibun being returned to power in April 1948. This move came at the start of the Cold War, when Phibun's policies set them as opponents of the communist regimes and consequently in line with American foreign policy. The United States subsequently supported the regime with aid—starting a long tradition of American-backed military regimes in Thailand.

Phibun once again changed the name of the country to Thailand in 1949 and this time the change was to be permanent. Another significant event was the coronation of King Bhumibol on May 5, 1950. The people rejoiced as the new king made his solemn oath: "We will reign with righteousness for the benefit and happiness of the Siamese people."

However, some people were not happy with the way the country was being governed. Phibun's regime benefited many, but there was much dissatisfaction in poor rural areas, which led to increasing favor for left-wing ideologies. Political parties with communist leanings gained in popularity and received endorsement and support from other communist countries, with China and North Vietnam encouraging visits to pass on teachings and training. The danger was not unrecognized by Phibun, and the communist parties were banned in Thailand, only to reappear soon after under different guises.

Phibun was getting old now and some felt that he was not able to take effective control of the country given the increasing pressures, with a younger group of generals led by Sarit Thanarat eager to take control from him. The people were allowed to make the decision in 1957 when Phibun called an election, and they subsequently voted for him to continue as prime minister. But this was an unsatisfactory outcome for Sarit, who rejected the democratic choice of the people and staged a coup anyway. Thanom Kittikachorn was appointed as prime minister by Sarit, but after a few months Sarit seized direct power himself and maintained a five-year authoritarian rule, during which he banned all political parties and ordered the arrests of dissidents and the executions of communists. He sought to return to a social order that was more Thai in nature by shunning some of the Western ways of thinking favored by previous governments, though he did implement some sound financial policies and encouraged investment from foreign countries that further benefited the country's improving economy. Sarit died of cirrhosis in 1963, whereupon Thanom returned to power once again to develop his own style of totalitarian leadership.

The economic expansion continued apace in the cities and urban areas as a result of the previous regimes' policies, continuing high rice yields that still remained Thailand's most important export, and from continuing aid from the United States. And despite the instability of the country, tourists had also started to visit in relatively small numbers. In 1960 the number of visitors exceeded 100,000 for the first time, and the Tourist Authority of Thailand was created, charged with overseeing the expansion and development of what would prove to be a vital source of income for Thailand.

The communist problem continued to cause difficulties for the government throughout the 1960s despite the harsh penalties meted out by the Sarit regime. Political parties such as the Thai Patriotic Front were thinly veiled fronts for the old Communist Party, and they were working with Vietnamese communists carrying out armed attacks against government troops such as those stationed in Nakhon Pathom Province. The Vietnamese communists saw this as a way of attacking the Thai government for backing the United States in the Vietnam War and allowing American troops to be based there, and for their deployment of Thai troops in South Vietnam to fight alongside the Americans. The United States had made contributions of over $2 billion to the Thai coffers since 1950, which naturally encouraged good relationships with the Thai government.

The many American soldiers based in Thailand and traveling to and from Vietnam were granted time off for rest and recuperation, or R&R. The U Tapao airbase was at the frontline for operations and the towns close by soon became favorites with the off-duty soldiers, with the small seaside fishing town of Pattaya quickly becoming an official R&R resort. The need to release the stress of spending time in a war-zone such as Vietnam resulted in R&R duly becoming known as I&I, or intercourse and intoxication, and Pattaya promptly responded with many new bars opening to help with the intoxication. Their other needs were satisfied by women who had migrated to the town from other parts of the country, but predominantly from the poor northeast region, looking to either benefit financially in the short term, or maybe to find themselves a husband for the long term.

Despite the internal conflicts and the involvement with the rapidly escalating Vietnam War, Thailand's economy was still progressing strongly, and increasingly the surging trade and the aid from the United States exposed Thailand to levels of income that it had never experienced before. Traditional ways of life broke down in some areas as more people migrated to the cities, often to work as cheap labor on the many transport and construction projects. Better-educated people were attracted by the wider range of job opportunities available to them in the new economy, and as more professional jobs became available, there was a natural development of a Thai middle class between the military and political elite and the poorer working class.

These changes did nothing to relieve the growing dissatisfaction in poor rural areas. Land grabs by the rich and powerful had left up to 30 percent of people without land in the north and northeast of the country, and the corrupt police weren't much help. This led to the development of a peasants' activist movement, which joined with left-wing student activists and openly asked questions about the leadership of the government, matters of corruption, issues of poverty, and the relationship with the United States. When the business community started to demand answers to the questions as well, the government finally had to take action. A new constitution was agreed on in 1968 with elections in the following year. Thanom Kittikachorn won, allowing him to continue as prime minister, but now directly answerable to an elected Assembly.

The new members of parliament continued to pressure Thanom by constantly questioning government policies. In 1971 there was a distinct possibility that the military budget might be cut as a result of action taken by the MPs, and Thanom staged a military coup against his own government. This time there was no pretense of openness and consultation as parliament was dissolved, the cabinet disbanded, the constitution abandoned, and martial law declared. Thailand was a truly military state.

This did nothing to alleviate the ill feelings of the people, or to make the old problems go away. There were trade deficit problems with Japan, the communist insurgency escalated to helicopter attacks in the north, and rallies and demonstrations showed the people's displeasure. Thais were no longer as politically naive and unaware and they were prepared to stand up and make their voices heard. Even the king, who until now had interfered with his governments very little, spoke out against the methods employed by Thanom's regime.

The government constantly hunted down suspected insurgents, and towards the end of 1973 a group of students was accused of conspiracy and 13 were arrested. The student body protested, joined by growing numbers of disenfranchised workers and other citizens. On October 13, 1973, several hundred thousand people rallied in front of the Democracy Monument in the center of Bangkok to protest, and the arrested students were released. The rally broke up the next day and the protestors began to disperse quietly, but those heading south found themselves facing police who had cordoned off the exits the day before and not cleared them quickly enough. Tensions grew and the police panicked, first using tear gas on the protestors and then live ammo.

The military was called in to control the massive riot that ensued; tanks rolled down the streets of Bangkok while support helicopters flew overhead, firing down into Thammasat University. Thanom ordered the military action to be intensified to force the protestors into submission, but army commander Kris Sivara disagreed and countermanded the order by withdrawing the troops instead. After the smoke had cleared, it was officially announced that 77 people had been killed and 800 wounded, though unofficial figures put the numbers much higher. That night on national television, the king condemned the government's action and their inability to handle the situation, leading to the decision to exile Thanom and two of his close associates from Thailand.

An interim government was installed under the leadership of Professor Sanya Dharmasakti, a dean at the Thammasat University and someone more sympathetic to the students' and peasants' views than the previous government. The activist movements pressured him to introduce large-scale reforms quickly, and the period of unrest after the October 1973 massacre caused problems in the supply of basic commodities, causing prices to spiral, resulting in more general dissatisfaction. Soon the country was affected by the oil crisis, and the widespread price increases in 1974 led to rising inflation and a crippling recession. This led to an increase in anti-government activities and the government was viewed by many as weak and unable to rule. The country's political view polarized between those who appreciated the previous military government's economic policies and had benefited from their capitalist right-wing tendencies, and those who had suffered as a result of those policies and felt more socialist left-wing policies were needed.

Due to this polarization the next two elections failed to create a stable majority government. However, the success of communism in Laos, Cambodia, and Vietnam caused a massive influx of refugees to Thailand, and the public reacted against these unwanted immigrants by starting to display more right-wing views. The current government did not have the policies they wanted and so, in the 1976 elections, the right-wing conservatives gained power.

As the country moved more towards the right, news came that the chief antagonist in the October 1973 violence, former prime minister Thanom Kittikachorn, was to return to Thailand from exile to become a monk. The student activists organized protests, during which right-wing supporters beat to death two students who were putting up anti-Thanom posters in Nakhon Pathom. The students reacted angrily and it was reported by the media that during a subsequent protest they had used an effigy of the crown prince in a mock hanging.

This provoked fury from the right-wing elements, with a "cleansing killing" of students even being put forward as a solution by an extremist military radio station. Right-wing paramilitary groups stormed Thammasat University to vent their anger at what the media had said had happened, and the subsequent days saw the abduction, torture, and death of hundreds of students at the hands of these groups. The military didn't intervene, and in the aftermath they staged a coup, suspended the constitution, and promptly granted amnesties to those individuals involved in the killings, absolving them completely.

In October 1976 the ultra-conservative General Thanin Kraivixien was appointed as prime minister by coup leader Admiral Sangad Chalawyoo, and so began what has been described as the most oppressive regime in Thailand's modern history. Large numbers of students, intellectuals, and other left-thinking civilians feared for their lives as Thanin organized raids on universities and media offices looking for activists, who fled from Bangkok to join communist insurgents who were retaliating against Thanin. Conflicts between the armed forces and the insurgents became common in the northeast, and the economy suffered drastically.

The position was clearly untenable, and Admiral Sangad Chalawyoo staged another coup just one year later and installed General Kriangsak Chomanan as prime minister. To bolster trade and diplomatic relations, Kriangsak tried to repair old allegiances with China by allowing them to route supplies to the Khmer Rouge in Cambodia through Thailand. However, accounts of the atrocities carried out by the Khmer Rouge quickly became known and the Thai assistance was widely condemned. Kriangsak could not continue in his position after such a monumental error of judgment and so stepped down to be succeeded by General Prem Tinsulanonda in 1980.

Though more people were coming to Thailand as tourists, with 1.8 million visiting in 1980, the income generated was much less than the losses the country had suffered through falling demand and prices for Thailand's exports. But it could be said that the country was now more at ease. Prem was seen as a good, moderate man who had the support of the king and was prepared to work closely with him, the right-wing threat had been removed and so the insurgents had become somewhat calmed, and with the ending of wars elsewhere in Southeast Asia, there was now more peace in the region in general. The time was right for a new start.

Others thought the time was right for another coup. In April 1981 a group of junior army officers took control of Bangkok and stated their intention to form a new government under their control. But this time they did not have the support they needed from the military. The king and Prem presented a united front and as the majority of the armed forces remained loyal to them, Bangkok was quickly retaken and the coup dissolved.

Prem proved to be a competent leader by all accounts, and the people saw fit to re-elect him as prime minister in 1983 as the state of the country continued to improve. However, in November 1984, a massive devaluation of the baht in response to the soaring value of the United States dollar led to a change in economic fortune. The military expressed its dissatisfaction at the handling of the situation and strongly urged Prem to revise his cabinet. He refused and the ill feeling that remained ultimately led to another failed coup attempt in September 1985, which involved 10 hours of fighting on Bangkok streets between the two factions.

Prem was reelected once more in 1986 and so had continuously presided over a period of relative political stability, boosting foreign investment that had plummeted since the time of the Thanin regime, and encouraging more tourists to visit Thailand. In 1987 the Tourism Office of Thailand used the year of the king's 60th birthday to launch its first major promotion of the country with the "Visit Thailand Year." It had the desired result—3.5 million people visited Thailand, bringing 50 billion baht with them to boost the country's economy. This was a 34 percent increase in income from the previous year alone and now tourism income was approaching equal terms with agricultural exports on the country's balance sheet.

Economic growth and national stability continued under Prem, though he resigned as prime minister in 1988 to join the Privy Council, where he became a close adviser to the king. He was succeeded by Chatichai Choonhaven, who then lost power in a coup staged by Suchinda Kraprayoon in 1991. He promised a free election and claimed that he did not seek to gain power for himself, but when the election took place in April 1992, the new prime minister was declared to be none other than Suchinda Kraprayoon. The opposition demanded that an elected person should be appointed instead, seeing this purely as the start of another military dictatorship, and the voices of protest soon became louder.

Starting from May 17, 1992, people started to gather in Bangkok to demonstrate against Suchinda and to call for his resignation. As their numbers quickly swelled to around 200,000, the water cannons and clubs initially used against the protestors wielding stones and petrol bombs were soon exchanged for M16s. In an attempt to regain control of the situation, Suchinda declared a state of emergency and tanks were seen on the streets of Bangkok once again. The crowds would not back down and tensions mounted as the activists' leader, Chamlong Srimuang, was arrested. Live ammo was being used to subdue the protestors, and concerns over the enormity of what might happen became very real. On May 20 the royal family made their appeals on television for the confrontation to end. Suchinda released Chamlong, and in return Chamlong asked the crowds to disperse, which they did. Although 52 deaths were officially recorded, there were hundreds who were wounded, and over 3,500 were arrested, with many being tortured or treated inhumanely. Ultimately the protestors did achieve their aim, even if at a high cost. Suchinda resigned four days later and May 1992 became known as "Black May."

An interim government was followed by elections in 1995 and 1996. Then came the devastating financial crisis in Asia in 1997, in part initiated by the decision made to float the Thai baht instead of continuing to link its value to the U.S. dollar. The value of the baht plummeted, hurting companies' earnings and the country's ability to pay back foreign debt. Stock prices tumbled and the value of investments and real estate fell as investor confidence was weakened. Large amounts of funds were used by the Bank of Thailand to try to save the failing financial institutions, and as currency reserves fell, the treasury was unable to inject enough capital to improve the position of the baht. Combined with other factors, this had a subsequent effect throughout all of Southeast Asia, Asia, and finally the whole world, and the International Monetary Fund eventually had to step in with a US$17 billion emergency loan.

The boom of the previous years had also seen an increase in wage levels generally, and many people had utilized credit to improve their standard of living to enjoy this newfound wealth. Now construction work was ceasing, leaving numerous partly completed buildings littering the skyline of Bangkok; all manner of businesses were failing, and many people were put out of work. People who had enjoyed the benefits of the successful economy in the early 1990s found themselves in debt and jobless, and migrant laborers from the poorest regions had no work and were unable to support their families back home. The impact on the Thai people should not be underestimated; though the economy did recover slowly over the next few years, this was a bleak time for the people of Thailand, with many people still carrying the burden of these debts even today.

Thaksin Shinawatra, a former policeman who had built a US$2 billion empire from hotels and shipping, and had founded the software and telecommunications giants ShinCorp and AIS, entered into politics with the Thai Rak Thai (Thais Love Thais) party in 1998. His policies of cheap health care, development funds for each and every village in Thailand, debt relief for farmers, and a promise for a war on drugs were very different from those offered by the mainstream parties of the time, and he became the first prime minister voted into office with an absolute majority in 2001.

He declared that his party put the interests of the nation and its people first. Initially his policies focused on national self-reliance and reducing the high levels of foreign trade and investment that had led to such dire consequences in the 1997 crisis, but in the coming years he adapted this to accept a balance of open markets and foreign investment. His policies were at first successful but cracks soon began to show as questionable actions were taken and harsh criticism was made. In February 2003 action taken as part of the war on drugs led to 2,500 deaths, with the government admitting direct liability for up to one third but blaming the others on gang-related warfare. In October 2004, hundreds of rioting Muslims in the troubled deep south of the country were locked for hours in army trucks resulting in the deaths of at least 78 people. Thaksin was accused of treason, tax evasion, corruption, and control and manipulation of the media, and described as "a human rights abuser of the worst kind" by the Human Rights Watch.

However there was almost universal recognition of his strong leadership during the next crisis in Thailand. On December 26, 2004, an under-sea earthquake off the north coast of Indonesia resulted in a tsunami up to 30 meters high hitting Thailand at a speed of over 500 kilometers per hour. The southwest coastline of Thailand was devastated. Up to 8,000 people died; a similar number were injured and more than 4,000 people were lost and never found. Hundreds of thousands of people were affected in some way that day, whether through loss of family members, loss of homes, or loss of livelihoods.

© SUZANNE NAM

Citizens decorated tanks with flowers after the 2006 coup.

A pre-election campaign was underway at the time in Thailand, but this soon became unimportant as the magnitude of what had happened became apparent. The political parties supported Thaksin as he visited disaster zones, brought in troops and supplies, publicly berated his officials for not doing enough, and worked hard to make a difference where it mattered without wasting time on petty bureaucracy. Aid packages were developed for those affected to provide housing, rebuild damaged businesses, and replace fishing boats to help the Thai people gradually recover their shattered lives.

This display of strong leadership diverted attention from the troubling aspects of his administration and Thaksin successfully completed his full term of office, becoming the first elected prime minister in Thailand to do so. And his popularity at the time subsequently led to his reelection in February 2005, with Thai Rak Thai winning by a landslide. He was immensely popular with the rural population, having offered cheap loans as a way to boost the economy in their areas, but still he was not supported by the Muslims in the deep south. The unrest had been continuing for many years, with murders of school teachers and local officials occurring almost every day, and the public and troops were both regularly targeted by bombs. Nothing Thaksin had done had made any real difference to a large group of Thai people, and the deaths in October 2004 had not been forgotten.

Allegations of corruption and inappropriate business practices were being made once again, and in 2006 the final straw came when Thaksin sold shares in the companies he founded to Singaporean investment fund Temasak for

US$1.9 billion. There were demonstrations in Bangkok by tens of thousands of people in protest at his actions, two of his cabinet members resigned from their positions, and in February 2006 Thaksin responded by dissolving parliament and calling a snap election.

Thai Rak Thai won the election definitively (thanks in part to a boycott by the Democrat party). Thaksin said that he would not accept the position of prime minister, but would continue as caretaker prime minister for the time being, after which he delegated his responsibilities to his deputy and left the country on vacation. The election was invalidated in May following an investigation into the vote-rigging allegations, and this effectively returned Thaksin to the seat of power, even though he still remained out of the country.

In September 2006, the military took control once more as Thaksin was in New York City preparing for a United Nations meeting. A coup headed by Sonthi Boonyaratglin was successful and martial law was declared again. This time the mood was almost jubilant in Bangkok as some supported the move, and many of them provided food to the soldiers who stood next to their tanks, as grinning tourists posed for photographs around them. The constitution was once again abolished and a retired general, Surayud Chulanon, was installed as a temporary Prime Minister. It was stated that the previous government had abused its power in such a way that it had effectively become undemocratic, that a new constitution would be written with the cooperation of the people, and that democratic elections would take place within 12 months to select a new government.

Over the next few months the criticisms of the interim government became louder. The process of redrawing the constitution was taking too long, and when the initial draft was produced, it was felt to be weak and many changes were demanded. Some unpopular laws were also passed, such as those concerning the privatization of universities and the censorship of entertainment media and the Internet; free-speech was being limited as criticism of the new regime was disallowed, and radio stations run by supporters of Thaksin were closed down. Protests by people in the rural areas that still supported Thaksin were restricted and many areas of the country remained under martial law long after the coup had taken place.

The originally stated aims of the coup leaders now seemed to be coming to fruition as a date for the new election was finally announced: December 23, 2007. A new constitution was agreed to and accepted by the people in a national referendum. Investigations into Thaksin's government had continued, leading to the Thai Rak Thai party being found guilty of election fraud in April 2007, and they had been banned from participating in government for five years. But this did not stop their MPs from being active in politics, and at election time the main candidates consisted of the long-standing Democrat party who had been in opposition while Thaksin had been in government, and the newly formed People's Power Party who were made up of many former MPs from Thai Rak Thai and were openly declared by their leader, Samak Sundavavej, to be a proxy party for the deposed Thaksin. In the election the voters polarized between the two, with the Democrats generally receiving the support from Bangkok and the south, and PPP winning more seats in the poorer north and northeast.

After much wrangling, the PPP entered into a coalition government with a group of seven minor parties, and together they elected Samak as Prime Minister at the end of January 2008. The military leaders announced the dissolution of their council when they made a statement that there would be no more coups, declaring that "the military should not be involved in politics and politicians should not interfere with the military."

Shortly afterward, Samak was kicked out of office not by a coup but by a a court, which ruled that he violated conflict-of-interest laws by taking compensation for appearing on his cooking show. After Samak came Somchai Wongsawat, another PPP leader and Thaksin's brother-in-law. He lasted barely two months before "yellow shirts," pro-Democrat activists, stormed the Bangkok airport and demanded that he leave office. At the same time, a coalition of smaller parties were able to take advantage of a power vacuum. The PPP was dissolved by the courts for electoral fraud and many of its members banned from office for five years.

The coalition prime minister, Abhisit Vejjajiva, a U.K.-born Eton and Oxford educated Chinese-Thai, assumed office in December 2008. Since then, tens of thousands of the country's rural poor, mostly from Isan, have expressed their dissatisfaction with the political process, questioned the legitimacy of the Abhisit government, and demanded new elections. Although many members of this group, called the "red shirts" because of their clothing, still support Thaksin Shinawatra, many say they are dissatisfied because Thailand's politics are dominated by elites and their votes don't count. Tens of thousands of red shirt protesters gathered in Bangkok in the early part of 2010. After a standoff with the government, which would not agree to new elections, the military came in to disperse protesters, killing more then 50, plus at least two foreign journalists.

Government

In 1932 Thailand was changed from an absolute monarchy to a constitutional monarchy, allowing the king to remain as head of state but stripping him of his absolute governing powers. Although the king has had some executive legislative powers in the successive constitutions that have followed since the end of the absolute monarchy, he holds moral sway over the population of the country. Generally the king has remained quiet on political matters, though after more than 60 years on the throne, he is much respected by the people and perceived as a moral leader. It could be said that his opinions can affect the direction that his country takes, and there is a certain degree of reassurance provided when major governmental changes are made with royal assent.

The country has only recently returned to a democratically elected government following a military coup in September 2006. After over a year of military rule, a new constitution was approved in 2007, shortly after which parliamentary elections were held, with Samak Sundaravej elected prime minister and forming his cabinet in December 2008. Samak lost the post just four months later and Abhisit Vejjajiva became prime minister.

ORGANIZATION

The executive branch essentially consists of the king, the prime minister, and the other ministers who do not necessarily have to be elected members of parliament. The Council of Ministers, or Cabinet, are in day-to-day control of the government and all of its activities, except those of the legislature itself and the separate entity of the courts and judicial system, and they meet regularly to establish government policy and prepare budgets for due consideration by the legislature. Along with their deputies, ministers head their respective departments and give policy direction to the permanent agency officials who supervise the actual work done by regular employees of the agency.

The legislative branch, otherwise known as Parliament or the National Assembly, has the primary responsibility of adopting laws to regulate Thai society, although all bills must be signed into law by the king. It consists of two bodies, the Senate and the House of Representatives, each with their own secondary responsibilities and duties.

The Senate consists of 150 members, 74 of whom are appointed by a subcommittee of the Electoral Commission from about 500 applicants from a variety of professions, and 76 of whom are democratically elected to represent the 76 provinces of Thailand. They consider laws and bills previously approved in

LONGEST REINING MONARCH

On June 9, 2006, the entire country came to a standstill to celebrate the 60th anniversary of King Bhumibol's coronation. For days before and afterward almost everyone in the country wore shirts, scarves, or hats in yellow, the color signifying the day of the week the king was born. Twenty-five foreign kings, queens, princes, princesses, sheiks, and sultans, including Emperor Akihito and Empress Michiko of Japan, Prince Albert of Monaco, Britain's Prince Andrew, and Crown Prince Jigme Khesar of Bhutan, traveled to Thailand to join in the celebration of the king's reign, at 60 years the longest-reigning monarch alive today.

Unsurprisingly, the festivities were fit for a king. In an amazing display, the Royal Barges, 52 elegant wooden boats elaborated carved to resemble mythical creatures and manned by more than 2,000 oarsmen, proceeded in perfect formation along the Chao Phraya for the first time in decades. The king's public address from the balcony of the Anantasamakom Throne Hall was attended by an estimated 1 million Thais, all wearing yellow and shouting "Long live the king." The adoration of the monarch reached a near fever pitch at all levels of society.

Bhumibol was born in Cambridge, Massachusetts, when his father, a prince and half-brother of King Rama VI, was studying public health at Harvard University. Never a likely candidate for the throne, he spent most of his early life studying in Switzerland and learning to play the saxophone. His older brother, Rama VIII, took the throne at age nine shortly after Thailand became a constitutional monarchy, but when he mysteriously died of a gunshot wound to the head in 1946, Bhumibol, just 18 at the time and still in college in Lausanne, became king. He switched his courses from sciences to political science and law, finished his degree, and returned to Thailand to assume his duties as king.

Though there were two kings before him who ruled briefly as constitutional monarchs, it has been King Bhumibol who has shaped the role that the Thai monarchy plays in a democratic society. With limited political powers, his time on the throne has been largely dedicated to the development of rural Thailand and to improving the lives of the country's poor. He has often traveled throughout the country visiting remote villages and promoting sustainable development projects, work that recently earned him a United Nations Human Development Lifetime Achievement Award. In the portraits that adorn the walls of nearly every home and businesses in Thailand, the king is often pictured not in full regalia

the lower House of Representatives, inspect and control the administration of state affairs, and approve or remove people in higher positions of power.

The House of Representatives contains 480 seats, with 400 occupied by members of parliament democratically elected from electoral constituencies and 80 based on proportional party lists from groupings of votes in the provinces. One party sits in sole majority or in coalition with other parties, and the opposition is any parties not in the governing party or coalition. The house

© SUZANNE NAM

King Bhumibol is revered in Thailand.

but rather dressed normally, out in the countryside talking to villagers, pencil in hand and camera around his neck.

It is perhaps for this reason that the king, despite having little political power, has become such an important figure in Thai life. He has rarely involved himself in political matters or even offered an opinion on whether prime ministers or military coup-makers were taking the country down the right path, and it is often said that the king is "above politics." During times of political crisis, however, he has played a critical role: In 1973 and 1992 he intervened to end violence during uprisings against military rulers.

People differ in their political ideologies, on whether the most recent coup d'état was a good thing or a bad thing, and whether Thailand should be more protectionist or less so, but no one will ever criticize the king. The fact that it's illegal may be part of it; the Thai government recently blocked the popular video website YouTube because it contained material they deemed insulting to the king. But even in private, most people will point to everything he has done for the country in his lifetime.

selects a prime minister from among its members to administer state affairs. It has the general duties of approving legislation to be brought in front of the Senate, inspection and control of the administration of state affairs and expenditure, and representing the people.

The direct administration of Bangkok and Pattaya come under elected governors, whilst appointed governors administer the other 74 provinces, with these being broken down into districts, sub-districts and villages for purposes of local management. At the village level, a mayor or *poo yai baan* will be elected by the people subject to approval by the central government, and often they are the first contact for settlement of minor disputes within the community before the matter is brought to the attention of the higher authorities.

POLITICAL PARTIES

At the present time the dominant party is the People's Power Party, which was formed from the ashes of the Thai Rak Thai party, the political party of the previously deposed prime minister, Thaksin Shinawatra. Despite questions over Thaksin's administration, Thai Rak Thai attracted a great deal of support among the people due to its populist policies, including debt suspension and universal health care for the poor, low-cost housing for those with low incomes, and the prosperous economy under his leadership.

The leader of the People's Power Party, Samak Sundaravej, openly declared himself to be Thaksin's proxy and so won a considerable amount of support from fans of Thaksin, though this was still insufficient for him to take an outright majority in the December 2007 elections. A coalition was eventually

IS THAILAND SAFE?

Since the 2006 coup d'état made headlines around the world, people have been wondering if Thailand is still a safe place to live. While it's true that Thailand has been undergoing a period of sustained intense political instability that started in 2005 and has shown no signs of stopping, protests and demonstrations have been remarkably peaceful, and violent incidents few and far between. Even the November 2008 storming of the airport by then-government opposition members (whose politicians are currently in power and are the subject of major opposition demonstrations themselves), while disruptive and inconvenient for Thais and foreigners, was relatively peaceful.

While there is no guarantee that the situation won't take a turn for the worse, bear in mind that foreigners have never been targeted by anyone involved in the unrest. However, during the protests in early 2010, the U.S. State Department advised Americans that they should not travel to Bangkok unless absolutely necessary.

As a foreigner and someone who probably does not speak Thai fluently, it is important to keep abreast of local politics enough to know when and where political demonstrations will be and whether there are any legitimate safety concerns. Both the *Bangkok Post* and the *Nation* cover politics and current events, and while neither can be considered an objective news source, scanning the headlines will give you a good sense of what's going on. Also, make sure to register with your embassy (if you have privacy concerns, you do not need to give your real name) online so that you will receive email updates and warnings.

formed with a number of smaller parties, and Thaksin's populist projects continued, along with drives to improve the economy through making the country's production sector more competitive, laying a strong social foundation for the future, and an unequivocal war on drugs.

The party's coalition partners were smaller parties receiving between 2 percent and 10 percent of the overall votes; most had similar election platforms of populist policies with core conservative and royalist ideals.

Thailand's political parties are currently in a state of flux. The People's Power Party, which was formed from the ashes of the Thai Rak Thai Party, was dissolved by the Constitutional Court in December 2008 because of instances of electoral fraud in a verdict that many outside of Thailand viewed as suspiciously well-timed considering the political turmoil the country was undergoing at the time.

Many of the party's MPs were also banned from holding political office for five years in that same ruling. Pheu Thai (meaning for Thais), which was formed just a couple of months before the court ruling, is the successor party to the People's Power Party and most of the MPs who were not banned from holding office have switched their affiliation to that party.

As a result of the banning of many of the People's Power Party MPs from office, the current ruling party is now the Democrat Party, led by Abhisit Vejjajiva. The Democrat party rules as the result of a coalition of smaller parties, many of whom had been in coalition with the People's Power Party before.

The Royalist People's Party, Thais United National Development Party, and Neutral Democrats Party were formed mostly by former allies of Thaksin, reflected in their very similar platforms to the People's Power Party. The For the Motherland Party was formed by a combination of Thaksin's opponents and supporters and has a much more centrist manifesto with the slogan "Bring happiness and well-being to the people." The Thai Nation Party has a longer history than most and had been part of a coalition with Thai Rak Thai in 2001, but they fiercely opposed Thai Rak Thai in later years. Prior to the election there had been talk of mergers among some of these parties, so the coalition was not too surprising, but the Thai Nation Party in particular found themselves heavily criticized by voters when they joined the coalition in apparent defiance of their stated position against Thaksin and his cohorts.

Though the Democrat Party shares the populist policies and royalist conservative ideology of many other parties, they have remained steadfast in opposing much of what Thaksin stood for and what he has been accused of. In doing so they have won the support of areas of the country that did not directly benefit from Thaksin's policies, such as Bangkok and the south, but they have alienated voters in the poorer north and northeast.

POLITICAL ISSUES

Though there were clearly problems within the political processes in Thailand prior to the September 2006 coup, the army's action was met with a mixed response within Thailand and some condemnation from the international community. As democracy had been upheld in Thailand since the events of Black May in 1992, it was felt that the coup was a step backward.

The United Nations raised concerns over human rights, and the United States, the United Kingdom, the European Union, Australia, Malaysia, and New Zealand all voiced their misgivings. Others, including Japan and South Korea, looked for a successful resolution and a return to democracy, and China seemed almost unconcerned.

With the return to a democratically elected government in 2007, Thailand has once again become a full member of the international community, with previously suspended aid restarted and diplomatic relations reestablished. The prime minister is keen to foster strong relations with Thailand's neighbors and has already made visits to countries in the ASEAN group, including Cambodia and Laos, to introduce himself and his government's foreign policies, but he has yet to make an appearance on a broader world stage to further cement international relations.

Currently, Thailand's biggest trading partner is the United States, and the slowdown in the U.S. economy amid the ongoing credit crisis is having repercussions for Thailand. This is exacerbated by the soaring value of the baht, making exports more expensive and vastly reducing the spending power of tourists. The Thai economy is also affected by the increase in the price of oil. Though the government had stated that it is dedicated to creating a balanced economy immune to these troubles, by ensuring sustainable growth while improving the confidence of Thai and foreign investors, continued political instability has undermined the country's ability to achieve its growth potential.

Current proposals include hefty investments in Thailand's infrastructure, including improvements to Bangkok's mass transit system and a thorough overhaul of the national rail network, improvements to seaports and airports, and major irrigation projects. Domestic consumption is to be aided by funds allocated for the development of villages, an amendment to the lottery scheme to help raise capital, educational loans to poor students, debt assistance to farmers, guaranteed commodity prices, and increased protection against natural disasters. Analysts feel this will boost the economy but runs the risk of fueling inflation, which has not been well controlled for the last two years, and so the government might find itself walking a dangerous line in the short term.

Internal problems also remain, most notably the armed conflict in the far south, where more than 2,900 people have died in the last four years, making this the most lethal conflict in Southeast Asia at present. Political measures taken by previous governments have been considered ineffective, and military action has sometimes been considered brutal, but the conflict is no closer to resolution and rumors abound that the insurgents will take their action to more northerly provinces to make their voices heard.

The government has clearly stated its intention to resolve the unrest but without putting forward any specific proposals. Members of the government have suggested that some form of self-rule may be a possibility, but the possibility is minimal for regional autonomy in the near future.

In many ways, there is a feeling of rebirth around the governance of Thailand these days, even though many of the faces returning to positions of power have been seen before in the political arena. There is an opportunity for a fresh start and a move into a more stable political era, but there is just as much likelihood that old mistakes will be repeated and the latest round of changes will be little more than a false start.

JUDICIAL AND PENAL SYSTEMS

The Courts of First Instance deal with all legal matters in Thailand, with civil, criminal, and provincial courts adjudicating on general matters, issues involving juveniles and family concerns, and specialized areas such as bankruptcy and taxes. Bangkok has many district courts dealing with criminal cases as well as three main civil courts, including municipal courts that deal only with minor cases that can be handled quickly. All other provinces have at least one provincial court that exercises unlimited jurisdiction, and all cases in the province are considered there. At least one judge presides over a case with no supporting jury, though in some matters a quorum of up to four judges may be established, depending on the severity and complexity of the case.

Each region also has a Court of Appeal, and a quorum of three judges, including one Chief Justice, will hear every case. The next and last step is for a case to be referred to the Supreme Court, where a quorum of three judges presides, with the president of the Supreme Court playing a personal role in some judicial matters.

It is widely understood that any prison sentence in Thailand is a very unpleasant experience, and the bookstores at the airports will usually have a few first-hand accounts of the treatment that can be expected. The notorious

© SUZANNE NAM

Government House in Bangkok, where the country's parliament meets

Bangkwang jail, or Bangkok Hilton, houses a number of long-term foreign prisoners who are often there as a result of drug offenses, sometimes with sentences of over 50 years. They live alongside Thai murderers and drug dealers who have avoided the death sentence, which is often meted out but usually commuted except in severe or high-profile cases.

The effectiveness of policing at the local level varies. Thailand has recently been at the center of some internationally coordinated arrests, and there is no doubt that the very highest standards of policing can be seen here. It also should be remembered that the average salary of a local police officer is relatively low, and that stories of on-the-spot fines or outright solicitations for bribes are common. Consequently it can seem that crimes at almost any level can be paid off with a substantial donation to the police or, where appropriate, even to the victim's family.

Although this does little to encourage a sense of justice being done, it does mean that it is possible to pay for minor misdemeanors to be overlooked. Police in tourist areas have understood this for many years, and tourists faced with the official 50,000-baht fine and deportation or even a jail sentence for a minor drug bust might prefer to take the option of a large cash fine. However, unsuccessfully attempting to bribe a police officer would probably have very dire consequences, and this course of action is not recommended.

Economy

Thailand's economy experienced unprecedented growth in the 1960s and 1970s, making it one of the world's fastest-growing economies at that time, laying the foundation for a diversified open-market capitalist economy and propelling the country from underdeveloped to middle-income status by the 1990s.

Although the days of the "Asian Tiger" economy and the high growth rates that went with it are over, Thailand's economy is still one of the strongest in Southeast Asia, with its per capita GDP topped only by Singapore, Malaysia, and Hong Kong. Much of the economic growth has been export driven, and the country has moved from agriculture and relatively cheap, unskilled labor–intensive manufacturing to more sophisticated, value-added exports (although labor-intensive manufacturing still makes up a significant portion of the economy). The Asian Financial Crisis of 1997 stalled development—the devaluation of the baht on June 30, 1997, triggered the region-wide financial collapse—but after massive debt restructuring and a US$17 billion helping hand from the International Monetary Fund, Thailand's economy was able to bounce back and has continued to grow at average yearly rates above 5 percent despite high oil prices, the political uncertainty that began in 2006, and the global economic downturn that started in late 2008.

During the decades of significant growth, the government of Thailand also began tackling income disparity (though critics say they haven't done enough),

© SUZANNE NAM

Despite development, much of the country gets by on a few dollars a day

expanding social services and building infrastructure. While income disparity is extreme and there are millions living on barely enough to get by, Thai citizens have universal access to public education through high school and access to inexpensive government medical care. Most communities are served by the country's well-maintained and efficient highway system and have clean running water and other basic infrastructure.

Agriculture continues to dominate the country's economy, and nearly 50 percent of GDP comes from the farming of rice, sugarcane, tapioca, rubber, soybeans, coconuts, and other agricultural products. Thailand is one of the world's largest exporters of rice and a lead producer of fisheries products, including shrimp and canned tuna. Other natural resources such as natural gas also contribute significantly to the country's GDP.

In 2008 unemployment was reported at just 1.4 percent of the labor force, making it one of the strongest economies in the world in those terms, but that number is misleading: Much of the work force is employed informally, so true unemployment is most likely significantly higher.

PEOPLE AND CULTURE

One of Thailand's many strengths as a home away from home is the exuberance with which most Thai people approach life and the relaxed, welcoming way they deal with foreigners. Visitors who come to Thailand on vacation are often charmed by Thai culture and Thai people. Visitors who relocate here find them that much more alluring. In fact, the few gripes you may hear about Thailand, such as scams and aggressive touting, won't be a problem at all if you're here to live rather than on vacation.

Generalizations are tempting, and there are many to be made about Thai people and Thai culture, such as that everyone is Buddhist, that the culture is permissive, and that they can't "handle" Western-style democracy. On the surface, these may all seem true, but as in any culture, things aren't as simple or transparent as they appear on the surface. Thailand is predominantly Buddhist, but the Buddhism practiced by most is deeply entwined with Hinduism and animism, and the far south of the country is predominantly Muslim. Thais seem to turn a blind eye toward the strip clubs and go-go bars that flagrantly

© SUZANNE NAM

violate the law, yet across social classes most Thais are conservative in dress and behavior. Thailand has suffered from decades of political instability and coup d'état after coup d'état, but never has the citizenry been as politically well informed as it is today.

As you get to know the country, draw conclusions carefully. Just as it would be difficult to understand the culture and people of the United States by observing New York City for a few months, Thai culture has many facets. Foreigners who make blanket statements about Thai people or Thai culture after having lived here for only a short time are often wrong.

People

Current estimates place the population of Thailand around 65 million, with 31 percent of those living in urban areas while the remainder live in poorer rural areas around the country. The area around Bangkok officially contains some 10 million residents, and the city itself claims to be home to around 6 million Bangkokians, making it by far the most populous place in Thailand, well ahead of Chiang Mai, which has around 250,000 city inhabitants and 1.3 million in the surrounding province.

The population is split almost evenly between men and women, though the spread widens in the older population, with 55 percent of over-65s being female. This is reflected in mean life expectancies: Men live an average 70.2 years, women generally outlive them by nearly half a decade to 75.0 years. During their lives the average woman will give birth to 1.64 children, providing an annual population growth of just 0.626 percent. This has declined dramatically from 3.1 percent in 1960, particularly in the last few years. For now, nearly 25 percent of the population is under age 15, but in due course decreasing birthrates will create an aging population.

Though the average annual wage is officially quoted as 250,000 baht, the legal minimum wage can be as low as 55,000 baht per year. In addition, the fact that the minimum legal wage is not always paid results in unskilled workers in impoverished regions working full days of heavy labor for as little as 100 baht a day. Officially, 10 percent of the population lives in poverty and just 1.4 percent are classed as being unemployed, and there are currently no standard government subsidies to help them.

IMMIGRATION

The Indians were the first visitors from distant lands who settled here in the 1st century A.D. as merchants and to spread the Buddhist religion; the next major influx was in the 13th century when Chinese from Yunnan fled the threat of the Mongol empire and settled under the protection of the Thai king. These migrations were nothing, however, compared to the numbers of Chinese who arrived between 18th century and the 1920s: More than 100,000 were settling in Thailand each year, and stricter immigration laws had to be introduced. Nowadays migrant workers come from Burma, China, Cambodia, and Laos to work in factories, agriculture, and homes, with around 1.3 million working legally and up to 700,000 working without permits.

The wars in Southeast Asia from the 1960s led to large-scale refugee issues, with 600,000 Cambodians, 320,000 Laotians, and 158,000 Vietnamese displaced and seeking asylum in Thailand. Nearly all of them were eventually repatriated or settled in other countries, but a small number still remain. More recently, refugees from persecution have been arriving from Burma, with nearly 150,000 of the Karen people currently living long-term in refugee camps near the Burmese border. These people are part of a larger group of ethnic minorities that live in Thailand, including the various hill groups in the north of the country whose somewhat nomadic lifestyle has been restricted both by tighter border controls and an unwelcoming attitude from other Thais and people in neighboring countries.

Thais do chose to migrate from Thailand; this practice essentially started in the 1970s, when professionals could earn much higher salaries in more developed countries such as the United States, and it continued through the 1980s when skilled workers were attracted by the opportunities available in the oil-producing regions of the Middle East. More recently the draw has been for Thai people at all levels to work in the prospering industrialized countries of Southeast Asia, with Taiwan in particular attracting professionals, semiskilled workers from fields such as transport, and even unskilled workers to work as domestic help. Large Thai communities have developed outside of Thailand, most notably in Los Angeles, which has a Thai population of around 200,000 and is jokingly referred to as "the 77th province of Thailand."

YOUNG THAIS

All Thais now receive free education for 12 years, with nine years' attendance being compulsory. This has resulted in the literacy levels of 15-year-olds improving from 71 percent in 1960 to 92 percent today. University education

THE SEX INDUSTRY

Although prostitution in Thailand is illegal, it's impossible not to notice the red-light districts, go-go bars, and sex workers (often referred to as "bar girls") populating many of the nightlife spots in Bangkok. The blind eye that authorities seem to turn to these activities has become something more like a full face-mask. There are rarely crackdowns or arrests; neighborhoods such as Phat Phong, Nana, and Soi Cowboy seem to exist solely to cater to prurient interests; and there are no signs that anything will change any time soon.

Bangkok gained its notorious reputation during the Vietnam War, when the city became an R&R spot for U.S. servicemen on leave. It was during this period that Phat Phong went from a normal commercial neighborhood to one filled with massage parlors and hostess bars. Sex is still big business here, as is evident in the hordes of tourists who flock to these places on a nightly basis.

Dancers working in the go-go bars and strip clubs in Bangkok typically earn a salary of about 6,000 baht per month, which is augmented by tips and whatever else they can earn; the women working in bars earn significantly less. Most emigrated from Isan and other poorer rural parts of Thailand looking for an opportunity to make more money, and they often support whole families back home from the money they earn.

The problem is not one solely created by foreigners, however. Prostitution existed in Thailand long before any Western influence arrived, and it flourishes in areas where there are no foreigners. Whether this is due to the money it generates, the permissive nature of Buddhism, or other cultural factors is up for debate. What is not up for debate is that despite all indications to the contrary, it is illegal in Thailand.

is not individually subsidized, apart from some scholarships that are offered, and it remains prohibitively expensive for many, with associated costs of 150,000 baht per year. Nevertheless, around 12 percent of students go on to complete the minimum four years for a graduate degree, which is almost essential for any progressive career in social sciences or business. These lines of work account for some 37 percent of regular employment, with industry accounting for around 14 percent, and the remaining 49 percent associated with agriculture.

With a lack of work experience, income levels depend greatly on qualifications. Young unskilled workers receive as little as 3,500 baht per month, skilled workers can earn up to 5,000 baht, police and teachers start at 6,500 baht, and a new university graduate could realistically earn 8,000 baht or more in Bangkok. Employment in the capital, however, involves higher living costs, with a minimum apartment rent around 5,000 baht per month, compared to less than 2,000 baht in rural towns. Alternatively, nearly every

Thai male has the opportunity to enter the armed forces either as a volunteer or as a conscript, although this is only really a viable long-term career path for commissioned officers.

Young people are particularly at risk from untimely death: Motorcycle accidents account for over 30 deaths and 400 injuries every day, with most of these being young males, and 1.3 percent of the population under the age of 25 has HIV/AIDS, resulting in around 50,000 deaths every year. These numbers have fallen greatly following past government campaigns, and now the government is looking at other problems that may affect youth. Alcohol advertising has essentially been banned, and alcohol sales are becoming more restricted, which is also the case with cigarettes. The war on drugs has recently been resurrected, with the main target being cheap methamphetamine from Burma and Cambodia, called *yah bah,* which is becoming increasingly available and popular.

WESTERNIZATION

Since the years after World War II, Thailand has seen an increase in the influence of the West and a corresponding decline in traditional Thai ways of life. Financial aid from the United States started in the 1950s and helped to accelerate economic development, but this led to an increase in people leaving their home villages and migrating to urban areas to work. One eventual effect of rapid economic growth was a greater reliance on money rather than the produce of the land, and a corresponding increase in personal debt. Neither of these could be sustained when the economic problems of the 1990s arrived; this period saw migrant workers losing their jobs and families losing their land to bank foreclosures. The bigger problem for Thailand is that although agriculture accounts for nearly half of the economy, as the country grows richer, few people want to continue working as subsistence farmers without accumulating wealth and moving up the

Westerners have difficulty integrating fully into Thai society.

social ladder. This dissatisfaction goes hand in hand with development, but the government is still struggling to provide the right mix of policies to maintain balance.

Tourism started to bring different influences in the 1960s, which also saw an increased presence of U.S. troops in certain areas, which further shaped the development of the country. Both generated income in different ways and in greater amounts than ever before, with tourism becoming a vital part of Thailand's economy over the subsequent 30 years.

This had a profound effect on seaside villages that had subsisted on fishing for hundreds of years; villagers now finding their homes quickly being transformed. People who had led simple lives and were deeply reserved in many ways were suddenly exposed to the money and morals of a significantly different group of people: foreign tourists.

As beautiful areas of Thailand have been paved over with concrete and English has almost taken over as the most common language in some places, many argue that some element of the people of Thailand has been lost. Others would say that these changes are inevitable in a globalizing world, that people constantly adjust their ways—not always a bad thing—and that ultimately we should look to the people themselves to see how they feel about the changes to their lives.

And though some Thais may complain and some may be regretful, many more accept the way life has changed and just get on with things in a happy and carefree way—as you'd expect in a country known as the Land of Smiles.

Ethnicity and Class

ETHNICITY

At present, 75 percent of the population of Thailand consider themselves to be of Thai descent; 14 percent are of Chinese heritage; 3 percent are Malays, who make up the majority of the population in the far south; and 8 percent are others, including people of Khmer descent and the smaller ethnic groups that live in northern Thailand.

To most Westerners, especially those who have not spent much time in Asia, Thailand appears to be a very ethnically homogeneous place where everyone just looks "Thai." As you spend more time in the country, however, and look more closely at the people of Thailand, ethnic differences become more evident. Thailand is less a homogeneous society and more a variegated mixture of cultures and ethnicities from across the region. Some Thai people have broad features characteristic of Khmer people, some are quite fair and tall, others have darker complexions and are smaller in stature.

Initially you may not notice these differences, but you can bet that everyone in Thailand is aware of them. The country is not entirely stratified by ethnicity, but ethnicity does influence the way some people think about individuals, and there are plenty of ethnic stereotypes and prejudices kicking around Thailand.

Chinese Thais make up a significant portion of the population, and their influence is felt all over the country.

Like many other countries in the region, a fair complexion is considered attractive, and at any drugstore or beauty counter you'll find a confusing array of "whitening" creams, lotions, and treatments designed to keep the skin from looking too brown. Men aren't immune either: There are even whitening deodorants marketed to them.

SOCIAL CLASS

Given that Thailand evolved from an aristocratic society with peasants and slaves into a democracy over the past 100 years, it's not surprising that the country has a stratified class structure that is influenced to some extent by ethnicity. The aristocracy in Thailand still exists, and certain family names, typically those that start with "Na," are connected in some way to the monarchy. Unsurprisingly, these families tend to have significant accumulated wealth and property compared to the rest of the society. They are also more likely to be involved in government than the average Thai.

Class issues have played a significant role in the political instability that Thailand has been dealing with since the 2006 coup d'état that ousted Prime Minister Thaksin Shinawatra. Wildly popular Thaksin was seen by his supporters as pro-poor and pro–working class. His opposition, who ultimately engineered his downfall, is seen as elites, aristocrats, and urbanites who meddle with the democratic process if things don't turn out the way they want. Whether any or all of this is true isn't as important as the social rift that appears to be deepening.

Although social classes are not entirely rigid, for many in the lower classes, social mobility is nonexistent. There are a few stories of entrepreneurs who started as street vendors and became millionaires; for the most part, laborers and other unskilled workers have little hope of moving beyond those professions. Worse off are the migrant workers in Thailand, mostly from Burma, who work illegally at very low wages paid under the table. This is really Thailand's underclass; they have little legal protection and no right to education for their children, who often come with them.

OUTSIDERS

In everyday casual interactions, Thai people treat Westerners with a degree of openness not seen in most other parts of the world. Walk into any bar full of locals in the middle of Thailand and you'll most likely get smiles and curious questions. If you're friendly, by the time the night is over, someone will have bought you a drink. Attempting to speak Thai, even poorly, will get you accolades and encouragement (and perhaps a few giggles). It's not that Thai people aren't proud of being Thai, but they are not jingoistic or suspicious of the rest of the world.

If you're interested in fully integrating into Thai society, though, you will hit many obstacles. To draw a very broad generalization, Thai people still consider themselves Thai and the rest of the world not Thai. If you are a white non-Buddhist Westerner, no one will ever think of you as Thai (only a handful of foreigners have ever become Thai citizens), and most will keep you at some distance socially or emotionally. This might be one of the hardest challenges of living in Thailand for an extended period of time. It's difficult to make close friends among Thai people who aren't already somewhat internationalized.

Customs and Etiquette

SOCIAL BEHAVIOR
The *Wai*

You can't go more than 10 minutes in Thailand without noticing people putting their hands together in a prayer-like gesture and bowing their heads to each other. Although this isn't a casual greeting, it is a sign of respect and will almost always be used to greet elders, teachers, bosses, and even hotel guests. The *wai* is an important social gesture, and for a Thai person, the absence of a *wai* when otherwise called for can be taken as a serious breach of etiquette. As a foreigner you won't necessarily be expected to use it in business situations where it would otherwise be appropriate—a handshake works fine—but if you visit someone's home and meet their parents, talk to a monk, or find yourself in a similar situation, make sure to *wai* as a greeting. Though a basic *wai* is easy to do, the level at which you hold your hands will vary depending on the amount of respect you want to show the recipient. Until you understand the nuances of the motion, it is best to keep the *wai* somewhere around face level. In general, only *wai* people who are older than you or otherwise should be accorded respect; *wai*-ing little children in response to their *wai* is a bit of a social gaffe. What if your hands are full? There is no need to drop your bags, but make the gesture even if it's imperfect. Remember, though, that Thai Muslims for the most part do not *wai*.

Daily Conduct

Another thing you'll notice immediately upon arriving (well, maybe once you leave the airport) is the general level of politeness in the country. The use of polite particles *ka* and *kap* is nearly universal; people will greet you when you walk into a restaurant or step into a taxi; and when someone bumps into you on a crowded street or even in a nightclub, chances are they'll say "excuse me" or apologize with a smile. A *mai pen rai* attitude, which

Even Ronald *wais* in Thailand.

© SUZANNE NAM

THAI NAMES

In Thailand, everyone from your building manager to the CEO of the company you work for is on a first-name basis. While you may be used to referring to people in formal situations as "Mr." and "Ms.," in Thailand referring to someone by their last name would just be considered strange.

There are still some very important rules of etiquette to observe when addressing people. As a general rule, put the word *khun* before anyone's first name, whether you are addressing them directly or in the third person. If the person is older than you, use *pi* before their name, and if the person is younger, use *nong*. If you don't know the person's name (if you're addressing a shop clerk, waitress, etc.) use either *pi* or *nong* on its own. All of these rules apply for both men and women.

To make things more confusing, nearly everyone in Thailand has a nickname. You may have a nickname too, but it's probably a diminutive of your formal name, so it's pretty easy to figure out who you are on the office contact list. In Thailand, nicknames often have absolutely nothing to do with full names. So your colleague Boom may really be named Gannita, but everyone will call her Boom (or Khun Boom, Pi Boom, or Nong Boom), and that's how she'll introduce herself. This isn't really a problem until you need to send someone an email and realize you have no idea what the recipient's formal name is!

loosely translates as "no worries," pervades casual social interactions, and acting aggressive and impatient will generally get you nowhere fast.

Although it's difficult to make generalizations and exceptions always occur, Thais are extremely friendly, social, and curious people, especially when it comes to foreigners. Don't be surprised if the taxi driver you just met wants to know whether you're married, how many children you have, even your salary. There's no offense meant—it is just friendly banter, and you should take the opportunity to ask questions about the other person's life too.

It might seem counterintuitive if you've ever seen a Thai go-go bar, but Thais are usually reserved and conservative in their behavior in public. *Conformist* may be too strong a word, but there is a propensity to behave in a manner that does not rock the boat. Very strange behavior or dress can make people uncomfortable, although they may be too polite to express that discomfort to you.

Etiquette

There are a few important etiquette rules you need to remember when living in Thailand besides general politeness and respect. Do not criticize the monarchy or have more than a basic conversation about the king. In a small circle of close friends you would be able to have such a discussion, but most people will take great offense. The king is generally revered, it is illegal to speak out against him, and foreigners are not above prosecution. Twice a day, at 8 A.M. and 6 P.M., the king's anthem is played on loudspeakers in every city. Do as those around you do, and stop where you are until the music is finished. If you go to a movie in a cinema, you are required to stand when the brief film about the king is played.

Also refrain from pointing your feet at anyone, especially at an image of Buddha in a temple, and don't touch anyone on the head except for small children. Finally, you are expected to give up your seat to

© SUZANNE NAM

Take your shoes off before entering temples and most people's homes.

a monk if you are riding on public transportation, and there are even some reserved seats for them on trains and boats. Women are not allowed to touch monks, or vice versa, but the onus will fall on you to get out of the way if contact seems imminent.

Public Displays of Affection

In general, Thais are very affectionate in public but not in a sexual manner. It's quite common to see two girls holding hands, even in their teens; parents hugging and kissing kids; and friends with their arms around each other. What is not common is seeing people hugging and kissing in a nonplatonic way.

SOCIAL CUSTOMS
Meals

Thailand's love affair with food ensures that you can generally eat whenever you want to without worrying about offending anyone (the one place you can't eat, however, is on the Bangkok subway or Skytrain). **Breakfast** is available anytime from 7 A.M. onward. For locals, this may consist of a bowl of *jok* with crispy fried cruller slices, a soft-boiled egg, cilantro, and slivers of ginger or some noodles, although lots of people will take a more Western-style coffee and baked item instead, and you'll find plenty of street vendors in big cities selling sweet waffles and other familiar breakfast treats.

Lunch is generally eaten between 11 A.M. and 2 P.M. If it's a workday and you happen to be in a city around this time, you'll notice throngs of people coming out of their offices for their afternoon meal. It's almost unheard of for Thais to pack a lunch. And why would you? Chances are there's plenty of food to choose from. During the week, lunch is often a social event, and casual restaurants and street vendors' tables will be full of work colleagues or groups of college students enjoying a meal together.

Dinner is as important as lunch, and you'll also find popular street food areas packed full of families and friends from around 7 P.M. on. In larger cities you can get a meal in a restaurant any time between 6 P.M. and midnight, but places in more rural or less populated areas will probably close earlier.

Snacking is nearly a national pastime. If you drop into anyone's office, you'll probably see a little corner set aside just for snacks, which can range from grilled fish balls to cookies to traditional *khanom Thai.* You'll also find food vendors around the office throughout the day. In many offices, people bring snacks to share with their colleagues, and there is almost always a designated spot in the kitchen or break room where communal snacks go. A small gesture can go a long way in creating bonds with workmates and subordinates, so bring treats for the office at least once in a while.

© SUZANNE NAM

Food is an essential part of Thai culture; you can't go far without finding a place to eat.

Gender Roles

Thailand is a traditional but increasingly progressive society when it comes to gender roles. Thai women hold cabinet positions and seats in the legislature; they are the country's scientists, doctors, and engineers; and they work in finance and business. Pass any construction site and you're likely to see women digging trenches, hauling sand, or engaging in other forms of manual labor that some might consider "man's work." Women have equal access to education and enroll and complete programs through graduate school at nearly the same rate as men. But, they're also usually the primary caregivers of children and of elderly parents. Women manage the household and, of course, are expected to look pretty and feminine. While many career paths are open to women, there are few female chief executives of large companies or managing directors of banks. The military, an important political institution in Thailand, is virtually all male at the upper echelons. In sum, Thai women face the same issues that women all over the world face.

There are also some peculiarly Asian gender issues in Thailand. Job applicants are asked to submit photographs and provide height and weight information, and some help-wanted advertisements will even specify that female applicants should be slender and not wear glasses. Although the practice is less and less common (and is illegal), wealthier men will sometimes take more than one wife or have long-term mistresses, while women are not socially permitted more than one husband. Prostitution is not uncommon in Thailand, and it exists not just in touristed areas frequented by foreigners.

GAY AND LESBIAN CULTURE

Thailand has an extremely progressive and tolerant view toward homosexuality, and it may be one of the most open societies in the world when it comes to transsexuality. Especially in urban areas, it is completely ordinary to see same-sex couples walking hand in hand, and many gays and lesbians, especially in the younger generation, don't often feel compelled to hide their sexual orientation from their friends or families. For whatever reason, the creative sector tends to attract a large number of gay men. There are numerous clubs and neighborhoods in all major cities that are either completely gay or mixed, and in general, no one at any "straight" club will bat an eye if a same-sex couple enters.

Transsexuality is common in Thailand, and you're likely to see *katoey* (the Thai word for a transsexual male) working as waitresses, store clerks, travel agents, and in other service-oriented businesses. Many *katoey* go to great lengths to look very feminine, to the point that it is difficult for most people to tell

LADYBOYS

Dressed to perfection with silky, shiny hair down to her shoulders, a miniskirt up to her thighs, and an enchanting smile accentuated with just the right touch of makeup, the sexy, ultrafeminine waitress serving you dinner is getting stares from every guy in the room. On closer inspection, the waitress seems a little taller than the average woman, her hips a little slimmer, her presentation a little more perfected...her voice a little deeper. Could it be that the woman everyone is looking at is actually a man? In Bangkok, the answer is an unqualified "yes."

Though no one knows the exact numbers, it's safe to say Bangkok is home to thousands of *katoey* or *ladyboys*, men who either live as women, are in the process of undergoing gender reassignment, or have completed the transformation. *Katoey* take women's names and will always use the feminine particle *ka* instead of the masculine *kap* when speaking.

While there are transvestites all over the world, the extent of the phenomenon is unique to Thailand. Homosexuality is generally well tolerated, especially in the big cities, and won't be viewed as out of the ordinary by many people. Open transsexuality, still taboo in many cultures, is also far more accepted here, and it's more commonplace in Bangkok than in any other city in the world. Discrimination still exists, but you are likely to see *katoey* working in retail shops, in offices, and in hotels and restaurants.

The art of illusion is particularly well practiced in Thailand, where some of the biggest and most prestigious hospitals offer a myriad of procedures to transform men into women. As a result, many of the *ladyboys* in the city are amazingly beautiful and convincing.

Despite the widespread practice and general level of acceptance, it would be inaccurate to say that the life of a *katoey* is not filled with challenges. The movie *Beautiful Boxer,* based on the life of *muay Thai* champion Parinya Charoenphol, is a wonderful, heartbreaking, and uplifting story about a young boy in the provinces born believing he was meant to be a woman. By chance he turns to kickboxing as a way to earn enough money to become a woman, but learns that he loves the sport and remains a fighter through the transition. The international award-winning, beautifully filmed film chronicles his emotional journey from he to she set against a backdrop of kickboxing rounds and cabaret performances.

the difference. In fact, Thailand is the world leader in gender-reassignment surgery, and people travel here from all over the world for it.

Despite Thailand's tolerant stance on homosexuality, there is still some discrimination and prejudice towards gays, lesbians, and *katoey*. Few of the country's business and civic leaders are openly gay (and none are *katoey*), and some Thais in the older generation view anyone who isn't heterosexual as abnormal.

Religion

Buddhism is the dominant religion in Thailand, and nearly 95 percent of the country's population consider themselves Buddhists. Nearly all Thai Budhist men enter a monastery at some point in their lives to live as monks and strictly follow the tenets of Buddhism; most do it for just a month in their teens or early twenties. If you happen to be out between 5 A.M. and 7 A.M. any morning, you're likely to see monks clad in orange robes walking the streets and receiving donations of food from area residents. There are temples all over the country, and you'd be hard-pressed to find even a small village without one within walking distance or a quick ride. They can play a big role in the community, not only as places to practice Buddhism but as congregation points.

Buddhism pervades everyday life in Thailand, both in a physical sense because of its influence on art and architecture and in its influence on norms and behaviors. It is not the official religion, however, as Thailand is a secular state.

Islam is another significant religion in Thailand, and although Muslims make up less than 5 percent of the population, in the far south they outnumber Buddhists. There are also large populations of Muslims in other parts of southern Thailand and in Bangkok. Islam in Thailand traces its roots back to the 13th century, and Thai Muslims are overwhelmingly Sunni.

© SUZANNE NAM

Many Thai men enter the monastery at some point in their lives, even if just for a month.

The Arts

Throughout Thailand's long and diverse history, art has always played a key role in society, providing outlets for worship, educating the masses on Buddhist values, or glorifying national achievements. By looking at the country's varied artistic and architectural forms, one can trace Thai history back through the ages, with two major sources of inspiration—religion and monarchy—playing a continuous role, while a diverse mix of foreign influences have also slipped in. Even the tiniest temple in a rural village is often home to a wealth of artistic treasures, such as priceless Buddhist sculptures and murals depicting deeply entrenched religious beliefs.

Temples were the main source of art in Thailand for about 800 years, as every royal court made it a priority to build these ubiquitous religious structures to enshrine statues of Buddha. The walls were decorated with murals and intricate wooden carvings and lacquer work, reflecting the complex court culture and its heavy Indian influences. Today the nucleus of Thai art is Bangkok, where several quality museums feature classic and contemporary art from Thailand and abroad. Chiang Mai is becoming a major center for the arts in its own right, highlighted by collections of Lanna pieces from past and present depicting the unique culture of the region.

MAJOR ART EPOCHS
Mon Dvaravati Period

The Mon Dvaravati period is particularly notable, as it planted the first artistic seed in Thailand, influencing the various styles that would later emerge. Dvaravati art was the product of the Mon communities that ruled Thailand from the 7th through the 11th centuries, prior to the arrival of the Khmers. Most art forms produced during this period were sculptures made of stone, terra-cotta, bronze, and stucco, influenced by Hinayana and Mahayana Buddhist and Hindu religious subjects. Perhaps the most distinctive Dvaravati sculpture is the Wheel of Law, a symbol of the Buddha's first sermon erected on high pillars that is still today placed in temple compounds. Fine examples of Dvaravati art can be found in Bangkok's National Museum and the Jim Thompson Museum.

Sukhothai Period

One of the most prominent Thai kingdoms was Sukhothai, established in 1238. Its art was heavily influenced by Theravada Buddhism, merging human form with the spiritual. Images of Buddha and ceramics were the most popular art

© SUZANNE NAM

Much of Thailand's art is devotional in nature.

forms, and sculptures were characterized by elegant bodies and slender oval faces. Emphasizing the spiritual aspect of Buddha by leaving out anatomical details, the effect was enhanced by casting images in metal as opposed to carving them. Brick and stucco images of Buddha can still be found in the ruins of the Sukhothai Historical Park, while many examples of art from this period were moved to the National Museum in Bangkok.

Ayutthaya Period

An era spanning 400 years, from 1351 to 1767, the Ayutthaya kingdom spawned a wide variety of art forms, influenced by everyone from the Khmers and Chinese to the Japanese and Europeans, a by-product of mid-16th-century trade and diplomacy. The early Ayutthaya period reflects Dvaravati and Lopburi influences, featuring images of Buddha carved primarily of stone, while paintings featured only red, black, and white coloring with rows of juxtaposed Buddhas. Due to the destruction and pilfering of the Ayutthaya kingdom by the Burmese, few artifacts of this period remain, however some examples of Ayutthaya art can be found at the Suan Pakkad Palace and National Museum in Bangkok, as well as Wat Rajaburana in Ayutthaya.

Lanna Period

In the 15th century, the northern region of Thailand began to flourish in what is referred to as the Lanna era. This was the golden age of Chiang Mai, when King Tilokaraja ruled and great emphasis was placed on the arts. The word lanna translates to "land of 1 million rice fields," and its art is characterized by Burmese, Laotian, and Sukhothai influences, though it boasts a distinct identity of its own. Lanna people were considered a gentle and sweet group, a stereotype that remains today. Many works are based on the artists' natural surroundings and feature paintings of flowers, leaves, and outdoor scenes. Lanna murals depict cultural traditions, including ceremonies, festivals, and ordinary activities in the village as well as religious Dharma images. Local artisans today keep the Lanna tradition alive by creating reproductions; workshops and retailers can be found throughout Chiang Mai.

Rattanakosin Period

The Rattanakosin period—also referred to as the Bangkok era—was born with the Chakri Dynasty that still rules today, founded after the collapse of Ayutthaya in 1767. Art from this era is characterized by two themes: the promotion of the classical Siamese traditions under the reigns of three kings, Rama I, II, and III, followed by the rule of Rama IV, when Western elements found their way into Thai art. Initially the art scene during the Bangkok era was focused on salvaging what was left from the pillaged war-ravaged areas, and new pieces of art continued in this vein. Later, however, ornamentation became a dominant factor, and images became more realistic. Murals began to flourish, as did the ornamentation of temples with colorful gilded images, statues, and intricate designs. For the best examples of art from the early Rattanakosin period, visit Wat Phra Kaeo and the Grand Palace in Bangkok.

Contemporary Art

Interestingly, the father of modern Thai art is actually a foreigner, an Italian sculptor named Corrado Feroci who was invited to Thailand by King Rama VI in 1924. Feroci created bronze statues of Thailand's past heroes, and in 1933 was asked to establish an institute of fine arts to instruct a new generation of artists in modern art. The school eventually became a university called the Silpakorn (Fine Arts) University, and Feroci's own name was changed to Silpa Bhirasri. He remained in Thailand until his death in 1962. With the introduction of modern art, painters began experimenting with impressionism and a bit of cubism. Today, Thailand's contemporary art scene is centered around Bangkok, with an increasing variety of works available on the market. Although many younger artists have departed from the religious themes of the past, there are still some who remain influenced by traditional Buddhist values, which tend to be more popular among the general public. Much to the dismay of the traditionalists, there are some Thai artists breaking away from these norms by addressing more controversial issues in their work, often stirring up public controversy in the process.

Famous Thai Artists

While few Thai artists have made a name for themselves on the international stage, there are several notable individuals who led the Thai art scene into uncharted territory, such as Angkarn Kalayanapongsa (born 1926) and Misiem Yipintsoi (1906–1988). Chakrabhand Posayakrit (born 1943) is also a groundbreaking artist, painting portraits that interpret classical themes in soft colors. Montien Boonma (1953–2000) was one of the only Thai artists to create a buzz overseas, his works appearing in many international exhibitions. Works by Montien reflect sections of Thai life that have undergone rapid change, and they employ local materials and motifs in an incredibly unique style. Most Thais will also recognize the name Chalermchai Kositpipat (born 1955), Thailand's most successful painter today. The Chiang Rai native's works have been exhibited worldwide, and in his art he is known for his innovative use of images of Buddha that often have raised eyebrows. Some say he has lost his confrontational edge, but nonetheless he is still admired by many high-profile clients, including His Majesty the King Bhumibol Adulyadej.

ARCHITECTURE

Fabulous teak mansions built high on stilts, golden palaces, colorful *wats,* and even quaint rows of shophouses built by Chinese immigrants are all major hues in Thailand's architectural palate. The country's history is heavily imprinted on its wide-ranging architectural gems, allowing for a developmental history of Thai society to be traced back in time. Because Thailand's capital kept changing location through the ages, several areas are home to the country's key architectural highlights, and contemporary architecture is mainly found in forward-thinking Bangkok.

Sukhothai

The Sukhothai period (13th–14th centuries) is regarded as the apex of Thai culture, advancing major achievements in architecture. During this period the mainstays of Thai temples were developed, including the *phra chedi* (stupa), *bot* (where an image of Buddha is enshrined), and *prasat* (castle). Khmer elements abound, while the Mons—dominant from the 6th to the 9th centuries—also provided Theravada Buddhist influences. Sukhothai-era houses and palaces built of wood have long since vanished, but ruins of stone and brick temples in the Sukhothai Historical Park—a UNESCO World Heritage Site—remain to provide evidence of the period's distinctive architecture.

Ayutthaya

Architecture of the Ayutthaya period (14th–18th centuries) was largely an extension of the Sukhothai style, but while Sukhothai laid the groundwork, Ayutthaya was the golden age. A rich and powerful city renowned for its military might, buildings erected during this period took on a royal grandeur, with golden temples and glittering palaces becom-

ruins at Sukhothai National Park

© SUZANNE NAM

ing a mainstay. During the Ayutthaya period there was also a Khmer revival, when kings built a number of neo-Khmer-style temples and edifices. During the 13th–15th centuries the influence of the Chinese appeared in the form of kilned ceramic roof tiles and mother-of-pearl inlay, while in the 16th–17th centuries European styles came in with the arrival of foreign diplomats and high-ranking officials. Much of the ancient city's architecture was destroyed in 1767 when Ayutthaya was sacked by the Burmese, however ruins of the ancient city remain and have been designated a UNESCO World Heritage Site.

Rattanakosin

For most travelers to Bangkok, their first views of historical Thai architecture come at Wat Pha Kaeo and the Grand Palace, two attractions that have shaped the architectural image of the country in the world's eye. Indeed, the Rattanakosin period is the most diverse of all Thailand's eras in terms of architecture, given that it began with the founding of Bangkok in 1782 and continues today. Much like the earlier art of this era, architecture was designed to mirror the dominant styles of the former capital, Ayutthaya, in the wake of its destruction. This meant incorporating Khmer elements (such as Wat Arun), Chinese elements, and a few Western elements into temples and palaces.

Traditional Thai styles began to decline around 1900, when buildings increasingly took on European forms. For craftspeople to be considered masters of their trade, they were required to learn Western techniques, hence the concepts of Frank Lloyd Wright and Mies van der Rohe were embraced by local architects. Neoclassical elements were incorporated, a fine example of this being Wat Benchamabophit (Marble Temple) in Bangkok, which was erected for King Chulalongkorn in 1900 and designed by his half-brother, Prince Naris. A few decades later, art deco became a key style, evident in buildings such as the Hualampong Train Station and buildings along Ratchadamnoen Avenue.

Starting a few decades ago, when Bangkok's urban center really began to grow, a sense of "anything goes" appears to have emerged, with elements of modernism, Greek revival, Bauhaus, sophisticated Chinese, and native Thai styles all mashed together in eclectic designs that are often quite eye-catching but occasionally quite garish. Today's urban architecture has few features to distinguish it from that of any other major international city, with glassy highrises, ritzy condominiums, and flashy shopping malls becoming the norm. That said, many government buildings and universities have been built combining Thai styles with sensible contemporary design, an eye-pleasing effect.

Traditional Thai structures can still be found in throughout the country, and even the simplest building can be a great source of beauty with uniquely Thai elements. There are elegant classic wooden houses on stilts with curved roofs, Malay-inspired buildings in the south, "raft" homes over the river, Chinese shophouses, and Sino-Portuguese buildings in areas like Phuket. It is in this diversity that Thailand's architectural beauty can be found, a stark contrast to the glittering high-rises that are becoming the mainstay in the capital.

PLANNING YOUR FACT-FINDING TRIP

Preparing to Leave

WHAT TO BRING

Clothing

Thailand's climate is hot and tropical (think Miami in August), so bear that in mind as you pack for your trip. If you'll just be exploring potential neighborhoods, house hunting, and generally getting a feel for the country, bring clothes that are loose, lightweight, and breathable. Tank tops and shorts are tempting, but in addition to looking a little too casual, they don't offer enough protection from the sun. Covering up your skin, so long as you do so with loose light fabrics, can actually keep you cooler in the long run. If you'll be spending a lot of time walking around outdoors, take a clue from the Thais

© SUZANNE NAM

© SUZANNE NAM

Local carriers have frequent flights to most parts of the country.

who work outside on a daily basis, and consider bringing or picking up a lightweight broad-brimmed hat. Laundry services are available at all levels of accommodations, from guesthouses to five-star hotels. If you are walking around a lot in the heat, your feet will sweat and swell, and you are far more likely to have blisters, so comfortable shoes are essential. Unless you'll be moving around a lot, three or four changes of clothing should be sufficient for your trip. But bring extra underwear, as you will most likely be showering more than once a day.

In major cities in Thailand, people general dress nicely, and even those just running errands or hanging out at the mall on a Saturday will seldom be seen looking too sloppy or unkempt (if you walk around most residential areas in the evening, you'll see folks hanging around or running to the store in their pajamas, but that's a different story). People will also generally make assumptions about you based on the way you are dressed, so unless you want to be treated like a backpacking tourist when you're house hunting or looking at schools for your kids, ditch the flip-flops and ratty cargo shorts. You will almost always be treated better if you are dressed well. It almost goes without saying that any meetings with government officials, even if you're just stopping into the immigration office to extend your tourist visa, things will go more smoothly if you are dressed more formally. For men, khakis and polo shirts are acceptable if you're just walking around, or even for casual meetings with real estate agents. Women have more options but you should avoid looking like you're going to the beach. If you are going to the beach, or exploring Thailand's beaches as possible places to move, don't worry about the flip flops or shorts; those are fine in beach areas.

PROFESSIONAL DRESS

If you are coming to Thailand for meetings with other professionals or you'll be networking, or interviewing for jobs, you'll most likely be expected to dress in business attire. For men this means suits, ties, and dress shoes, even though the thermometer could be in the 30s Celsius (90s Fahrenheit) while you're in town. Depending on the types of meetings you'll be having and the people you'll be meeting with, you may be able to get away with not wearing a tie, and you can even take your jacket off quickly after you've arrived, but you should gauge the level of formality carefully and err on the side of being overdressed. Some professionals, such as teachers, are a little more casual, but you'll still be expected to wear a button-down shirt and long pants.

Women have a little more leeway in that they don't absolutely have to wear business suits, but you will still be expected to wear professional-looking clothing (i.e., a button-down blouse and skirt or slacks, or a dress) if you are in business meetings or interviewing. Though many professional women do wear pantyhose in Thailand, it is not considered taboo to skip them. Women can also get away with open-toed shoes and even sandals in all but the highest positions or the most formal offices. In the past, women in Thailand did not wear sleeveless tops in professional environments, but this is changing, and it is not uncommon to see women wearing sleeveless dresses or sleeveless blouses to work, although spaghetti-straps, halter tops, and tube tops are a no-no. Bring a light cardigan with you in case you are meeting with more formal people, as well as to protect you from icy-cold air-conditioning.

Toiletries and First-Aid Supplies

You can find nearly everything you need in Thailand at a reasonable price, including international health and beauty brands such as Dove, Pantene, Nivea, and others, so don't waste space in your luggage for shampoo, contact lens solution, or other toiletries. Over-the-counter medications are usually cheaper in Thailand than they are back at home (Tylenol, for example, is about half the price here) and the most popular ones are easy to find. Consider it an opportunity to do some research by visiting drug stores and supermarkets while you're here.

Computers and Mobile Phones

If you are here doing research, meeting people, and looking for a place to live, being connected either by phone or by email will make it much easier to get things done. Nearly every hotel or guesthouse in any popular area of Thailand has Internet access, and many also have Wi-Fi. If the place you are staying doesn't have it, there are also usually coffee shops and Internet cafés that provide access, so if you bring along your computer you should not have a problem finding a connection.

Telephone service is a little more difficult. Even if your mobile phone uses the same frequency bands available in Thailand, international roaming charges will be exorbitant (especially if you use data roaming). If you have an unlocked phone with a removable SIM card, just pick up a Thai SIM card at any 7-Eleven and sign up for a prepaid plan, in which you buy credits as you need them. If your current phone doesn't have those capabilities, you can pick up an inexpensive second-hand phone for under 1,400 baht while you are here. You can rent a Thai phone at the airport, but it will cost significantly more than buying one outright.

Currency

Thailand's currency is the baht, abbreviated as ฿. In early 2010 the official exchange rate was 33 baht to the U.S. dollar, and the rate has fluctuated between 41 and 31 baht to the dollar over the past five years. Baht bills come in denominations of 20, 50, 100, 500, and 1,000, although you'll see an old 10 baht note once in a while. Coins come in denominations of 1, 2, 5, and 10 baht plus 25 and 50 Jatang coins, though those are uncommon except at supermarkets.

You can change dollars to baht at nearly any bank, but you may be asked to present your passport. Exchange rates will be clearly marked, and most banks do not charge a fee for the transaction. There are also some money changers around in touristy areas, and most high-end hotels offer the service as well. Banks almost always give the best rates if you are changing cash, but

Thailand's major banks post exchange rates.

© SUZANNE NAM

NATIONAL HOLIDAYS

Many of the Buddhist holidays celebrated in Thailand are governed by the lunar calendar, and specific dates will change every year.

Date	Holiday
January 1	New Year's Day (international calendar)
February	Makha Bucha Day
April 6	Chakri Day
April 13-15	Songkran
May 5	Coronation Day
May	Royal Plowing Ceremony
May	Wisaka Bucha Day
July	Asana Bucha Day
July	Khao Pansa
August 12	Queen's Birthday/Mother's Day
October 23	Chulalongkorn Day
December 5	King's Birthday/Father's Day
December 10	Constitution Day

you'll usually get the absolute best deal if you just withdraw money from an ATM. Recently banks have begun charging a fee for foreign bank withdrawals though many U.S. banks will refund ATM fees. When you factor that in, it's almost the same as changing cash; but it's still more convenient to use ATMs than to bring large amounts of cash with you.

HOW MUCH MONEY TO TAKE?

Thailand has a huge range of accommodations options and is generally an inexpensive country, so how much you budget for your trip depends entirely on how you want to live while you're here. If you are on a very tight budget, you can eat, sleep and get around for under 650 baht per day. It's not difficult to find accommodations from 250 to 400 baht per night, depending on where you are staying. Small cities in Isan will have substantially cheaper guesthouses than Phuket, but even there you can find a guesthouse for 400 baht per night or less if you're willing to sacrifice some comforts and stay in Phuket Town instead of on the beach. Food in Thailand can likewise be very inexpensive. Street food or a dish from a casual chophouse will cost less than

50 baht per meal, a little more if you add in beverages, so you can realistically eat three meals a day for 160 baht.

If your budget is a little bigger, you can find comfortable, well-located basic hotels in most parts of the country for under 1,000 baht per night. Restaurant meals at local restaurants will run under 200 baht per meal, so you won't suffer much if you budget 1,700 baht per day.

Transportation can add substantially to your budget but depends on where you are and how much time you have. Public transportation is the cheapest way to get around, but in some areas it's not a feasible option. Places such as Phuket have limited public transportation and expensive taxis, while Bangkok has decent public trains and buses and inexpensive taxis. If you're outside of any major metropolitan area, you'll need your own transportation unless you're really good at navigating local buses and have plenty of time to wait for them. Renting a car will cost 1,300 baht per day and up. Make sure to budget for gasoline, which cost about 25 baht per liter (99 baht per gallon) in early 2010.

WHEN TO GO

Thailand's best weather is in the **cool season, November through February.** This is when temperatures across the country drop into the low 20s Celsius (70s Fahrenheit), the humidity becomes far less oppressive, and the weather feels downright pleasant. This is the most popular time for tourists to visit; you'll see plenty of other foreign visitors and peak pricing, especially around Christmas or New Years, so if you're in the country trying to get things done on a short timeline, it may not be the best time of year in terms of efficiency. Although Thailand is a Buddhist country, business tends to slow down from mid-December to early January. Businesses will remain open, but things may not happen as quickly as at other times of the year. The **rainy season** is generally **July to October,** when Bangkok is subject to monsoon rains. Don't write this season off completely, as it doesn't rain all day or even every day, and it rains significantly less in certain parts of the country. If you don't mind a few downpours and occasional street flooding, you'll pay significantly less for accommodations during this time, and unless the rains are really bad, it won't interfere with your ability to meet with people, visit schools, or go house hunting. The **hot season (March–May)** means higher temperatures, lots of humidity, and occasional storms. There's a reason for the expression "Bangkok blanket." Again, it won't interfere with your fact-finding, but it might feel uncomfortable if you are not accustomed to blazing sun and sticky humidity. If you're planning a move here, you might as well get used to it now.

In mid-April the whole country celebrates **Songkran,** or Buddhist New Year, and this is the only time when it's probably not a good idea to visit Thailand with the intention of getting anything done. Many people take off the entire week surrounding the holiday, and some restaurants and shops close.

Arriving in Thailand

VISAS AND PASSPORTS

Visitors from most countries do not need to apply for a visa before arriving in Thailand, and will be granted a 30-day visa waiver on arrival. If you're planning on being in Thailand for more than a month, you can apply for a longer tourist visa at your local Thai consulate or embassy. In either case, make sure you have a passport valid for at least six months from the date you arrive in the country.

TRANSPORTATION

If you're flying in from abroad, you'll most likely be arriving at **Suvarnab-humi International Airport,** just outside of Bangkok. The most convenient way into town is to take a taxi; a ride to most central locations will be under 350 baht. If you're on a tight budget or don't want to add to the pollution in the city, you can take an express bus from the airport to many of the most popular neighborhoods and hotels. The airport rail link is scheduled to open in mid-2010, and it will take you straight to the Skytrain.

© SUZANNE NAM

Make hotel reservations in advance, especially for popular areas.

Sample Itineraries

If you're moving to Thailand and have the luxury of choice about where to relocate, spend as much time here as you can before making any decisions about where to live. If you are retiring or coming here to teach English, you will have many more options than those who are moving here for a specific job or to set up a company. You may have had your heart set on Ko Samui before you arrived, but after visiting Chiang Mai, realize daily life will be much more enjoyable and living expenses much lower in the laid-back north of Thailand. You won't know unless you visit.

Figure out the most efficient way to get from one place to another in Bangkok and other major cities with terrible traffic.

The following sample itineraries assume you have some flexibility in where you'll be living and cover the areas the majority of foreigners move to in Thailand. In a week, you won't be able to see all of the most popular areas, but you will get a chance to see a couple of major areas and to spend some time looking at apartments or houses, looking at schools if necessary, visiting supermarkets, and otherwise generally getting a sense of what life will be like here. With a couple of weeks, you'll be able to hit the country's four most popular areas for foreigners, albeit briefly. In a month, you'll be able to visit these areas and also spend substantial time in each, investigating different neighborhoods and understanding the way of life.

ONE WEEK

If you're in Thailand for just a week, you'll realistically only be able to see a couple of major areas. Use Bangkok as your base for exploration and, after spending a few days in the capital, venture out into one of the other popular living areas for another few days to see a totally different side of the country. If you're not interested in living in Bangkok, skip the city entirely and add one of the alternate side trips instead.

© SUZANNE NAM

Take a peek at Thailand's beaches, even if you're not considering life on the coast.

Days 1-4:

Land in Bangkok, and after you pass through immigration and customs, take a taxi directly to your hotel (take the airport rail link if it is finally up and running, you don't have too much luggage, and you're staying near a Skytrain or subway station). If you've arrived during the day, take a quick shower and then grab a map and head out to explore the neighborhood surrounding your hotel to get a feel for Bangkok. After shaking off jet lag, spend the next three full days exploring the central part of the capital. On day 2, your first full day in Bangkok, pick two neighborhoods you're most interested in living in and begin exploring them by car or, preferably, on foot. The areas around Ploenchit and Victory Monument are both very popular expat neighborhoods. They're very different from each other and offer a good contrast. If you're hungry, stop at one of the many noodle stands on the streets of either neighborhood for a quick bowl of noodle soup. Return to the Victory Monument area for dinner at one of the many street stalls around the Victory Monument rotary.

Make sure to arrange some meetings with local real estate agents for day 3 so that you have a chance to know what you'd like to see beforehand. If you have school-age children, arrange school visits on day 2 and day 3, as these often take at least a few hours with commuting time. If you're considering studying while you're here, use that time to visit some of the universities in Bangkok, such as Chulalongkorn and Thamasat. If you're planning on teaching English, make appointments beforehand with potential employers instead. On day 3, spend the morning looking at potential schools, universities, or jobs, and the afternoon visiting various apartments and houses with a real estate agent. In the evening, head back to the central part of the city and spend an hour at Chitlom or

Ploenchit, the megamalls near Siam Square. Aside from window-shopping and people-watching, visit the high-end international supermarkets to see what your grocery shopping options will be like. Plan on having dinner at either one of the food courts or at one of the many restaurants inside the malls. On day 4, head out of the center of the city, either to one of the suburban neighborhoods such as Bangkapi, with large housing estates and easy access to international schools, or to one of the urban neighborhoods such as Dusit, which is not as well served by public transportation but offers less-expensive housing and a chance to live more locally. Wherever you go, plan to go in the morning, during rush hour, so you get a good idea of what it's like to commute in Bangkok.

Days 5-7

Wake up early and take the first morning flight to your next destination, either Chiang Mai, Khorat, or Phuket (if you're heading to Khorat, you'll need to pick up a rental car). If you're exploring northern Thailand, once you land in Chiang Mai, go directly to your hotel or guesthouse to check in (or leave your bag if you can't get early check-in) and then spend the first half of the day walking around Chiang Mai town. Stop in the afternoon for a quick bowl of fragrant *khao soy* noodles in curry broth. In the late afternoon and evening, head out to the Nimmenhamen neighborhood to get a feel for the younger, funkier side of Chiang Mai. Make sure to stop into one of the many coffee shops for an iced coffee made from local beans and to chat with the folks behind the counter, who will most likely speak enough English to have a conversation and will offer friendly advice about apartments and living in Chiang Mai. Plan ahead so that you can spend day 6 looking at apartments in and around central Chiang Mai. Take a break in late afternoon by heading up to Wat Doi Suthep for a great view of the city and an opportunity to visit one of the region's most important Buddhist temples. Take note of the way the city is laid out and how it spreads; it'll help you determine whether you want to live in the center or would prefer living on the periphery. On day 7, head out on a rented motorbike or car to explore the suburbs of Chiang Mai. If you can, make appointments beforehand to see some of the housing developments a few miles outside the center of the city. Otherwise just drive up and ask the security guards if you can view any vacant houses. Pad your schedule so you have time to drive out into the mountains and see how lovely the region is.

Day 8

Return to Bangkok in the morning and spend a few hours exploring one more potential neighborhood, such as Thong Lor. Arrange your plans so you can take the Skytrain instead of a taxi and then walk from the Skytrain stop down Soi Thong Lor. It's a long, hot walk, and most locals use taxis or motorcycle taxis for the last leg of the journey. If you're feeling brave, give it a try. Pop into one of the neighborhood's grocery stores and then grab a late lunch at one of the many Japanese restaurants before heading back to your hotel to pack up for your trip home.

TWO WEEKS

This itinerary is designed to give you a fast and furious overview of the four most popular regions in Thailand for foreigners to live. You'll be covering a lot of ground, but you can take advantage of Thailand's reliable, inexpensive domestic flights to get around quickly. You'll spend the first seven days of your trip using the itinerary above. The second week, you'll split your time between Isan and Phuket.

Day 8-10

Return to Bangkok on an early flight and pick up a rental car at the airport as you'll spend the next few days driving around northeast Thailand. Your first stop will be Nakhon Ratchasima (Khorat), Thailand's sixth largest city, about four hours by car from Bang-kok. Spend the afternoon exploring central Khorat. Though it's not the most picturesque part of the region, it's a good place to look for a job if you are a teacher as there are many universities and private schools look-ing for qualified instructors. In the evening, head to the Mall, Khorat's largest shopping mall, for dinner at one of the many uniquely Thai chain restaurants. The next day, spend the morning visiting some of the city's universities and visit a few apartments in Khorat. In the late afternoon, drive out to see what the suburbs look like. Joho, on the main road out of town, is very popu-lar with expats who work in the area but don't want to live right in the

Sampling street food is an essential part of research.

city. At night, head to one of the city's popular expat hangouts, such as George and Dragon, to chat with foreigners who've been in the city for a while, and have a cold beer (don't be surprised if most of the expats are men and many of them seem disgruntled). On day 10, set out in the morning for a road trip to Phimai. It's less than 40 miles from Khorat and is home to Thailand's best Khmer ruins. You're not just visiting for the sightseeing but to get a chance to see what country life looks like, as even 60 kilometers (40 miles) outside of Khorat, life changes dramatically. In the late afternoon, head back to Bangkok, where you'll spend the night before setting off on the final leg of your trip.

Days 11-13

Take an early morning flight from Bangkok to Phuket, where you'll get a chance to see a little bit of southern Thailand. When you arrive, take a taxi to your hotel or pick up a rental car at the airport. If you're not renting a car, considering renting a motorbike since you'll need your own wheels to get around the island quickly. Check in at your guesthouse, drop off your bags, and spend the next couple of hours driving up and down the island's west coast to get a feel for the different beach areas on Phuket. If you are looking for schools for your kids, spend half of day 12 visiting one or two of the island's international schools. Otherwise arrange some meetings with real estate agents and then take a break later in the day for an afternoon swim on one of the island's beautiful beaches, such as Patong Beach or Karon Beach. In the evening head out to Patong Beach once again to experience the island's nightlife.

Day 13

Spend your last day on Phuket away from the beaches in the suburbs, where many foreigners live, or in the area surrounding Phuket Town. If you have time, arrange to see a couple of apartments or houses before heading to the airport to return to Bangkok before flying home.

ONE MONTH

A full month in Thailand will give you a chance not only to see all the major areas but to start to understand Thai culture, get to know the people of Thailand, and even begin to climb all the bureaucratic hurdles you'll face as you set up your home here. This will be a busy month, and you'll do plenty of traveling from one region to another and spend plenty of time traveling around each region, but make sure you also give yourself some time to get into the rhythm of everyday life, and remind yourself that you're very lucky to be moving here. Spend an early morning walking through one of Bangkok's many meat and produce markets trying to identify all of the different kinds of fruits and vegetables on sale. In Chiang Mai head up to Wat Doi Suthep to visit the many faces of the Buddha and observe the devout. On the islands, head to the beach for an afternoon to take in some sun and fun. Wherever you are, if you find yourself with spare time or energy, set out for a couple of hours with no purpose other than to wander around and people-watch.

Use your time in each of the regions not only to get a broad idea of what each area is like but also to take an in-depth look at parts of the country. In Bangkok, walk around as many neighborhoods as you can. In northern Thailand, make the drive from Chiang Mai to Chiang Rai, then arrange a two-day trek out into the jungle. In southern Thailand, spend a few days in Phuket, then travel to some of the region's other amazing beaches and islands.

Days 1-7:

Whether you ultimately settle down in Bangkok or not, it's still an important city to get to know and spend some time in, and it will give you valuable insights into what modern Thailand is all about. In a full week, you have time to explore most of the city's central neighborhoods, spend a day in the suburbs, meet with real estate agents, visit some of the international schools, seek legal or business expertise, and even spend some time at the many expat hangouts talking to foreigners who've been living in Bangkok for years. Even though being a tourist isn't your priority, you'll have time to take a ferry on the Chao Phraya to visit a couple of the country's most important historical sites and even take in a museum.

Days 8-14

Spend the next week in northern Thailand. It's a big region, and traveling around involves lots of driving through the mountains, so you won't be able to see everything in a week, but you will be able to see the most popular urban areas and the smaller villages in between. While you're in the north, do a hiking trip from either Chiang Mai or Chiang Rai. Either will take you into the beautiful mountainous jungles of the region, and some will also give you a chance to do some white-water rafting and visit remote villages. Don't forget to indulge a little bit in all the wonderful things Chiang Mai has to offer, including beautiful handicrafts, delicious regional cuisine, and charming guesthouses.

Days 15-21

Head to Isan for this leg of your trip, and plan on doing a loose loop around the region. Start out in Bangkok and cross the lower part of the region

Check out the local markets in areas you are interested in living in.

before heading north from Ubon Ratchathani to Udon Thani before circling back through Khon Kaen. You'll be doing a lot of driving from one city to another as you visit the region's primary urban areas of Khorat, Ubon Ratchathani, and Udon Thani. Along the way you'll spend a lot of time looking at fields and water buffalo, but that's what life is like in this part of the country. Make sure to stop at some of the smaller cities in northeast Thailand, including Suring and Khon Kaen. On your road trip, spend a few hours just getting lost so that you'll get a chance to visit some of the smaller villages and to interact with people (if you're worried about getting lost, get a GPS-equipped rental car). Return your rental car to Bangkok before heading to Phuket by air.

Days 21-27

Use Phuket as your home base to explore not only the country's most popular tourist destination but also the surrounding provinces of Phang Nga and Krabi; if you have more time, you could also spend a week exploring other parts of the country along the coast, and even hop over the isthmus to visit the Ko Samui archipelago in the Gulf of Siam. After you arrive in Phuket, spend a couple of days on the island getting a feel for it and gauging whether you would enjoy living in such a bustling, developing environment. If you're looking for something a little less touristy, head north to Phang Nga Province. The area has some gorgeous beaches, and the tourism industry is just starting to explode, but it's still relatively quiet and laid-back. Spend another couple of days island-hopping in Phang Nga Bay, which separates Phuket from Krabi province. There are some gorgeous islands, from underdeveloped and quiet to built-up. If you don't want to arrange the travel yourself, an easy way to see many of the most popular islands is to take a group snorkeling trip. Travel agents all over the region sell tickets, and tour operators will arrange pick-up and delivery at your hotel or guesthouse.

Practicalities

The following list of places to sleep and eat will help you enjoy your time in the country, and they represent some of the best choices in different price ranges. The list was put together with convenience in mind, not sightseeing, so in most cases these guesthouses, hotels, markets, and restaurants will be located in central areas where you're most likely to be apartment hunting or networking, not necessarily where you'd stay if you were here visiting temples and going to museums. Use the restaurant listings as a starting point, but as you walk around scoping out neighborhoods and looking for places to live, ask the real estate agent, security guard, school principal, or potential colleague you've just met to recommend great places to eat in the vicinity. Thailand is a food lover's paradise, and there's a delicious bowl of noodles or amazing curry to be found in every neighborhood.

ACCOMMODATIONS
Bangkok

In an area full of five-star hotels and embassies, **Golden House** (1025/5–9 Ploenchit Rd., Skytrain: Ploenchit, 02/520-9535, www.goldenhouses.net, 750 baht) stands out as one of the few low-priced options until you get into more touristy areas to the north and east. Simple, clean rooms and bathrooms are a bargain, especially if you get a room facing the garden in the back. The best part is the location, just a two-minute walk to the Skytrain and a 10-minute walk to the U.S. embassy. If you want to spend a little more, there are plenty of five-star options in the neighborhood. If you need to be in the Old City while you're visiting, **Navalai River Resort** (45/1 Phra Athit Rd., ferry: Phra Athit, 02/280-9955, www.navalairiverresort.com, 2,500 baht) is a good balance between backpacker guesthouse and boutique hotel. Rooms are pleasant, clean, and modern, and the hotel is right on the Chao Phraya River and just a two-minute walk to the river ferry stop.

If you're basing yourself in the Silom area of the city and want to see Bangkok's funky, artsy side, **Lub d** (Decho Rd., Skytrain: Chong Nonsi, 02/680-9999, www.lubd.com, 600 baht) offers inexpensive rooms, fun design, and a good location close to the city's banking district. Stay in one of the dormitories if you want to really save cash (there's also a women-only dorm), or reserve one of the private rooms with en-suite bathrooms. In the same neighborhood but closer to the river is the area's best high-end hotel, **Lebua at State Tower** (1055 Silom Rd., 02/624-9999, http://bangkok.lebua.com, 3,500 baht). Five-star luxury, stunning views, and a great location make this all-suite hotel a top choice for business visitors and families, since the suites are spacious and there are two- and three-bedroom units. The **Pullman Bangkok King Power** (8/2 Rangnam Rd., Skytrain: Victory Monument or Phayathai, 02/680-9999, www.pullmanbangkokkingpower.com, 3,500 baht), just adjacent to the King Power shopping complex, is a great place to base yourself if you're considering living in the Victory Monument or Phayathai areas. The hotel has five-star amenities, beautiful modern rooms, and very good on-site dining options, but it is much more reasonably priced than larger international luxury chains.

Chiang Mai

Central Chiang Mai has scores of hotels and guesthouses to choose from. If you want something inexpensive but convenient to Chiang Mai's old city, **Buri Gallery House** (102 Rachadamnoen Rd., tel. 05/341-6500, www.burigalleryhouse.com, 1,000 baht) is a newer hotel in an amazing location. Housed in a beautiful Thai-style wooden house designed as a small modern hotel, some rooms are very small, but the service is excellent. Breakfast is included, and there is an outdoor seating area, a massage parlor right in the lobby, and free Internet if you need to check your email. The top-notch charming service and beautiful lobby send many visitors home happy after staying at **3 Sis Bed & Breakfast** (1 Phra Pokklao Soi 8, tel. 05/327-3243, www.3sisbedandbreakfast.com, 1,300 baht), which makes for a pleasant stay right in the old city a block away from some of the city's most significant Buddhist *wats*. A very chic café serving Thai and Western dishes (with ingredients from the three sisters' father's

© SUZANNE NAM

3 Sis Bed & Breakfast in Chiang Mai is a perfect place to base yourself.

organic farm) is downstairs. Rooms are very comfortable, the bathrooms are particularly plush for the price, and there's free Wi-Fi throughout the hotel.

Just beyond the center of town on the Ping River, the **River Ping Palace** (385/2 Charoen Phratet Rd., tel. 05/327-4932, http://riverpingpalace.tripod. com, 1,500 baht) is a great little guesthouse for those exploring the area just outside the old city. The small complex of old wooden houses is decorated with antiques, and the breezy dining area overlooking the river is a lovely place to enjoy a slow breakfast before heading out to research Chiang Mai. Rooms are comfortable but very basic, as are the bathrooms. **Tamarind Village** (50/1 Ratchadomnoen Rd., tel. 05/341-8896, www.tamarindvillage.com, 6,000 baht) is an oasis in the middle of the old city. This boutique hotel, set in a large walled-in lush green space, somehow manages to create an aura of true peace and quiet right in the middle of backpackers and *tuk tuks*. Rooms are rustic in that they have more classic than modern design elements, but they're also spacious, clean, and luxuriously appointed.

If you are looking for absolute luxury and want to get a feel for suburban Chiang Mai, the **Four Seasons Chiang Mai** (Mae Rim-Samoeng Kao Rd., tel. 05/329-8181, www.fourseasons.com, 13,000 baht) has enormous stand-alone villas set on a lush green rice paddy. The property is outside of the city but convenient to the main thoroughfare.

Phuket

If you want something cheap and reliable away from the beach areas, **Talang Guesthouse** (37 Thanon Thalang, tel. 07/621-4225, 350 baht) is a good choice: a comfortable, inexpensive place to sleep with quite a bit of character. Some rooms have air-conditioning, and all have private bathrooms, but the property is definitely showing its age. Nevertheless it is a friendly place to stay, conveniently located, and quite inexpensive. With all of the development going on, it's surprising that simple beach accommodations such as **Mai Khao Beach Bungalows** (Mai Khao Beach, tel. 08/1895-1233, http:// mai-khao-beach.com, 800 baht) still exist. The basic thatched-roof huts don't have air-conditioning, only fans, but they do have basic bathrooms with cold showers. Mai Khao Beach is a quiet spot with limited amenities, but there is a beachfront restaurant on the premises serving good inexpensive Thai food. There's also camping available, and the bungalows close during low season (May–November).

Situated in Surin, just across from the beach, **Twin Palms** (106/46 Moo 3, Srisoonthorn Rd., Cherngtalay, Thalang, tel. 07/631-6500, 8,200 baht) is the perfect blend of urban chic and tropical resort and is a good base if you're exploring that part of the island. The guest rooms look over two large beautiful pools and perfectly landscaped grounds; inside is a blend of dark wood and clean whites. A great option in Patong, if you don't want to stay in the thick of it all and don't want to sleep in a generic or messy guesthouse, is the **Little Buddha Guesthouse** (74/31 Nanai Rd., Patong Beach, tel. 07/629-6148, www. littlebuddhaphuket.com, 500 baht). Rates are an exceptionally good value considering the superclean rooms, nice bathrooms, and tasteful furnishings. There's even a small lobby done in muted colors and natural materials. The hotel is located behind the Jungceylon Mall, so make sure to stop in and see the supermarket, megamarket, and shopping while you're there.

Karon Café (526/17 Soi Islandia Park Resort, Karon Beach, tel. 07/639-6217, 800 baht) is a typical Karon beach guesthouse, set inland a few minutes from the beach on the upper floors of a commercial shophouse. Rooms are clean and well-furnished and come with hot showers, air-conditioning, cable TV, and refrigerators. There are also larger family rooms available if you need to sleep more than two people. If you're considering living in one of the villages adjacent to the beaches, staying here will give you a good opportunity to see what life is like.

Khorat and Vicinity

If you just want a cheap, clean place to base yourself as you explore northeast Thailand, **San Sabai** (335 Thanon Suranari, tel. 04/425-5144 or 08/1547-3066, 350 baht) is all you need. The small guesthouse is within walking distance of the city sights and has air-conditioning and televisions in every room. The decor leaves much to be desired, and the rooms are not spacious, but in this price category it's as good as it gets. If you have a rental car or other means of getting around on your own, the **Dusit Princess** (1137 Thanon Suranarai, tel. 02/636-3333, www.dusit.com, 1,700 baht) just outside of the city center, is an excellent value. Part of the luxury Dusit chain (though less than half the price of what you'd pay in Bangkok), the hotel has beautiful grounds and well-furnished, spacious rooms with cable TV, Internet, and other modern amenities. Just one step below the Dusit is the **Sima Thani Hotel** (2112/2 Mittraphap Rd., tel. 04/421-3100, www.simathani.com, 1,600 baht), offering most of the same amenities, including plenty of restaurants to choose from, a nice pool, and modern rooms. It's not quite a five-star, and the furnishings might feel a little more run-down than at the Dusit, but the property is still far superior to most other options in Khorat.

Overlooking a lagoon amid rice fields, **Tanita Lagoon Resort** (113 Baan Nong Huaw Mue, Nadee, Muang, Udon Thani, tel. 081/884-6334 or

086/654-6334, tanitaresort@gmail.com, www.tanitaresort.com/lagoon.htm, 1,200 baht) is an interesting place to stay about 15 minutes by car outside the center of Udon Thani and will really give you a sense of what rural life in the region is like. Although there's a restaurant on the premises and all of the accommodations are in old teak houses, it's not quite a resort, and you're certainly not paying resort prices. Rooms and attached bathrooms are clean, and although not exceptionally well decorated, white duvet covers and little extras such as slippers make them a step above basic rooms.

Ban Prasat Homestay is perhaps one of the best ways to experience life in Thailand and to be certain that the money you spend is going to the people around you. The villagers of Ban Prasat have been hosting visitors since 1993, shortly after exploration of the pits was completed. The project started with just Thai and foreign archeology students but was quickly expanded to tourists with the help of the Tourism Authority. To arrange a visit, call the village headman at 04/436-7075 or the regional TAT office at 04/421-3666. You'll be matched with a family who will invite you into their home, feed you, and bring you to see such things as silk weaving, basket making, and traditional food preparation. For around 400 baht per night, this is an amazing bargain and a once-in-a-lifetime opportunity. About 24 kilometers (15 miles) south of Udon Thani is **Gecko Villa** (126 Moo 13, Baan Um Jaan, Prajak Sinlapakom, tel. 08/1918-0500, www.geckovilla.com, 5,500 baht), an exceptional little retreat that stands head and shoulders above everything else in the region. The accommodations are set in a traditional wooden home with modern amenities, a lovely swimming pool, and lush green grounds surrounded by rice paddies. Rooms are all nicely furnished with traditional and modern Thai elements, and you'll feel like you're a guest in someone's very nice home in Isan. Staff will also give impromptu cooking lessons if you're interested in learning how to make traditional Isan fare or other Thai dishes (all of which is included in the cost of your stay).

Pattaya

Pattaya's accommodations options typically run from cheap guesthouses in the thick of the party zone to high-end resorts on the beach. **Jomtien's RS Seaside** (125/9 Moo 10 Jomtien Beach Rd., Bang Lamung, Chonburi tel. 03/823-1867, www.rs-seaside.com, some rooms from 660 baht, but most in the 1,100–2,300 baht range) is located at the south end of the beach strip. It's renowned for offering a good value, although room rates have been creeping up. The rooms are clean and well-lit, and at the top range you'll get views of the sea. There's also a pool and a central seating area, a Jacuzzi, and an espresso bar. **DD Inn** (410/50 Moo 12, Jomtien Beach Rd., tel. 03/823-2995, www.jomtienbeachhotel.com, 500–600 baht), in Jomtien Beach, is a good pick for budget travelers looking for basic, tidy lodgings. Most of the rooms at this Australian-run guesthouse consist solely of beds, desks, TVs, and white walls, but for 500–600 baht, that's not bad.

Green Jomtien Studios (217/1 Soi 15 Thep Prassit Rd., tel. 03/830-3941, 500 baht) is the place to go if you'd prefer to hang your hat far away from the typical Pattaya scene while you research the area. It's located one kilometer (0.6 miles) from Jomtien Beach in a quiet area. The long-stay hotel's rooms are fully furnished, and the wooden furniture is handmade in traditional Thai style. The posh **Royal Cliff Beach Resort** (353 Phra Tamnuk Rd., tel. 03/825-0421, www.royalcliff.com, 6,120 baht), at the southern end of Pattaya Bay, features various types of rooms and has a special family-friendly section of the hotel. The **Cabbages & Condoms Resort/Birds & Bees Resort** (Phra Tamnak Soi 4, tel. 03/825-0035, www.cabbagesandcondoms.co.th, 2,500 baht) not only has 50 rooms set on grounds with streams and ponds, its own beach, and a swimming pool, it is also a resort with a noble mission: It provides financial support for Thailand's Population and Community Development Association (PDA). The PDA teaches the importance of condoms in preventing the spread of HIV/AIDS and does other rural development work in Thailand. The individually decorated rooms have Thai motifs like elephant prints on the walls.

FOOD
Bangkok

Tucked away on a small street off of Thanao Road is **Chote Chit** (146 Prang Pu Thorn, 02/221-4082, Mon.–Sat. 11 A.M.–11 P.M.), one of the oldest restaurants in Bangkok at more than 80 years old, although the owner, Krachoichuli Kimangsawat, is not exactly sure when her grandfather originally opened the place. She says the recipes here haven't really changed in all that time, and you'll find some things on the menu that you rarely see in other restaurants, such as banana-flower salad. There is a gigantic selection in this humble spot, but it is better just to ask Khun Krachoichuli what she recommends. For more upscale modern Thai fare, visit **Nara** (Erawan Bangkok Mall, 494 Ploenchit Rd., Skytrain: Chitlom or Rajadamri, 02/250-7707, daily 10 A.M.–10 P.M.) on the ground floor of the posh Erawan Mall. The restaurant looks far more expensive than it is; staff are attentive and friendly; and the decor is casual, elegant, and subtly Thai, but the quality of the food makes it sometimes impossible to get a seat here during lunchtime (call ahead for a reservation). *Som*

© MONIKA MURPHY

Street food vendors sell everything from snacks to meals in Thailand.

tam mu krop, traditional *som tam* topped with crispy fried pork, brings new life to a near-staple dish; the fresh spring rolls wrapped in crepe are another standout. The best dish is also one of the cheapest on the menu, at 80 baht—the Sukhothai noodles, a sweet, spicy noodle soup with ground pork and crispy fried vegetables. Try a bowl even if you're full; it's as good as it gets. Another favorite among expats in Bangkok is **Jay Kee's Fried Chicken** (137/1–3 Soi Polo, Wireless Rd., subway: Lumphini, 02/251-2772, daily 10 A.M.–10 P.M.). Sometimes called Polo Chicken, this stuff is so good you may find yourself ordering more after you've finished the first plate. It starts off as juicy, crispy fried chicken but is then coated with mounds of fried garlic and served with spicy and smoky dipping sauces, sticky rice, and whatever other Isan side dishes you choose.

For some good fast food and a chance to see how regular working folks eat lunch, head to the **Siam Square Food Court** (Siam Square alley behind the Lido Cinema, Skytrain: Siam, daily 10 A.M.–4 P.M.). There are 80 stalls selling everything from noodle soups to sweet drinks to *khaokamu* (braised pork leg in gravy), and tables and chairs to sit at. The best place to enter is adjacent to the Lido Cinema. To see how the young and hip like to eat, have lunch or dinner at **Another Hound Café** (Siam Paragon Mall, 1st fl., 991/1 Rama I Rd., Skytrain: Siam, 02/129-4409, daily 11 A.M.–10:30 P.M.). In addition to spicy pastas featuring Thai flavors, there are some interesting takes on Thai fried chicken, mango salad, and *larb* (which is served as a bruschetta). Though the dining room is predominantly decorated in grays and blacks, nothing about the interior is subdued thanks to oversized chandeliers and sleek modern furniture. Prices aren't exorbitant and the restaurant is casual, but this is definitely a place to be seen.

Chiang Mai

To get a sense of the city of Chiang Mai, head to one of the many night markets for a meal. The **Chiang Mai Night Bazaar** has food stalls interwoven with the crafts and trinkets, including lots of satay and even *khao mok gai kai* (chicken and yellow rice). **Anusarn Market,** on the corner of Sri Dornchai and Chang Klan, has plenty of local Thai and Chinese food stalls that offer excellent inexpensive food, as do the **Saturday Market, Sunday Market,** and **Worowot Warorot Market.** Expect to spend 10–30 baht per dish.

If you're not in the Kao Soi Lam Duan neighborhood, head for the nameless restaurant with the yellow sign reading **Kaow Soi** in Latin letters (Phra Pokklao Rd., across from Three Kings' Monument, tel. 08/5618-1041, 6 A.M.–3 P.M., 30 baht). This is a very casual local place serving *khao soi,* soups, and garlic rice, a great accompaniment to the traditional dish. This may not be the most beautiful restaurant in the city, but their *khao soi* is among the best. **Den Duang Restaurant** (147/1 Changklan Rd., Tel. 05/327-5333, 10 A.M.–10 P.M., 70 baht) has mostly Thai patrons. If it is delectable Thai food you are after, grab a seat and check out their comprehensive Thai menu, with meat and fish and seafood dishes alongside the regular tourist-friendly *pad Phat thai* and stir-fries. They have a few Western dishes as well (think spaghetti). The one thing you wouldn't expect from this Thai-oriented menu is the serious array of drinks—they have coffees, teas, and trendy cocktails.

Just across from Nimanheminsoi 1 is the **Hong Tauw Inn** (95/16–17 Nimanhemin Rd., tel. 05/321-8333, daily 11 A.M.–midnight, 150 baht), which translates to "shophouse." Full of quirky decorations and funky clocks, this restaurant offers a wide range of classic Thai dishes along with quite a few set-menu options for 2–4 people, which is perfect if you're new to Thai food or if you like to share. Another helpful feature is that the menu is written in romanized Thai coupled with English descriptions, so you can order your favorites *and* practice your Thai. Fitting right into the Nimanhemin neighborhood, **Khun Nai Teun Sai** (Soi 11, Nimanhemin Rd., tel. 05/322-2208, daily 5:30 P.M.–midnight, 150 baht) is a casual but elegant place for dinner. The modern restaurant, decorated with modern art, offers well-prepared typical Thai dishes such as spring rolls and *satay,* but it is more about atmosphere.

This is a great place for couples or groups of adults, but it may feel a little less comfortable with children.

Phuket

Right on Surin Beach are a number of small restaurants serving up seaside meals and offering both Thai and Western food. Everything is predictably decent and inexpensive. If you come around dusk and sit at one of the tables on the beach, you'll feel like you're dining like a king regardless of what you're eating—the view from the tables is magnificent during sunset. In the parking lot of the beach, a number of street vendors begin setting up in the late afternoon, and there is plenty to choose from if you're looking for something more casual.

Right in the center of all of the action in Patong, across the street from the beach, is the **Ban Thai Restaurant** (94 Thaveewong Rd., Patong Beach, tel. 07/634-0850, 11 A.M.–1 A.M., 500 baht). The outdoor dining area is lovelier than one would expect in the middle of such a crowded touristy beach, and the seafood is fresh and well prepared. The restaurant is great for people-watching; it's not, however, a place for a quiet dinner—there's often loud live music and plenty of commotion from the streets of Patong. If you're looking for authentic Thai food and are not too picky about where you eat, venture over to the **night market** on Rat-U-Thit Road, parallel to the beach, between Soi Bangla and Sawatdirak Road. You'll find plenty of seafood and other stalls set up, catering to hungry tourists and locals alike.

For something a little more chic, with a great view and a relaxed vibe, **Joe's Downstairs** (223 Prabaramee Rd., Patong, Kathu, tel. 07/634-4254, daily noon–1 A.M., 600 baht), right below Baan Rim Pa, is a fun tapas bar, cocktail lounge, and restaurant with an international menu. The white modern interior is a nice backdrop to the view of the ocean and the colorful, artfully arranged dishes. The stately, expansive **Baan Klung Jinda Restaurant** (158 Yaowarat Rd., Phuket Town, 07/622-1777, Mon.–Sat. 11 A.M.–2 P.M. and 5–10 P.M., 350 baht) is set in an old colonial-style house complete with porticos and shuttered windows—a definite step up from most of the dining options on the island. Inside, the menu is deliberately traditional and typical, although there are some more exotic ingredients such as venison. Expect to find lots of curry and seafood dishes, all well prepared and presented. The restaurant also has a good wine selection, another plus if you're looking for a special place to dine.

Khorat

The best food in Isan is found in casual restaurants and in markets where vendors sell *som tam* and *gai yang* from makeshift street stalls. Finding small restaurants can be a little tricky in Khorat, as few of the best local joints have English menus, phone numbers, or even names you'll be able to identify. Luckily, Khorat has two different night markets right in the center of town to choose from if you're looking for some regional cuisine for dinner. The **Night Bazaar** (Thanon Manat, between Thanon Chomphon and Thanon Mahathai, daily 6–10 P.M., 30 baht) has food stalls selling quick, cheap meals as well as lots of low-end T-shirts, sneakers, and clothing. If you're feeling really brave, try some *menda tot,* or fried waterbugs, sold by one of the many fried-bug sellers you'll see at the market. The smaller **Wat Boon Market** (Thanon Chumphon near Thanon Kudan, across from Wat Boon, daily 6 P.M.–10 P.M., 30 baht) has fewer shopping stalls but more food, including non-Isan dishes such as *pad thai* and noodle soups.

Khorat also has a good selection of midrange sit-down restaurants to choose from. Although you will encounter inevitable language challenges, don't be discouraged—people are generally patient and friendly even in the city. **Baan Lan Look Mai** (309 Soi Savai Lieng, Thanon Mukkhamontri, tel. 04/425-3281, daily 11 A.M.–11 P.M., 200 baht) offers excellent Thai dishes in a charming old-fashioned house and garden setting. Dishes here range from traditional and reliable Isan regulars to innovative and unexpected flavors. For a bit of the latter, try the duck curry with grapes. The Population and Community Development Association of Thailand, a local NGO dedicated to community health and population control, opened **Cabbages and Condoms** (86/1 Serbsiri Rd., tel. 04/425-8100, 150 baht) to support the organization's mission. The extensive menu covers Thai regional dishes from across the country in addition to Isan specialties. The restaurant is brightly decorated (with, of course, a condom motif), and it is a step above most basic restaurants in the area, though still a comfortable place if you're looking for something relaxed and casual. All profits from the restaurant, as in the other locations throughout the country, help fund the organization.

Gai yang (grilled chicken) is one of the most popular dishes in the city, and you can't miss the plentiful small shops and stalls selling it. **Kai Yang Wat Pa Salawan** (Soi 3, Sueb Siri Rd., nearby Wat Pa Salawan, no phone, 10 A.M.–7 P.M., 100 baht) is a very casual canteen-style sit-down chicken shop that also serves Isan favorites such as *laab moo* and sticky rice.

Pattaya

Mantra (at the extreme northern end of Pattaya Beach Rd., tel. 03/842-9591, www.mantra-pattaya.com, daily 5 P.M.–1 A.M., 300–1,000 baht) is the current "it" restaurant in Pattaya—everyone's buzzing about its well-executed pan-Asian dishes and its very slick design. Indeed, the sparkling new restaurant has brought a much-needed breath of fresh air to the city's dining scene. The place serves Indian, Japanese, and Thai fusion, and it does all of them quite well. The interior features bold colors and is a sight to behold. The bar area makes for a comfy place for a drink or two in a swanky environment, while the interior dining area is sprawling and also very cool. The basic Indian food—naan, Samosas, and dal, especially—is particularly delectable. **Symphony Brasserie** (Pattaya 2nd Rd. between Soi 7 and 8, tel. 03/842-0939, www.symphony-pattaya.com, daily 5–11 P.M., 600 baht and up) is a popular choice for Thai and European cuisine. The award-winning establishment has an upscale atmosphere with white tablecloths and soft lighting. The menu runs the gamut from pan-fried frog's legs in a curry sauce to escargot to pasta, steaks, lamb, and seafood.

As is the case all over Thailand, casual street food is always a good bet for savory cheap eats. Food stands can be found all over the city, including an agglomeration of vendors along Pattaya Beach Road. And while high-quality grub and food courts are mutually exclusive in the West, that's not the case in Thailand; if you're looking to sample a wide variety of authentic Thai food, head to the food court in the **Carrefour** (Pattaya Klang Rd., daily 11 A.M.–10 P.M., 100 baht and up). The Hypermart as well as Tesco Lotus are popular destinations for Thais looking for good cheap eats; you can get rice and noodle dishes as well as fish and other meat curries.

DAILY LIFE

© SUZANNE NAM

MAKING THE MOVE

You've made the decision to move to Thailand. Now what? A surprising number of people just pack a bag and arrive in Thailand with vague plans, little cash, no job, and no visa, and a surprising number of them figure out how to make it work. Thailand has relatively permissive immigration laws that allow visitors to remain in the country (with some bureaucratic hassle) for months on end, and that's often enough time to figure out how to earn an income and get settled for the long term. If you don't have the constitution for that type of lifestyle, or if your company is moving you over, there are plenty of things you can do ahead of time to make the transition less stressful.

© SUZANNE NAM

Immigration and Visas

If you hold a passport from North America, the European Union, or most Asian and Latin American countries, the easiest way to enter Thailand is on a 30-day visa waiver that you can get when you arrive in the country. This is often called a tourist visa-on-arrival, but technically it's not a visa. Almost everyone who will be studying in Thailand, has a job here, or is looking for employment as a teacher enters the country this way. Once you're here, you have to gather the necessary paperwork for your visa, then leave the country again to visit a Thai embassy or consulate abroad to apply for an entry permit, which you then need to bring to an immigration office in Thailand to have converted to an actual visa. Most people go to either Penang or Kuala Lumpur in Malaysia, but any embassy or consulate can process the paperwork and grant your entry permit, usually in 24 hours. Although it is possible to have the paperwork completed before you arrive—you can have it delivered to you and then use it to pick up your entry permit in your home country's Thai consulate or embassy, thus avoiding another trip—few employers will do this. Though it does seem inefficient to arrive only to have to turn around and leave again, make the most of it by enjoying the fact that you've got an excuse to visit a neighboring country for a day or two.

Once you have the entry visa in your passport, you must go in person to an area immigration office and convert it into a visa that allows you to remain in the country. Depending on the immigration office you go to, this process can take from a couple of hours to all day. The default visa is single entry visa, but if you are planning on leaving the country for any reason while your visa is valid, you must apply for a multiple entry visa and pay an additional fee. Otherwise your visa will cease to be valid once you depart. Foreigners are required to report to the immigration office every 90 days. However, if you leave the country (assuming you have a proper multiple-entry visa) and return, you are considered to have checked in with immigration. In some provinces, you can do this reporting by mail, although that rule seems to change frequently.

The good news is that once you've done this the first time, you will not have to leave Thailand again for your visa renewal, although you will have to go back to an immigration office to have it renewed.

If you've arrived without a visa and don't qualify for one, you are allowed to get up to three 30-day visa waivers in any six-month period. You cannot do this inside Thailand. You must leave the country, have your passport stamped, and then return. There are numerous companies in Bangkok and some in other parts of the country that arrange these so-called "visa runs." Typically, you arrive at a meeting place very early in the morning and board a bus or van with other people doing the same thing. You'll be driven to a land border crossing point (from Bangkok, this is usually the border at Poi Pet, Cambodia), leave Thailand and enter the neighboring country, then turn around and reenter Thailand with a new 30-day stamp in your passport. The whole process takes a full day to complete. If you're interested in staying in Thailand for more than three months, consider applying for an ED Visa; it will give you a convenient excuse to learn Thai.

TYPES OF VISAS

There are many types of nonimmigrant visas issued by the Thai government to foreigners, including visas for journalists, missionaries, researchers, and skilled specialists. Most visas, at least initially, are valid for a one-year period. These are the most common visas.

B Visa

The B Visa is issued for work or business, and it is the visa you'll get if you've got a job in Thailand and your employer is sponsoring you. You can also get a B visa if you are a qualified investor evaluating investment opportunities in the country. The paperwork required for a B Visa is voluminous and includes certified financial statements and other corporate documents from your company. It's not the type of visa you can realistically get on your own, but if you are working for a company here in Thailand, they will produce the materials for you and usher you through the visa process. If you are on a company-sponsored visa, you will lose it immediately if you leave your job, with just a 24-hour grace period.

ED Visa

The ED Visa (education visa) is issued to people studying in Thailand at qualified educational institutions.

Many schools offer education visas.

GRAY-MARKET VISAS

There are a handful of companies in Thailand that offer "gray-market" visas. They're not counterfeit, but they aren't really legitimate since they often require that you sign documents saying that you are in the country as a potential investor. Costs for these visas run around 10,000 baht plus any fees you need to pay to the Thai government and are generally valid for one year. Applicants typically get a one-year multiple-entry B Visa that allows you to stay in the country but does not allow you to work here.

In order to obtain one of these visas, you'll need to process your paperwork outside the country at an embassy or consulate. Some embassies and consulates are on to this scam and will reject these applications. The visa provider will generally know which countries have the highest likelihood of success.

You can find these visa providers by searching for "one-year visa Thailand" on any Internet search engine.

These visas are a little shady, and if there is a crackdown by the immigration department, such visas may not be available anymore. If you need a visa and don't have a job, consider an education visa instead. The requirements are not burdensome, and the visa is completely legitimate.

You must be enrolled in a study program, but you do not need to be studying full-time or pursing an academic degree. You can qualify for an ED Visa if you are studying Thai and take a few hours of classes per week, which makes this visa an excellent option if you want to stay in the country but don't have anyone to sponsor you for a B Visa.

O Visa

The O Visa is a catchall visa for those who have family in the country, are getting medical treatment here, or are retired. If you marry a Thai national, you will qualify for an O Visa. Retirees must be at least 50 years old and show proof of at least 800,000 baht in a Thai bank account or a monthly income of at least 65,000 baht to qualify.

WORK PERMITS

If you are going to be doing anything in Thailand that produces income, the law requires that you have a work permit. In order to get a work permit, you need to have a job first, and many employers, especially those in the English-teaching business, won't even consider hiring you until you're in the country. The general practice is for employers to hire you first and even allow you to start working before processing all of the work-permit documents.

In almost all cases, your employer will handle the work permit application process for you, although they may not necessarily pay all the fees involved.

BEING AN EXPAT MOM

Canadian Karla Cripps, 32, has been married to 29-year-old Thai national Tou Patumsuwon for three years. They have two boys, ages two and one. Karla has been living in Thailand for six years and is the Bangkok editor of the regional travel and leisure website CNNGo.com. Tou was born and raised in Bangkok and is a small-business owner, a freelance photographer, and a design project manager.

How did you meet your husband?
We have mutual friends who, I'm somewhat ashamed to say, introduced us at a bar on Khao San Road. When I first met him, I thought he talked too much and was way too forward. Then he grew on me.

What is the biggest challenge of living in Thailand as a foreigner married to a Thai?
At home we have our fair share of cultural differences that arise, especially when it comes to raising the children in terms of rules, schedules, and limits. It also took a while for me to get used to the fact that in Thai-

land, the in-laws are around a whole lot more than they would be back in Canada. Although now that we have two toddlers, I welcome their help with open arms. Also, I'd say one of the biggest challenges is getting used to the unwanted attention when you're not in the tourist-frequented parts of the city. There aren't that many foreign women married to Thai men, so it's a bit of a novelty for some who can't help but stare at us when we enter a restaurant or other public place. One issue I will never get used to is all the strangers who try to pick up my kids, give them candies or treats, etc., when we're out somewhere. I'm told this is culturally acceptable behavior among Thais, but I find it unsettling.

What are the biggest rewards?
Life is never boring. Every day brings something new, whether I'm learning something fascinating about the religion and culture or trying a new Thai dish at some hidden restaurant. Also, my husband is a very patient man who cares for

Having your employer onboard is absolutely essential, as much of the documentation required involves financial and corporate information you would not otherwise have access to.

Thailand, like most countries, has a policy of not granting work permits for positions that can be filled by its own citizens. Most of the professions for which foreigners seek work permits in Thailand—teaching English, highly skilled managerial jobs, and so on—are not a problem, but if you are looking for a job that could easily be filled by a Thai, make sure you ask prospective employers if they will be able to get you a work permit before investing too much time and effort in the process.

Having a work permit not only entitles you to work legally in Thailand, it's also an essential document if you want to open a bank account, get a nonprepaid mobile phone, get a driver's license, and many other small necessities. If

everyone, attributes that I've tried to emulate. I also love the fact that my children are being brought up in a multicultural environment. We're fortunate enough to travel back to Canada every year, and we try to raise them by incorporating the best of both cultures.

Do you speak Thai?
I'm no expert, but I can get by all right in Thai and carry on conversations with those around me. (My in-laws and nanny don't speak any English.) I'm still learning new words every day, though, more so now that my oldest son is starting to talk quite a bit.

Which language do your children speak?
They speak and understand both Thai and English as we try to follow the "one parent, one language" rule. It's phenomenal to see my two-year-old son switch between languages with ease, depending on who he is addressing.

Where will you send them to school?

I have chosen a bilingual school near our home where the instruction is 80 percent English and 20 percent Thai. There are some great – but very expensive – international schools in Bangkok that we'll consider when they're older, but I want to make sure they have a strong Thai foundation first.

Do you have a nanny?
Yes. She's more like a live-in nanny-maid. I find it actually gives me more quality time with my kids. Because I don't have to spend my time cooking and cleaning, I can devote my nonwork time to them.

How did you find her?
She's a 20-year-old migrant worker from a Karen village in Burma that my cousin-in-law's nanny recommended. Amazingly, she traveled 12 hours in the trunk of a car to find work in Bangkok to support her family. Fortunately we were able to register her, so she's now a legal worker here. She's a part of our family, and I can't imagine life without her now that I'm working full time.

you are considering taking a position without a work permit or doing consulting or other "informal" work without a Thai-based employer, factor in the inconvenience of not having the permit for banking and other basic transactions—and the fact that you will be working illegally.

Since work permits are attached to specific employers, your work permit and visa will be canceled immediately upon termination. This means you have 24 hours to get out of the country. You can do a quick border run to get an additional 30 days to figure out your next step.

WHAT ABOUT THE REST OF THE FAMILY?

Spouses and children of employees on B Visas are routinely granted visas that allow them to stay in Thailand. If you are getting a B Visa as an investor, you must have additional funds available depending on the number of family members you are seeking visas for. Coming in on an ED Visa, your spouse and children are not granted visas. Children enrolled in full-time school while in Thailand will usually qualify for their own ED Visa if necessary.

Spouses and children are not granted work permits regardless of their visa status.

Moving with Children

Bringing children to Thailand offers some excellent perks and a few challenges. The perks are significant, especially for parents used to coming from places where child care is expensive. Hiring a full-time nanny is exorbitantly expensive for most people in the United States, but in Thailand it will cost just a few hundred dollars per month. In general, Thai people are very child-friendly, and it's rare to see anyone frown upon small children running around shops or restaurants. And, of course, your children will get to grow up exposed to different cultures and languages. For many parents, these three perks outweigh any of the obstacles.

Public play space is limited in big cities.

Many families who come to Thailand as expats have lived in other countries before and will move to another foreign country after they leave. All this change can be difficult for children, but they are usually more resilient and flexible than adults. Bangkok has a very international population, and the international schools see students come and go every year, so if you live in the capital, your kids will have plenty of peers who are in the same boat and will feel quite "normal" despite being in such an extraordinary situation.

The biggest challenge parents face on a daily basis is ensuring their children's safety. Although you can find child car seats in some large shops, some taxis don't even have seatbelts in the back. Medicines and common household chemicals rarely have child-safety caps, and crosswalks are routinely ignored by drivers. Unless you want your kids to live in a bubble, as they get older and more independent you will need to train them (and their child-care providers) carefully so they know how to avoid common dangers.

Finding the right schooling can be difficult. Although some parents (especially in families where one parent is Thai) enroll their children in public schools, they are on average inferior to public schools back home. In Bangkok there are many international schools offering U.S., British, or international curricula and instruction in English or French, but these schools can be as expensive as private schools are in the United States, and if you're in a smaller city or a rural area, you have fewer schools to choose from.

Moving with Pets

While having domestic animals in the home wasn't popular here a couple of decades ago, dog and cat ownership increases every year. You will be able to find a veterinarian, pet food, and even kennels in many parts of the country. Many apartment buildings will allow cats, but dogs, especially large ones, are more of a challenge: Not every building prohibits dogs, but more do than don't. It's not impossible to have a dog here, although it's not the most dog-friendly country. Dogs aren't allowed on public transport and in most public parks, and it's hard even to find a taxi to take a large dog anywhere.

Bringing a dog or cat into Thailand is not difficult. Although the Department of Livestock Development has the right to quarantine incoming dogs and cats for up to 30 days, if your paperwork is in order and your pet is in good health, you should be able to go through the whole inspection process at the airport and take your pet home with you that day. Check with the Department of Livestock Development before you make your travel arrangements, as flights from abroad sometimes land in the middle of the night and officials are not at the airport 24 hours a day to do inspections. If you arrive in the middle of the night when no veterinarian is available to inspect your pet, you will have to wait until they arrive before you can leave the airport. Occasionally, unscrupulous officials will attempt to shake down pet owners coming into the country, and there are stories circulating of owners who've paid as much as US$1,000 to "clear" customs before they can get their pets. At most you should pay a few thousand baht for paperwork. If you are charged more than this, stand your ground. You can also hire an agent in Bangkok who will meet you at the airport and shuffle you and your pet through the process quickly.

OPTIONS FOR PET TRANSPORT

Hundreds of pets are moved in and out of Thailand every year. The happiness and sense of normalcy that your pet provides you and your family is worth the trouble and expense of bringing it along, but you should be fully informed of the procedures and aware of all your options so you can avoid potential pitfalls. If a move to Thailand is in your pet's future, there are some important things you need to know – even before you begin your adventure.

Freight Forwarders and Moving Companies

Freight forwarders often handle pet transportation. The upside of this option is that you will be relieved of the worry and trouble of handling the paperwork during the move. The downside is that most cargo companies are used to moving inanimate objects – not living beloved members of the family. If you must use a freight forwarder or moving company, realize that conditions on the departure and arrival ends of the flight are often unsuitable for animals, and there may be long delays in transit or clearing customs and quarantine.

Pet Movers

Pet moving companies specialize in moving animals across borders and generally take special care to ensure that your pet arrives safely. Beware of cargo companies masquerading as pet movers, as your pet may get no better care than a piece of luggage – and at many times the price. Ensure you get an itemized quotation for the service and a detailed itinerary. If there are stops on the way, will anyone be there to walk and water your pet? Will your pet be accompanied before and after the flight during any warehouse stays?

D.I.Y.

If you have the time and patience to plan and perform the move on your own, you will need to know the export regulations of the country you are departing from. The United States does not require any documentation or permits, but many other countries require an export permit certifying that your pet has had all necessary vaccinations, is microchipped, and is healthy enough for air travel.

To import an animal into Thailand, make sure you follow these rules:

- You will need a health certificate in English stating the animal's species, breed, sex, age, and color or other identifying features.

- Your animal must be in good health.

- The country you are coming from must have been free from rabies for at least the past 12 months, *or* the animal must have a proof of a rabies vaccination not less than 21 days before your departure.

- If you are bringing a dog, it must have been vaccinated against leptospirosis at least 21 days before your departure or have had a lepto-

DAILY LIFE

Next, you will need to know the airline regulations related to your pet's trip. Airline regulations vary from carrier to carrier, and many airline staff are not familiar with their own company's regulations. Contact your airline and get them to provide you with their pet-moving regulations in writing. Make certain that you follow the regulations to the letter and that you inform the airline that your pet will be traveling well in advance of the departure date.

Airlines have varying policies on how pets are allowed to travel. Some airlines allow small dogs to ride in the cabin with their owners. Other airlines only allow pets as "accompanied baggage," and others only allow animals to travel as cargo.

Finally, you'll need to obtain an import permit from the Department of Livestock and Animal Husbandry in Thailand. You can get this in advance by sending a copy of your pet's veterinary records and the Export Permit issued by the country of departure. Once all this red tape is handled, your pet is ready to fly.

Patrick Bundock
Patrick is a 20-year resident of Thailand who has operated a dog-training school and boarding facility in Bangkok for 15 years. He advises Thais and expats on pet related issues. You can contact him at train@ k9bangkok.com.

CUSTOMS AND QUARANTINE IN THAILAND
Customs and Quarantine at Thailand's international airport run hot and cold. Depending on your arrival time in Thailand and whether there are any quarantine staff on duty, your pet may be held for inspection. In the last year I have heard three nightmare stories of dogs being held for more than 10 hours at the customs warehouse or hefty duties being levied on owners – even for mixed breeds. Ensure that all of your pet's paperwork is in order, but if you do run into problems at customs, be polite and respectful and reason with the inspectors to the best of your ability to have your pet cleared without delay.

spirosis test with a negative result not more than 30 days before your departure.

· All animals must also have proof of vaccination against other "significant infectious or contagious diseases" such as distemper, hepatitis, and parvovirus at least 21 days before your departure.

· The animals must be conveyed in nose- and paw-proof crates designed to avoid any risk of injury or unnecessary suffering.

The more difficult part is getting your animal to Thailand if you are coming from North America. Flights are long and often involve transfers, so make sure you plan your itinerary carefully. Small dogs and cats are allowed on some international flights, but animals over 22 pounds must go below. Even if you take a direct flight from Los Angeles to Bangkok, your pet will spend nearly 20 hours in the cargo hold without a walk. If you are transiting through another country, make sure to talk to the airline about any additional documentation you may need to provide.

What to Take

Housing options run the gamut from tiny studios to single-family homes with expansive grounds, but wherever you end up, keep in mind that many homes and apartments in the capital and on the islands are rented furnished with beds, dining room tables, and living room furniture, and that you can find nearly any household goods you could want or need in Thailand when you arrive. If you are moving out into the country, your housing will most likely not be furnished, but even if your shipping costs are paid for as part of a relocation package, you may not want to bring too much.

WHAT YOU MAY MISS

There is abundant shopping in Thailand, but there are a few things you won't be able to find or that will be inordinately expensive compared to the prices back home because they have to be specially imported for a very small market. Here are some common items to consider packing or shipping:

- Books in English, especially unpopular or uncommon titles
- Board games
- Bikes (you can find inexpensive bicycles and very expensive imported bicycles in Thailand, but nothing in between)
- Barbecue utensils
- Maple syrup
- Decaffeinated coffee
- Hair dye—it is available, but often just in dark colors
- Vitamins and supplements (many are available in Bangkok but are very expensive)

MONEY

Bringing a big stack of cash to Thailand to get yourself settled probably isn't necessary, nor is it wise, since you can use your ATM card at most of the country's big banks; and once you open a bank account here, you can transfer money fairly easily. You'll be subject to a daily maximum and may have to pay some additional fees, but it is still more economical than changing money in the country. Most apartments require first month, last month, and a security deposit, but serviced apartments, which are common in Thailand, require little upfront cash.

Appliances and housewares are readily available.

ELECTRONICS

Although electrical outlets in Thailand take either two round prongs or two flat blades as in the United States, Thailand's electricity runs on 220 volts, not the American 120 volts. If you make the mistake of plugging your U.S. appliances or electronics into the wall, you'll fry them quickly and without fail. Step-down transformers are available at some hardware stores if you must bring electronics from abroad. Most electronics with rechargeable batteries, such as laptops and mobile phones, have built-in transformers and can be used worldwide without problems.

Electronics stores are abundant in Thailand, and televisions, DVD players, and home appliances are priced on par with or cheaper than similar products back home. If you have a large collection of DVDs, you may want to consider bringing your DVD player (and purchasing a transformer). There are plenty available in Thailand, but most will only play Region 3 DVDs, not the Region 1 DVDs sold in the United States. You can also find universal DVD players, although they are more expensive.

MOBILE PHONES

If your mobile phone operates on a CDMA or GSM standard (this covers all tri-band and quad-band phones), is unlocked, and has a removable SIM

© SUZANNE NAM

Mobile phones are the best way to keep in touch in Thailand.

card, you can bring it to Thailand and get a SIM card here from one of the country's mobile phone service providers. If you can take the SIM card out but your phone has been locked by your existing service provider, bring it anyway; there are plenty of shops in Thailand that will unlock it for you for a small fee. You'll most likely void the warranty, but given how quickly mobile phone technology changes and the fact that you'll be overseas anyway, there's nothing to lose. If you need to pick up a mobile phone here, you'll find plenty of options across all price ranges, and sometimes more advanced technology than is available in the United States.

MEDICATIONS AND PERSONAL CARE PRODUCTS

Thailand offers a wide variety of prescription and over-the-counter drugs, beauty products, and vitamins, so if you expect you'll just need Tylenol, vitamin C, and sunscreen, don't worry about stocking up before you arrive. Many popular personal-care and beauty-product brands, such as Nivea, Dove, MAC, Chanel, and others, are easy to find in bigger cities. Many drugs that require a prescription back home, such as antibiotics and oral contraceptives, are available at drug stores and are inexpensive. Drug formulas vary, however, so if there's a particular brand you can't live without, bring an ample supply with you and make arrangements to have more shipped over. Popular brands of contact lenses are available without a prescription, and they are less expensive in Thailand than in the United States.

Pharmacies stock over-the-counter drugs and can dispense controlled drugs.

CLOTHING AND SHOES

There are plenty of locally made and imported clothes and shoes to buy in Thailand, and international brands such as Zara and Mango in Bangkok, but larger sizes are difficult to find. If you're a woman who wears anything larger than a U.S. size 10 or are a taller-than-average man or woman, you might want to bring the clothes you'll need while you are here. It's easy to get relatively inexpensive custom-made clothing regardless of your size, but it will be tough to get jeans, khakis, and other casual wear. Even international chains stock very few pieces in sizes larger than a U.S. women's size 6. Finding good underwear is also tricky. Department stores and shops are filled with cute, sexy, and comfortable bras and underwear, but if you're larger than a 34B, you'll have a tough time finding things that fit. If your shoe size is larger than a U.S. size 8 for women or 10 for men, you should bring shoes too.

Bras and underwear are plentiful, if you happen to wear small sizes.

COMFORT FOOD

Bangkok's international supermarkets stock everything from Vermont maple syrup to microwave popcorn, so if you are living in the city, you will not have trouble finding most popular American, Australian, European, and Japanese foods. You can even find turkeys for Thanksgiving. There's only one food that's tough to find here—decaffeinated coffee. It's extremely expensive at local Starbucks and not always available in supermarkets, so if you are a dedicated decaf drinker, it might be worth it to pack some and have friends bring bags of it when they visit. If you must have Marshmallow Fluff or a particular brand of organic peanut butter, bring it along too. If you are living outside Bangkok and away from heavily touristed areas, you won't have access to as many international foods, but you don't need to bring them all the way from home when you can just stock up whenever you pass through the capital.

SHIPPING OPTIONS

Thailand has nearly everything you'll need to set up a comfortable home, so it really is feasible just to pack a couple of suitcases with the clothing, documents, and books you'll need and get everything else while you're here. This will also save you money when you leave the country, as you won't have to pay to ship things back and can sell whatever you've purchased on Craigslist, to friends, or by some other method.

If you need to ship things here and your company isn't arranging it for you, bear in mind that most items will be shipped by sea as part of a large container shipment and will take at least a few weeks, and usually more than a month, to arrive. The cost of shipping the contents of your home across the globe isn't astronomical, but it will cost thousands of dollars. Although there are scores of shipping companies offering overseas services, they aren't the folks actually moving your stuff to Asia. They facilitate obtaining space in a shipping container, pick up your stuff, help you with customs and insurance forms, and then find an agent here Thailand to help you navigate customs and deliver your things to you when they arrive.

CUSTOMS

If you are moving to Thailand and have a nonimmigrant visa that allows you to stay in the country for at least a year, you are allowed to bring your household effects into the country duty-free, but there are some important rules that apply. The duty-free exemption is meant to cover a reasonable amount of household items that you have already been using. It does not apply to new items you buy just before relocating. The customs department is also pretty strict about their "one item" rule, meaning that you are allowed one blender, one television, one microwave, etc. Relocating families are allowed duplicate items within reason. The exemption technically only applies if your goods arrive in the window one month before to six months after you get here, and there is significant paperwork that must be completed before shipping and upon arrival. Almost everyone hires a customs broker to deal with the paperwork and customs officials.

CARS

Used personal cars are not exempt from duty, which can be as high as 100 percent of the cost of the vehicle, making importing a car into Thailand prohibitively expensive for most people. United Nations employees, embassy employees from most countries, and employees of some international agencies do enjoy a car-import exemption. Check with your employer for specifics and logistics of importation under these circumstances. Bear in mind that in Thailand, people drive on the left side of the road and the steering wheel is on the right side of the car. It is not illegal to drive a left-hand-drive car in Thailand, but it can be more difficult in terms of visibility.

DAILY LIFE

HOUSING CONSIDERATIONS

Thailand has always been considered an inexpensive place to live, but that's not true across the board. Rental costs vary significantly depending on where you live and what you want. If you have the cash and the desire, your daily experience could be very similar to the one you are leaving. You can live in a modern Western-style apartment in Bangkok, surround yourself with super-markets that sell Jiffy peanut butter and French cheese, and stop into the local Starbucks for a latte every morning before heading to your office on the city's modern subway. But bear in mind that people who choose to live in more local areas with mostly Thai neighbors typically end up picking up the language faster and connecting to everyday Thai culture more than those who live in areas or buildings populated mostly by foreigners and wealthy Thais.

Luckily, if you're moving to Bangkok, housing options are myriad. Depending on your budget, you can find everything from furnished apartments

© SUZANNE NAM

that come with daily maid service and cost 30,000 baht per month to one-room coldwater-only studios in local neighborhoods for just a few thousand baht. Mid-range apartments, priced from 20,000 baht to 60,000 baht, make up the bulk of the market. In this price range you're likely to find modern, Western-style apartments in areas close to public transportation with swimming pools and parking.

As you begin to look for housing, make sure you know what you want. Do you want a house? A new condo you can customize? An apartment with a swimming pool? Maid service? A concierge? Restaurants and shopping close by or even in your building? Do you want to live in a building that houses mostly other foreigners, or one that's primarily Thais, or a mixed building with both? Do you need all of the amenities of a Western-style apartment? How much do you want to spend? In Bangkok and other locations popular with foreigners, the quality of housing tends to decline the farther you are from the city center (or the beach, as the case may be), so if you want a large, modern Western-style apartment on the outskirts, it will be tougher to find and in some cases just won't exist.

If your company is relocating you here, chances are they will help you find housing. You may find that the agent who has been hired to find you a house or apartment has some preconceived notions about the type of housing foreigners want and the neighborhoods they want to live in. Do not feel like you need to agree with their suggestions. Spend at least a couple of days getting to know your new city or town before making any decisions.

Once you've figured out a price range and determined what type of housing will suit you best, pick your location carefully. Public rapid transportation is limited, and traffic can be disastrous during rush hour. If you are looking for a place in central Bangkok and you'll be driving to work or driving the kids to school, test the commute before you commit. Some streets have easy access to the expressway and other major traffic arteries, but one block in any direction may add another 20 or 30 minutes to your ride.

Bangkok, Phuket, Samui and Pattaya have some very high-end housing, both for rent and for sale. There are plenty of apartments renting for 100,000 baht or more per month and selling for more than the equivalent of $1 million. At that level, you won't be spending any less per square foot than you would in most major cities in the United States.

There are amazingly cheap apartments to be had, but it's also easy to end up spending as much or more than you would back home on an apartment. At the low end, you can find very basic studio apartments in any urban area for just 3,000–5,000 baht per month. For that, you'll get a one-room apartment with about 250 square feet of space, a bathroom with a cold-water shower, and maybe a microwave and mini-fridge. If you're looking for one of these studios in Bangkok, you'll need to move to the outskirts of the city unless you're really lucky. In smaller cities, these apartments can be found in more central areas.

The downside to inexpensive local housing is that it may not be up to a standard you're accustomed to. The wiring can be downright scary; bathrooms don't have bathtubs, showers are simply a showerhead and a drain in the corner of the bathroom, and toilets are sometimes the squat variety or must be flushed using a bucket instead of a lever. Most regular Thai houses and apartments do not have hot water taps (although you can easily and inexpensively install a shower hot-water heater). If you did not grow up in a tropical climate, you'll probably find air-conditioning a necessity; it is not standard equipment or is only installed in bedrooms. Thai kitchens are almost never air-conditioned, and they consist of a sink, a propane range, and a refrigerator. You won't find an oven in a regular Thai kitchen either. The most difficult difference for many foreigners is the lack of natural light in apartments and houses. Blocking out the sun keeps things cooler, but it can feel a little depressing, especially with fluorescent lighting.

In Phuket, Samui, Chiang Mai, and other parts of the country that attract a lot of foreigners or have wealthy local populations, there is also a good range of housing options (and less traffic to contend with), although you won't find as much selection as in Bangkok. Because Phuket and Ko Samui are so popular with vacationers and, increasingly, retirees, the cost of housing isn't cheap, although you can still find houses near the beach to rent for the equivalent of US$1,000 per month and basic Western-style apartments for 15,000 baht per month. If you are moving to more rural and poorer parts of the country, there won't be many luxury apartments or furnished homes for foreigners available, but if you've chosen such an area to live in, chances are you don't want that anyway. In these areas it is possible to rent a whole house for less than 10,000 baht per month. There are fewer apartment buildings, but in areas where there are, Thai-style studios rent for as little as 3,000 baht per month. There aren't tons of real estate agents to work with, so your best bet is relying on word of mouth, talking to friends, and getting into a car or on a motorbike to look. Finding housing may be a little more involved, but most people in this situation end up experiencing a side of Thailand few foreigners get to see.

Housing costs in Thailand are far less expensive than living in New York, London, or Japan, but you can spend a substantial amount of money on your living quarters if you're living in Bangkok or opt for more luxurious digs than you'd have at home. Outside Bangkok, costs drop dramatically, and you'll find several thousand baht per month can be enough to cover your rent.

Renting

If you are moving to a big city or other area where there are many foreigners, you won't have difficulty finding an apartment, negotiating a price, signing a contract, and moving in. Tens of thousands of foreigners already live in Thailand, so people are used to renting to foreigners. Most housing marketed toward expats consists of higher-end furnished apartments with some services, such as cable television, already included. If you want convenience and don't want to deal with having your phone or cable hooked up, or even cleaning your apartment and changing your sheets, this is a great option. Those who are seeking a different experience in Thailand, or have a tighter budget, will have a harder time finding rental housing. It's not that it doesn't exist, but less-expensive apartments often aren't listed by real estate agents, and you will keep running into the language barrier as you search for a place, negotiate the lease, and move in.

Although the Internet is useful for seeing photos of houses and apartments and getting an idea of costs, resist the temptation to set up housing sight unseen before you arrive, unless you are moving to an area where options are

Landlords often post vacancies.

TYPICAL RENTAL COSTS IN BANGKOK, PHUKET, AND CHIANG MAI

The monthly cost to rent a modern two-bedroom apartment with a Western-style kitchen in the most desirable neighborhoods in three popular expat locations:

City	Neighborhood	Cost
Bangkok	Lang Suan	30,000 baht
Phuket	Patong	22,000 baht
Chiang Mai	Central	16,000 baht

extremely limited. Housing listed on the Internet tends to be more expensive than average, and if you don't know the area you are moving to and haven't seen other places, you will have no idea whether you are getting a good deal or even if it's the right place for you. In Bangkok, Chiang Mai, Phuket, and Samui, you can easily arrange to stay in a short-term serviced apartment for a week or two while you look for permanent housing. In other parts of the country you may need to find a hotel, but it's still worth the inconvenience to save yourself problems in the future.

FINDING THE RIGHT PLACE

Unfortunately, there is no central repository for housing listings in most places you will be house-hunting. There is a smattering of stuff on the Internet, some landlords simply put up signs in front of their buildings, and many apartments that might otherwise be totally suitable will be listed in Thai-language publications and difficult to identify. There are real estate agents in major cities that can help you find housing; they are often the best bet if you are looking

© SUZANNE NAM

Thai-style kitchens offer little more than a couple of burners, a sink, and a refrigerator.

COMMON HOUSING AND LAND TERMS

Most real estate agents and owners who market to foreigners use terms that will be easily understandable to most people, as homes are described based on the number of bedrooms and bathrooms and the floor area. Area is always expressed in square meters, not square feet, but as one square meter is equal to 10.8 square feet, the conversion is straightforward. Note that sizes often include attached balconies or other outdoor space.

Land sizes are expressed using the following terms in Thailand.

- *Ngan:* 400 square meters or 4,350 square feet
- *Rai:* 1,600 square meters, 17,200 square feet, or 0.4 acres
- *Talang wah:* 4 square meters or 43 square feet

for anything other than a typical serviced apartment but aren't looking for cheap local housing. The best way to find an apartment in any price range is to figure out which neighborhood or area you want to live in first, then spend a day walking or driving around, stopping into buildings and asking whether they have any apartments for rent. Security guards and building managers are generally happy to answer questions and will also arrange a quick tour of any vacant units on the spot. Even if you don't know any Thai phrases, you can have someone write a quick introduction in Thai for you to present. If you are looking for more traditional housing where there may be no one who speaks any English, bring along a friend, assistant, or other person who speaks Thai. This is a time-consuming and daunting process, but it really is the best way to find the right apartment and get to know the neighborhood you want to live in.

Serviced Apartments and Other Short-Term Rentals

Serviced apartments are furnished apartments with maid service, room service, laundry service, and other amenities one would typically find in a hotel. Although there aren't serviced apartments in every part of Thailand, they are easy to find in Bangkok and to a lesser extent Pattaya, Chiang Mai, Phuket, and Samui. They can be a very attractive option if you want luxury and convenience. The best thing about serviced apartments is that you won't need to sign a lease to move in, and you can stay for as little as a week or as long as a few years. You will pay for all that luxury, however—typically 30 percent more than you'd pay for a similarly sized regular apartment.

DAILY LIFE

SUCCESSFUL APARTMENT HUNTING

Marra Guttenplan recently moved to Thailand from New York City to spend a year working for the international development group Voluntary Services Overseas. Here's what she has to say about finding an apartment in Bangkok.

What type of housing were you looking for?

I was looking for either a studio apartment or a two-bedroom apartment that I would share with a woman I met through a Facebook group called Farang Girls in Bangkok. After looking around, it seemed as though I could get a lot more for my money in a two-bedroom apartment, and the woman I met seemed fun and normal, so I decided to go for it.

How did you narrow down potential neighborhoods?

I asked people from work and friends of friends that I was in touch with in Bangkok to suggest neighborhoods; I then walked around the various neighborhoods and decided on the Victory Monument–Phaya Thai–Ratchethewi area.

What made you pick that neighborhood?

It's close to the Skytrain, close to the center of town, relatively convenient to my office, and has lots of cute and affordable restaurants, bars, and noodle shops. I was told that a lot of NGO workers in Bangkok live around there and thought it would be a good place to meet new friends with common interests and budgets. I also saw several other foreigners my age when I was walking around.

Where else did you look?

The Sukhumvit area near Phloen Chit and Asok, which I found more expensive for both housing and food. I liked the Sukhumvit area, but it was a little too hectic, touristy, and dirty for me. I also looked at the Silom and Sathorn areas, which I found very expensive.

How did you look for an apartment?

I looked online, but mainly I just walked around the various neighborhoods and walked into buildings and asked if there were any apartments available to rent. I was able to do this in Thai, which definitely helped a lot, because many people did not speak any English.

What was your budget? Did you stick to it?

Long-Term Rentals

Rental terms for houses and apartments in Thailand are usually very similar to those in the United States. To rent most long-term apartments or houses, you will be required to sign a one-year lease and put down a security deposit equal to one month's rent. In many regular buildings there is either a building manager or a custodian on duty, so if you have any problems, you can immediately find someone to help you. Many long-term apartments and some houses are rented furnished, although it is possible to find unfurnished apartments, especially at the lower end of the price range.

I was hoping to spend 6,000 baht per month, but I was willing to go up to 10,000 baht. I will be spending 10,000 baht per month. I was also able to do this because my roommate will be staying in the larger bedroom and paying 13,000 baht per month.

Did you see many options in that price range?

I saw very few studio apartments for 6,000 baht but saw several for 7,000-14,000 baht. I also saw several two-bedroom apartments for 21,000-30,000 baht per month.

Did you negotiate with the landlord?

We did. The original price of the apartment was 26,000 baht per month, but we got it for 23,000. We also convinced the landlord to purchase a washing machine for the apartment and basic plates, silverware, glasses, and pots. Originally the landlord wanted three months' rent up front: a two-month deposit and the first month's rent. We negotiated to pay only the two-month deposit and to pay the first month's rent on December 1, when the lease starts.

Describe your apartment.

It's a two-bedroom, two-and-a-half bath, brand-new 65-square-meter (700-square-foot) apartment. It's fully furnished with new modern furniture, except for bedding and towels. There is a small gym and a pool, and there is a security guard and a key card to access the elevator bank.

Any pitfalls or advice?

If you're on a budget and want to live in a newer condo building, find a roommate!

A lot of buildings I looked at were full – it is probably better to look closer to the end of the month when the buildings will know whether or not they have availability for the next month.

Learn a few key phrases in Thai. It helps to find out about apartment availability and to negotiate with the owner.

I didn't go through a real estate broker. It might make the process a little easier, but I heard it increases the rent by about 2,000 baht per month.

Be prepared for several long, hot, sweaty days pounding the pavement and looking for apartments.

RENTAL AGENTS AND LEASES

In Thailand, rental agents are usually paid by the landlord, not the renter, so there is no downside to seeking help from a rental agent—except that the landlord may pass the cost along to you. Agents do not usually have listings at the very bottom end of the range, but depending on their specialty they can find you anything from a 15,000 baht-per-month studio in central Bangkok to a 150,000 baht-per-month house in the middle of the city. A lot of rental agents who deal with foreigners believe that they are all looking for luxurious serviced apartments in very international neighborhoods (probably because the majority of them are). Make sure your agent understands well what you are looking for so that you don't spend time viewing apartments and houses you would never live in.

Leases are almost always for one year, but the terms you negotiate for your lease depend on the person you are renting from. If you are renting from an individual homeowner, you may be able to negotiate a shorter lease. Even big buildings managed by professionals have some wiggle room. Basic lease terms are similar to those you will find in the United States. You are entitled to a quiet, safe home, and you must pay your rent on time and keep the home in reasonable condition while you are living there. In many cases you will get a lease in English, but if you get a lease in Thai, you must have it translated before signing it.

Not all apartments are listed, so spend time walking around the neighborhood you've chosen to live in.

Like anywhere else, resolving problems that may come up with your house or apartment is more about the reasonableness of your requests, the responsiveness of your landlord, and your relationship with him or her rather than the written terms of a contract. Goodwill goes a long way here, so take time to cultivate at least a civil relationship with your landlord, building manager, and anyone else working in your building. Taking a landlord to court in Thailand as a foreigner would be an expensive and difficult proposition.

Buying a Home

Under existing law, foreigners are not allowed to own land in Thailand, but they can buy condominiums. If fact, many condominium developments in Bangkok, Pattaya, Phuket, and Samui are built with foreign buyers in mind, and prices for these condominiums range from a few million to more than 30 million baht. Consider any decision to buy in Thailand carefully. Many people are under the misguided notion that buying condominiums in Thailand is an excellent investment. Whether this is true or not will depend largely on the location and condition of the building and unit. If you buy a new luxury condominium and don't expect to be living there for more than a few years before you try to sell it or rent it out, make sure you understand the market dynamics here. Thailand continues to develop, and newer, nicer, more luxurious condominiums are being built all the time. There's no shortage of buildable land, even on the islands, where inexpensive two-story concrete structures are

CAN FOREIGNERS OWN LAND IN THAILAND?

The short answer is no. Thailand prohibits foreigners from owning real property, so if you want to buy your home, you'll be limited to condominiums and other developments where legal title to the land does not rest with you.

There are some ways around this, although their validity has never been tested in a court of last resort and may not be airtight. Foreigners interested in buying land for their home or investing in land for development typically create Thai-domiciled companies that hold the title to the land. Since the Thai company cannot be foreign-owned and own land, some lawyers and advisers will create companies for you in which there is a nominal Thai owner who has 51 percent of the company's shares but does not have 51 percent control, nor 51 percent of the economic interest in whatever assets (the property) the company owns. Thousands of foreigners have set up these companies to own land in Thailand, and there are advisers and lawyers who can do this quickly and at relatively little cost.

Another option is to find a Thai partner who is willing to invest with you, but if you do, so you'll be giving up control of the company that owns the land. If you are married to a Thai national, it's possible to have your spouse own 51 percent of the company that owns land, but be warned that if things should not go as planned, you may not have much protection in a Thai court. Some legal advisers insist that if you go this route, you arrange for a long-term leaseback of the property so that at least you have the right to use it for the lease period (which can be up to 30 years and renewable).

The sky's the limit when it comes to luxury.

being replaced on a daily basis. By the time you decide to sell or rent, there may be a lot more competition in your neighborhood, and your property may not be considered as desirable anymore.

FINDING THE RIGHT PLACE

Much of the advice above about finding the right rental property holds true for condominiums. Pick potential neighborhoods and make sure you know what you want before you begin the search. If you know you will be in Thailand indefinitely, try to predict what your neighborhood will look like in five or 10 years. Are there more developments being planned, or empty plots of land where anything could be built?

Condominiums in Thailand are either freehold or leasehold, and this is an important distinction to keep in mind when you are looking. Freehold means you own the condominium forever. Leasehold means you'll own it for 30 years or more before ownership reverts back to the developer. Leasehold condominiums are less common outside very prime areas in Bangkok (or those where the developer is building based on his or her own leasehold rights), but some developers offer leasehold condominiums because foreigners aren't allowed to own more than half of any development. Leaseholds get around this requirement but leave foreign buyers with inferior property rights.

MORTGAGES

If you are buying property in Thailand as a foreigner, few banks will be able to offer you a normal mortgage with a competitive interest rate. There are some work-arounds that property developers have devised to encourage foreigners to buy, but they will routinely require significantly more than 20 percent of the purchase price to be paid in cash. Sometimes developers will offer to finance the purchase themselves, but typically do so only for a very short term—three or four years, after which you must pay off the loan in full.

Building a Home

Despite the fact that foreigners are prohibited from owning real property in Thailand, many foreigners figure out ways around the laws and decide to build their dream homes here. The first obstacle, how to ensure you have valid rights to the land, is tricky and requires good legal counsel and a stomach for risk. The second obstacle can also be formidable—how to ensure your home is being built to the specifications you desire. Thai and Western building standards vary tremendously, and many a homebuilder has a tale of woe about not getting what they wanted. In bigger cities it may be easier to identify building contractors who are accustomed to working with foreigners, but out in the country it will be much more difficult.

Thailand's nonstop building boom means there's no shortage of housing options.

Household Expenses

The basic cost of running a household in Thailand can be a lot cheaper than back home, but it can be easy to rack up additional expenses for things, particularly domestic help, that you never thought you needed until you arrived.

UTILITIES

If you are living in a fully serviced apartment, your primary utilities—water and electricity—will generally be paid by the landlord. If you are renting a normal apartment or a house, you will be responsible for water and electricity costs. If you live in a building, your landlord will bill you for them, and if you live in a house, townhouse, or other standalone unit, you will be billed directly and have to set up accounts with the water and electricity companies. Landlords will sometimes mark up the costs of water and electricity, so make sure you negotiate that up front when you move in.

Energy costs are less expensive here, but heavy reliance on air-conditioning can eat away at any substantial savings. Most homes are equipped with

MAE BAAN

Many foreigners living in Thailand hire *mae baan* to do domestic work in their homes. *Mae baan* literally means "house mother," and that's a good description of what *mae baan* are. They can cook, clean, do laundry, iron, run errands, grocery shopping, run interference between you and the rest of the world, and generally take care of you and your family. Many nicer apartments have maid's quarters (a small room, usually off of the kitchen, with an attached bathroom), but *mae baan* don't always live with the families they work for. Some, especially those who work part-time for several families, will just come in on appointed days. Others will stay during the week but return home for the weekend. All of this depends on the deal you negotiate. If you just need someone who is a house cleaner, you may

only need a part time *mae baan*. If you want someone to cook for you, do all the ironing, go grocery shopping, and even babysit once in a while, a full time *mae baan* might be necessary.

For what you're paying, which will be just several thousand baht per month for a full-time maid and nanny, you may not get someone who can do everything you want exactly the way you want it done. Housecleaning techniques, child-rearing philosophies, and even the way food is prepared are different in Thailand. The best relationships between families and *mae baan* are built on good communication, so make sure you explain what you want clearly. Don't forget that you're expected to pay an annual one-month bonus on Songkran, when your *mae baan* will most likely go home for a week.

propane gas ranges fueled by refillable metal tanks instead of gas piped into the house. Those tanks cost a few hundred baht to refill and will last a normal household months before they must be replaced. In an apartment building, your building manager will be able to replace the tank for you. Otherwise you will need to find a supplier, who will deliver replacement tanks to your door as necessary.

Cable television is included with most serviced apartments, but if you need it installed and will be paying for it yourself, expect to pay about 1,600 baht for installation and anywhere from 800 to 3,200 baht per month, depending on your package. High-speed Internet is available in almost every corner of the country and will cost about the same as cable television, depending on the speed of your connection. There are English-speaking agents at the major phone, cable, and Internet companies who will assist you in setting up your utilities and scheduling installation. You will probably spend 20 minutes on hold, and once you schedule your installation, be given a seven-hour window in which the technician will come to your house, but at least it feels just like it does back home.

Although it can be complicated to get your utilities hooked up initially, you can pay virtually all bills online through a Thai bank or at any 7-Eleven for a very small service fee. Since you probably won't bother ordering checks for your bank account, going to a 7-Eleven is the easiest way to take care of your bills. Just bring them into any shop along with enough cash to cover them. The clerk will run them through the computer, take your money, and give you a detailed receipt.

Tap water in Thailand is not potable, and nearly everyone drinks bottled water. You can buy it in 10-liter (2.5-gallon) bottles in any supermarket, but it's usually much easier to arrange to have it delivered. All apartment buildings already have the service set up; all you need to do is tell your landlord or the building manager how much water you need. It's usually delivered right to your door on a weekly basis. People living in houses can arrange water delivery directly with one of the many companies that perform the service. If you are living in a very rural part of the country, however, you may need to lug it home yourself from the supermarket.

DOMESTIC HELP

Most people who come to Thailand hire some sort of domestic help, whether it be a cleaning woman (and they are always women) who comes in a couple of days a week, a full-time maid, or something in between. For most people coming from the United States, having someone working in your home can

FINDING A NANNY

If you've never hired someone to look after your children, finding a nanny in Thailand will feel like a daunting task. Not only will you have to navigate the general difficulty finding someone you trust, but you'll be doing so in a foreign environment.

If all you want is a babysitter, it's not difficult to find someone to look after children. Ask your friends, neighbors, and colleagues, and you'll quickly have a few prospects to interview. But if you want someone to take care of them for hours a day who is bilingual and has some professional experience with children, it will be more difficult. Make sure you know exactly what you want before you begin the process. Do you want the caregiver to live in your home? Should she speak English, French, or Mandarin fluently? Is she to be available seven days a week? Does she also cook and clean? Once you've figured that out and started to ask around, go through a rigorous interview process and ask for references, then observe any potential nanny with your children for a few hours.

If you are in Bangkok, Bangkok Mothers and Babies International (www.bambiweb.org) has a listing service you can use to search for nannies looking for jobs; you can also post your own ad.

feel awkward at first as you navigate the type of relationship you want with your housekeeper, how much you pay them, and what type of boss you are. Since most Americans aren't used to having a maid and come from far more egalitarian societies, it can be tough to wrap your head around having someone come into your home to do your dishes and iron your clothes for just a few dollars a day. That's probably why foreigners are generally considered good bosses and tend to pay their domestic help better. Communication problems and unrealistic expectations are the source of most complaints that expats have about domestic help. Bear in mind that the person you hire is likely not going to speak a lot of English, nor is she going to be a professional trained housekeeper, even if she has years of experience. You must spend some time up front setting out a schedule of tasks and making expectations clear. It's also wise to walk your maid through how appliances are used and where things should go. If there are certain areas you don't want tidied up, such as your desk, make that clear too. If you're lucky, you'll find someone who can help you run your home more efficiently and keep you more organized, especially if you have children.

Some apartment buildings offer daily, bi-weekly, or weekly cleaning services for a fixed fee. If you are hiring someone yourself, your cost can vary dramatically depending on where you live. Some cleaning women will charge a few hundred baht per visit, and some 1,500 baht per week or more plus room and board. As you try to figure out how much you should pay, keep in mind that the current minimum wage is a little over 200 baht per day in Bangkok and less outside of the capital. Don't forget that in addition to whatever salary you agree on, it is expected that you will pay an additional month's salary right before the Thai New Year (Songkran) in April. Most Thais working as nannies, maids, drivers, and gardeners have families in other parts of the country and use those funds to visit them during the holiday and to support them throughout the year.

LANGUAGE AND EDUCATION

"Thai is so hard!" is the complaint many new residents have when they move to Thailand. It's not easy to learn the language, but if you calculate how much time and money you'll save by speaking passable Thai, you'll realize that it's worth the investment. Without doubt, learning some Thai will make your life easier.

Where to send your children to school isn't such an easy decision, however. The Thai public school system is not likely going to be an option for you, as your children may not speak any Thai or you won't be familiar enough with the system to feel you can confidently manage their education. International schools are plentiful in Bangkok, but as you move away from areas with large populations of foreigners, good options become fewer and farther between.

Learning Thai

Learn Thai. Don't be discouraged by people who tell you that Thai is an impossible language to learn or that you don't need to speak Thai to live in Thailand. You certainly don't need to be fluent, and you can survive here without much Thai at all if you happen to live in a part of the country where there are lots of foreigners or have a spouse or partner who's Thai; there are plenty of expats who have been here for years and can only say a few words. But, if you are going to be in Thailand for anything longer than a vacation, you'll find that learning a little bit of the language will help you tremendously in every aspect of your everyday life. You will have a much easier time meeting people and making friends in your community, and if you are working here, you will earn the respect of your Thai colleagues.

The Thai language isn't as difficult as some people believe. It is a tonal language, which is a challenge for most native English speakers, since English doesn't use tones to convey meaning, and initially English speakers often can't even hear the difference between a rising tone, a falling tone, a high tone, and a low tone. But training yourself to hear the tones and being able to mimic them actually happens quickly when you learn them in a structured environment. The other challenge is the writing system. Not only is Thai written in an entirely foreign script, there are 44 consonants and 15 vowels, which only sounds off-putting until you realize that many of those consonants make the same sounds. One of the reasons there are different ways to write a "d" sound is that each different written form, when combined with vowels and tone marks, indicates a different tone.

The good news is that you don't have to worry about conjugating verbs or using articles. And Thai people are usually very forgiving of your mistakes and very encouraging of foreigners' efforts to learn their language.

How much Thai do you need to speak? If you are living in Bangkok, Phuket, Pattaya, or another area that has a lot of international visitors, you'll find that you don't need much Thai to get by on a daily basis. Once you have mastered a few hundred words of vocabulary, you'll find that you are able to have basic conversations. You won't understand everything that is being said to you, but at least you'll be able to chat and make small talk. If you are moving out into more rural areas of Thailand, or smaller cities where foreigners don't typically travel, you'll really need to speak Thai with a level of fluency that will ensure not only that you can chat with your neighbors and colleagues but that you can obtain the things you need and are able to communicate in an emergency. Almost every major city has Thai language courses available, and a couple of months of part-time study will go a long way.

15 ABSOLUTELY ESSENTIAL THAI WORDS AND PHRASES

sawadee ka/kap – hello, goodbye
kap kun ka/kap – thank you
saibai dee mai? – How are you?
mai pen rai – no problem; no worries
saibai – good; fine; happy; relaxed; comfortable
mai put passa Thai – I don't speak Thai.
mai khao jai – I don't understand.
pai . . . – (I want to) go to . . .
tao rai? – How much? How many?
mai ow – I don't want that (thing)
mai dai – I can't/won't do that (action)
mai chai – no
gin khao – to eat (very informal but very widely used in colloquial
   conversation)
arroy – delicious
soi – side street

REGIONAL DIALECTS

Standard Thai is the predominant dialect of the Central Plains region, which includes Bangkok; it is also the country's official language and the language you'll hear on television, read in newspapers, and see is advertising. It is the dialect you'll learn in any structured Thai course and is sufficient to allow you to communicate with everyone in the country, with the exception of people from some of the ethnic groups that live along the borders of Burma.

Northern Thailand, southern Thailand, and northeast Thailand all have their own dialects, along with seven others spoken around the country. Although everyone should learn standard Thai, if you are living in Isan or southern Thailand, you will need to pick up some new vocabulary and expressions.

LANGUAGE SCHOOLS

There are hundreds of Thai language schools in Thailand. Most are for-profit affairs, although there are some academic programs at larger colleges and universities. Although you will find the largest number of language schools concentrated in Bangkok, at the very least you will find small schools in most major cities where foreigners live. Language schools use various methodologies, but most of the larger schools follow a similar format. Students are grouped by ability and taught in an immersive, interactive environment where little or no English is spoken. These courses are often scheduled as daily three- or four-hour classes Monday through Friday in monthlong modules, but there are some schools offering evening classes or classes once or twice a week instead of every day. Prices for structured programs with classes five days a week generally cost 4,000 baht and up.

The American University Alumni (A.U.A.) Language Center in Chiang Mai and Bangkok offers Thai programs that are well-regarded. Language Express, Union Language School, and Walen School of Thai in Bangkok are also recommended; Language Express and Walen offer education visas. Union Language School is affiliated with the Church of Christ, and many of the students are missionaries-in-training from the United States; but the school is open to everyone and course material is secular.

If the course schedule doesn't work for you, it's also easy to find a tutor who will come to your home or office. If you do go this route, make sure you discuss your tutor's methodology upfront and that you agree with it. The biggest risk you take if you hire a private tutor is that you'll get lazy. It's easy to reschedule classes or skip out on your homework. It's best to lay out a syllabus in the beginning and try to stick with it.

Most language schools can connect you with a tutor. You can also find tutors through friends and colleagues, but make sure the person who will be instructing you is qualified to do so.

Universities

For those truly serious about learning Thai and willing to invest time and money in their studies, there are a handful of very well-regarded Thai studies institutes at some of the country's universities. These courses are generally full-time, and some include substantial courses on Thai culture, society, and political science as well. In Bangkok, both Chulalongkorn University and Thammasat University have highly respected Thai programs. These are more expensive than nonacademic programs and attract highly motivated students. The only complaint some students have is that lessons can move quickly.

Khon Kaen University in Isan has a Thai studies program that some American universities use for their study-abroad programs, but it is open to other qualified people. Chiang Mai University has a Thai language institute, but it is not as rigorous as some, as classes only meet for four hours a week. A university can also help you obtain an education visa.

LEARNING TO READ AND WRITE

Most structured Thai language courses will teach you basic reading and writing in the midlevel and advanced classes. Again, don't believe anyone who says it's impossible to read Thai. Plenty of foreigners have managed to master it, and there are hundreds of thousands of six-year-olds who can read and write Thai. If you don't learn some Thai reading skills, you can get by, but most of your surroundings will be a mystery. You won't be able to read addresses, advertisements, bus routes, or menus. Even if you don't have the time to learn to read at a high level, you can learn the writing system in just a couple of days. Learning the basic sounds that each letter makes (without the tone rules) along with some common words will help you pick up additional vocabulary quickly.

Surprisingly, there are only a few Thai language workbooks available for English speakers who want to learn reading and writing on their own. None do a great job of demystifying the language, but they are decent references at the very least. Most of the major Thai language books have some reading and writing component. Workbooks designed for Thai children to learn the alphabet are great for learning the mechanics of writing, but because they have no English reference they're not useful for much more than that.

Education

If you're coming with school-age children, deciding how you will educate them is going to be the biggest challenge of moving to Thailand. There are many private-school options for your kids. In Bangkok, Chiang Mai, Phuket, Samui, and Isan, there are schools that follow a variety of different curricula, including British, American, and French, as well as religious schools that follow some form of international curriculum, but some parents find the level of instruction lacking. When you visit, sit in on classes, talk to teachers, and find out the makeup of the student body. Some schools that call themselves international in fact have instruction in Thai as well as English. Others follow an international curriculum and use English for instruction but have very few non-Thai students. High-achieving children who speak English as a first language may feel a little frustrated in this environment. English language, English literature, and other language-intensive courses may not be up to a level that parents find appropriate, since most of the other students will be working in their second language and might not be moving as quickly as your kids. Many children will get along just fine in this environment, and if they don't, parents often find other ways to augment their education, whether through tutoring or additional work at home. If you're only going to be in Thailand for a short time and your children will be returning to their school at home after that, talk to their teachers at home and ask what they'll be expected to know when they return. Talk to the headmaster and teachers at potential schools in Thailand to make sure those requirements are going to be met. Private schools in Thailand can be as expensive as those back home, running 300,000 baht and up per year.

The International Schools Association of Thailand has 75 member schools across the country and has uniform information about all of them on their website (www.isat.or.th).

COLLEGES AND UNIVERSITIES

There are hundreds of undergraduate and graduate programs in Thailand using English for instruction, so even without Thai language skills, you could come here to get a college degree or study for a semester or two; people from the United States, Europe, and other parts of the world do so. Most public and private colleges and universities in Thailand follow the American system, offering bachelor's, master's, and doctoral degrees. Most programs start in June and finish in March, although there are some that are on a September–May schedule. Some programs, such as the Sasin Graduate School of Business Administration at Chulalongkorn University in Bangkok, attract top-notch professors from all over the world. Unfortunately these programs can be pricey, even by American standards, as tuition for foreign students is higher than for Thai nationals.

HIGH SCHOOLS

If your children are of high school age and you'll be living in one of the prime living areas described in this book, there will be at least one international private high school available. The top international high schools are well funded and often have extensive extracurricular activities and large campuses with lots of sports facilities. They are also nearly as expensive as comparable schools back home, but many people coming in on expat packages will have tuition for their children covered by their employers. If you are coming from the United States and your children plan to attend college there, you're in luck, as more than half of the students at international high schools in Thailand go on to U.S. universities, and curricula are designed to prepare students for them.

INTERNATIONAL SECONDARY SCHOOL SYSTEMS

The international schools in Thailand use the following systems for secondary school study. The program you choose to enroll your children in will depend

HOMESCHOOLING

Jane is originally from the United States but moved to Thailand 10 years ago as a teacher. After getting a master's degree in Bangkok and marrying, she and her husband moved to Lopburi, 145 kilometers (90 miles) from Bangkok. Jane and her husband have three children, ages one, two, and four. She is homeschooling the eldest and plans to homeschool the others when they get older.

Why homeschooling?
Many reasons, including religion, my desire to maintain my role as the primary caregiver for my children, and cost. The first two are the most important, but as a single-income family on a local Thai salary, the cost of providing a comparable education through a private or international school would be prohibitive.

Will you have to go through many hoops to get your children's homeschooling program approved in Thailand?
As my oldest is just turning four, I have not had to do any of this yet, but I will be starting the process later this year. As I understand it, many Ministry of Education staff are unfamiliar with the requirements and procedures, particularly outside of Bangkok, but in a nutshell, they require basic information, your overall plan, and some curriculum particulars. Once you are approved, you have to keep the ministry informed of any changes. A Ministry of Education official will meet with you at least once a year. Officially, so long as the curriculum is comprehensive and covers the basics that would be covered in a traditional school, it is fine. But the language of the rules is very general, and I have heard that different officials interpret it a little differently.

Are there other parents in your community who are homeschooling, and do you ever pool resources?
Not here in Lopburi. When my kids are a little older, we will likely go to Bangkok occasionally to join in events and activities with the Bangkok Homeschoolers Association, who are mostly expats, and the Thai Homeschool Association, mostly Thais.

Are your children bilingual, and if so, how do you keep them learning in both languages?
My husband and I are both bilingual in Thai and English; Thai is his first language, and English is mine. At home we speak English, and when we are out and about we speak Thai. All three of the kids can speak and understand both. For the literacy element, I am just now beginning to work on letter recognition and beginning literacy things with my older two. While most of my materials are in English and designed for use with ABCs and such, so far I have been able to incorporate Thai language literacy easily as well. And they are doing fine with both.

on many factors, from the quality of instruction to the type of college or university your child wants to attend later.

International General Certificate of Secondary Education (IGCSE)

The IGCSE is an internationally recognized qualification generally for students aged 15 to 16. The qualification is based on the British GCSE and is a prerequisite to A Levels for students following the British system and an International Baccalaureate for students following the international system. Students who move from a British system to an American system will typically take AP courses after an IGCSE.

A Levels

A Level courses are generally in the last two years of a student's secondary schooling, just before entering a college or university. In the British system, A Levels are considered advanced and are preparatory for continuing study.

International Baccalaureate (IB)

This system was created by the University of Geneva in the 1960s and was intended to combine European and American education systems in a way that would make it easier for students to matriculate at any college or university around the world. IB courses are generally offered for the last two years of secondary school before entering a college or university.

Parents of nursery-school-age children have many options.

Advanced Placement

Under the advanced placement (AP) system, high school students take advanced, college-level courses and sit for exams that are independently graded by the American College Board in the United States. Many colleges and universities in the United States will accept AP credits (depending on scores) in lieu of university credit, as will some Canadian and European schools.

PRIMARY SCHOOLS

You will have a reasonable amount of choice about where you send your younger children to school if you're living in Bangkok or Phuket. In other popular parts of the country, there are some international primary schools, but not in every region. In Bangkok there are scores of private international primary schools, and throughout the country many of the international schools have classes from kindergarten through high school. Like private international high schools, primary schools can be expensive. In the lower grades they can also be competitive and tough to get into, so make sure to have some backup schools in mind.

Most schools do all their primary instruction in English, with some Thai culture and/or Thai language component. Nearly all schools enroll at least 25 percent of local students, with the balance made up of students from all over the world.

HEALTH

In Thailand you will have access to high-quality health care, but you'll also be exposed to new germs and environmental pollutants. Thailand is generally a very clean country in terms of food preparation, trash disposal, and personal hygiene, but it is by no means sterile or spotless. You'll routinely visit shophouse restaurants with cockroaches are running around on the floor and years of accumulated dirt on the walls. Some regard these as only cosmetic issues, as plates and silverware are always very clean, and food is fresh and safely prepared. Still, it may take some getting used to if you're a little squeamish.

Though coughs and colds tend to be less common here among foreigners, gastrointestinal problems will happen to everyone at some point. Diarrhea seems to be so common in Thailand that often the first question someone will ask you when you say you're not feeling well is *ton sia?* meaning, "diarrhea?"

© SUZANNE NAM

Health Care

Health care in Thailand is generally excellent and inexpensive. In fact, people from all over the world come here for everything from routine plastic surgery to complicated fertility treatments and chemotherapy. The nicest private hospitals in Bangkok look more like five-star hotels than health care facilities, and doctors often speak three or four languages and have been educated in the United States, Europe, or Japan as well as Thailand. In other major cities, you'll also often find good private hospitals with doctors who speak English.

Public hospitals are sufficient for many issues but are not always staffed with nurses and doctors that you will be able to communicate with. They may also seem substandard in terms of service and hygiene compared to health care at home and to the quality of care you'd receive in private hospitals. Unless you are really strapped for cash, use private medical facilities instead of public ones. International health insurance will almost always cover you at private hospitals. There are two exceptions to this rule. If you speak Thai well or have a partner who does, you may be able to navigate the public system sufficiently. In more rural areas, even where there are private hospitals, public ones may have better facilities or technology.

When you arrive here, before you get sick, find a hospital you are comfortable with and a doctor that you like. Ask colleagues and friends where they go and whether they can recommend any particular doctors. As with most other places in the world, the bedside manner of doctors in Thailand differs dramatically from stoic "just the facts" physicians to more sensitive types. You may find you don't need the most luxurious hospital and prefer a smaller, more local one. Or you may love that your hospital offers you tea in the waiting room. If you have a medical condition that requires a specialist, do some research before you arrive to identify some good candidates. If you're outside Bangkok, you may find you need to travel to the capital for treatment if you want the best-regarded specialty doctor.

© SUZANNE NAM

Not all hospitals have emergency rooms.

If you are pregnant or planning on getting pregnant in Thailand, there are excellent obstetricians all over the country and some very nice maternity units at higher-end hospitals; at some you can even rent suites so your partner can stay with you while you recover. Mothers accustomed to being shipped out after a couple of days will be pleasantly surprised by the amount of care given new moms, as the medical industry in Thailand focuses on plain old-fashioned caregiving as much as technology. Be warned that the majority of women in Thailand opt for cesarean births and will even schedule them with their doctors at convenient times for both the mom and the doctor. If you want a natural delivery, make sure that you select a doctor who has a lot of experience and is comfortable with your choice.

Types of Insurance

If you have health insurance through a foreign company doing business in Thailand, you will most likely be covered at private hospitals in Thailand, but you will have to pay out of pocket and seek reimbursement. Before you arrive, ask your insurance company for a list of accepted hospitals and the types of documents you will need to make any claim.

SELF-INSURING

Many foreigners in Thailand who are not covered by their employers decide to self-insure and have only high-deductible, low-cost insurance for catastrophic events. This is because health care costs are so much lower in Thailand that it may not make sense to pay for insurance for routine visits.

INTERNATIONAL COVERAGE

If you do decide to self-insure here, remember that when you go home to visit you won't have access to inexpensive health care. If something should happen that requires you to seek emergency medical treatment in the United States and you do not have insurance, your medical bills could be exorbitant. It's easy to get international catastrophic insurance to cover you when you go back home for visits or travel to other parts of the world, and it could save you a lot of money.

Pharmacies and Prescriptions

Many drugs that require a prescription in the United States are available over the counter in Thailand, including oral contraceptives, common blood pressure medications, and most antibiotics. Your prescription from home won't do you any good in Thailand, and you'll have to visit a doctor here to get medications that aren't available over the counter. Many common drugs are available in Thailand (pharmaceuticals are manufactured here for export) but might not be the same brand or dosage you've taken previously. Make sure to consult with a doctor here before switching to a new form of your medication.

There is a pharmacy in every town in Thailand and many in the cities. You can spot them by one of the universal symbols for pharmacy, a cross, in the window or on the store's sign. Smaller pharmacies won't stock uncommon drugs, and some medications are only dispensed in hospitals. If there's a medication you need and you think you won't be able to find it in Thailand, arrange to have it filled for three or six months before arriving. Some online pharmacies will ship medications, but only within the United States. In that case, you'll have to have someone at home forward them to you here. Make sure there is ample documentation enclosed in the package so that it's clear the drugs being mailed to you have been prescribed by a physician.

Doctors in Thailand tend to prescribe antibiotics far more frequently than they do back home, and it's pretty common to walk away from a doctor's appointment with some sort of broad-spectrum antibiotic for you or your

Medical beauty treatment centers can be found in any big city.

children. Part of this may stem from the fact that in Thai culture, some patients don't feel that they have been adequately treated unless they are given medication. Ask your doctor if the medication you are given is really necessary before taking it.

MEDICAL RECORDS

If you have a complicated medical history or are currently undergoing treatment, make sure to have copies of your medical records before you arrive so that your doctor in Thailand can review them. If you're using one of the country's private hospitals, you should have no problems finding a doctor who speaks and reads English.

Preventive Measures

VACCINATIONS

Anyone coming to Thailand should be vaccinated for hepatitis A and hepatitis B. These are routine vaccinations, and many people living in the United States get them even when they aren't planning to travel to foreign countries. Other vaccinations usually aren't necessary unless you will be living in a remote part of the country. Check the U.S. Centers for Disease Control and Prevention's travelers' advisory for Thailand (http://wwwn.cdc.gov/travel/destinations/thailand.aspx) for updates.

Traditional medicine is also an option.

ALTERNATIVE THERAPIES

So-called "alternative" therapies, including traditional Chinese medicine and acupuncture, are widely available in Thailand, where they are considered mainstream. There are still lots of old-fashioned Chinese apothecaries in Bangkok's Chinatown, and plenty of people visit for everything from aches and pains

© SUZANNE NAM

DAILY LIFE

to more serious diseases. It might be difficult to communicate with anyone in these shops, but some of the country's private hospitals have recently begun opening new alternative-medicine practices that offer everything from traditional Chinese medicine to yoga. These centers can be pricey, but the practitioners work in concert with doctors who practice Western medicine, so there is less risk of misdiagnosis or a treatment path that could harm you.

Environmental Factors

Thailand is no longer considered a developing country and has stepped up efforts to keep the air and water clean, but it still suffers from many of the pollution issues that plague industrial countries. There is a large and growing green movement that has a handful of champions in government, but the general attitude toward the environment is different from what you've probably experienced back home. People still throw trash on the street without suffering the shame and humiliation you might see in Japan or Germany. Burning trash and slash-and-burn agriculture are commonplace, especially in the countryside.

DISABLED ACCESS

Thailand is, unfortunately, an extremely difficult place to get around if you have difficulty walking or are otherwise physically impaired. Although some (not all) high-end housing is disabled-accessible, sidewalks in major cities are often torn up or uneven and lack curb cuts, and using public transportation or even crossing major streets requires that you climb stairs. Likewise, entering many office buildings, malls, supermarkets, and shops will often require some stair-climbing. In rural areas you may not even find sidewalks, making navigating a wheelchair almost impossible.

If you cannot walk easily, you will have to rely on automobiles to get around. Sadly there is no other option.

AIR QUALITY

Air quality in Bangkok is not perfect, but it's nothing like it was a decade ago, when the city was considered one of the most polluted in Asia. These days no smog blocks the blue sky, and the Air Quality Index generally hovers around "good" and "moderate." The air isn't considered unhealthy per se, but it's not perfect, and there are still plenty of cars and factories belching particulate matter on a daily basis. The hot and humid weather most of the year exacerbates

© SUZANNE NAM

Many of the country's cars and taxis run on natural gas, which has improved air quality.

the problem, making the air feel dirty and heavy, and you'll often see people walking around wearing face masks to keep out the pollution. If you suffer from asthma or have other respiratory problems, you should consider carefully whether Bangkok is the right city for you.

WATER QUALITY

Pollution of groundwater, surface water, and coastal water are all problems in Thailand that threaten not only the country's environment but its very livelihood. There have been efforts in the 1990s and 2000s to turn the tide, but for now water quality in Thailand remains a problem. Compromised water quality affects people living near or depending on water for their income in the long term, but it will not have a significant impact on the lives of those who live here for a few years.

In terms of precautions, most people in Thailand drink bottled water, and so should you. Avoid swimming in lakes and rivers unless you're confident that they are safe. Large rivers such as the Chao Phraya and the Tha Chin are extremely polluted in places and are not considered safe for swimming, despite the fact that many people use them for bathing and washing clothes.

SMOKING

Since the mid 2000s, Thailand has ramped up its antismoking efforts, prohibiting smoking in all indoor air-conditioned areas, including restaurants,

© SUZANNE NAM

Smoking is forbidden in most public places.

bars, and nightclubs. Though many thought the ban would be ignored, it hasn't been—there may be some small places that flout the law, but the vast majority of bars, restaurants, and clubs observe it. There has also been a big shift in the way people think about smoking. Plenty of people still smoke, but it's less socially acceptable than it used to be, and smokers are generally expected to be considerate of others and understand that their behavior is considered a nuisance.

SANITATION

Thailand generally has well-developed infrastructure, and although sanitation is not at the same level as in the United States, its quality and coverage are impressive. By some estimates, nearly 100 percent of the country's citizens have access to clean water in their homes and have sanitary toilet facilities. Those who do not have access to adequate sanitation tend to live in very rural areas or are part of ethnic groups that are underserved by the government.

Despite the wide coverage, Thailand's sanitization systems may be different from what you're used to. If you live in an expensive house or condo, you won't notice any difference, since newer buildings have modern Western plumbing. If you go out to a restaurant, travel, or visit friends, you'll see the way a typical Thai bathroom is set up. Many bathrooms still have squat toilets without any flushing mechanism; you need to scoop water from a reservoir and flush manually. There are also no bathtubs or separators between the toilet area and the shower. Some bathrooms do not have showers; instead people bathe using water they scoop from storage containers.

Thai sewers are also not as well equipped to handle paper waste as those back home. People do not flush toilet paper; instead they have a waste bin in the bathroom that is used to collect it. It's a difficult habit to get used to, but if you don't, you may be the cause of an embarrassing flood.

BUGS

Thailand is a tropical country, and there are bugs everywhere. The ones you'll see all the time are mosquitoes and cockroaches. Mosquitoes are more than a nuisance in Thailand, as some species carry Dengue fever, a debilitating disease that can take weeks or even months to recover from. Every year there are reported cases of Dengue in Bangkok, so it's not just a disease that strikes people in rural areas. Dengue-carrying mosquitoes tend to bite at dusk and dawn, and to safeguard yourself against the disease, you have to prevent the mosquito bites in the first place. Wearing a DEET-based repellent is the most effective way to do so, but it probably isn't realistic to do so every day. Instead, make sure you keep the screens closed when the windows are open, and do not give mosquitoes a chance to breed in your home. Mosquitoes breed in stagnant water, so make sure to remove any standing water or receptacles that could accumulate rainwater on balconies or near windows. The most common culprits are potted-plant plates and mop buckets. If you are out in areas where there are mosquitoes in the morning and evening, wear repellent or make sure your arms and legs are covered.

Cockroaches are essentially harmless, but they can be really disconcerting, as the Thai version are massive five-centimeter (two-inch) creatures that occasionally fly. Most apartment buildings do a good job exterminating, but if you live in a house or on the ground floor, you'll have to contend with insects in your home.

Safety

Just because most people in Thailand are friendly and laid-back doesn't mean you are always safe. Make sure to take commonsense precautions to protect yourself and your property. Purse-snatchings and muggings can and do happen, and comparatively wealthy foreigners are easy targets. Do not keep a lot of money on your person; it's better to take only what you need for the day from one of the thousands of ATMs. If you have to hit an ATM late at night, keep an eye out to make sure you're not being watched. Many 7-Elevens have ATMs just outside, and some have them inside the store, so no one can see how much money you've taken out or even that you've used the ATM. Women should always make sure to keep their bags close to their bodies, especially if you are walking in areas with lots of pedestrian and motorbike traffic. This isn't just to safeguard against getting your purse snatched; motorcycle drivers weave in and out of foot traffic, and your bag getting snagged on a passing bike can lead to serious injury for you or the driver.

Make sure you lock the door at home. Most apartment buildings hire security guards, but don't count on them to protect your belongings. They usually do look out for strangers entering the building or compound, but in larger buildings where people come and go frequently, or anywhere security guards are lax, there's no guarantee someone won't be able to get in.

If you are living in a single-family house, assess the type of theft protection you need. As you look around at homes in your neighborhood, you'll probably notice that even the humble ones have some sort of gate that can be locked to keep people out. Many homes also have bars on the windows of rooms on lower floors, and some also have electronic security alarms. Some people assume that foreigners are much wealthier than they are and have fewer qualms about burgling you than they would a fellow Thai.

If you have people coming into your home (or living there) to clean or take care of your children, don't leave valuables or cash around. Stash items in a small safe or a locked room. No one will take offense; it's common practice among Thais to do the same. As you establish a relationship with the people working in your home, you'll also gain trust, but it's something that takes time.

Harassment and Violence

Thai culture does not really condone or encourage aggressive behavior toward strangers, but some people do not feel that normal social rules apply to foreigners. Usually it's as innocent as a catcall or a comment about your body, but once in a while it can be a little more offensive. If someone says something to you, just ignore it and walk away. If you are in a crowded area, you have nothing to worry about.

Sexual assault and violence can happen in Thailand too, although rape specifically is not often talked about. You must exercise the same precautions you would at home. If you feel like someone is following you, immediately find other people. You may not be able to communicate the problem, but you can either just say "police" or stay with them until you are safe. Don't brush off an uncomfortable feeling out of embarrassment.

Be aware that nonverbal communication isn't the same in Thailand as it is in your home country. As a woman, it may be totally acceptable at home to hang out drinking beer with guys you've just met, and it doesn't mean you have any intentions or are open to their advances. In Thailand that's not necessarily true. While there are plenty of enlightened Thai guys who understand that men and women can be friends, some have a more traditional outlook. Until you can sort out the difference, try to stick to socializing in mixed groups.

POLICE

Despite all the talk about corrupt Thai police, they are often friendly and sincerely want to serve the public good. The phone number for the police nationwide is **191,** though you probably will not get someone on the phone who speaks English. To ensure you get someone that you can communicate with, call **1155,** the Tourist Police hotline. If you are the victim of a robbery or other

© SUZANNE NAM

Thai police officers keeping the peace

crime, you will usually have to go into the nearest police station to fill out a police report. Though it's unlikely that the police will recover your goods, you must have an official report to make any sort of insurance claim.

If you're on the other side of the law, expect humane treatment from the police, but don't expect any breaks for being a foreigner. Don't break the law in Thailand, especially any drug laws. Drug offenses carry very heavy penalties, including capital punishment for larger volumes. If you are caught in possession of drugs, there is likely nothing your embassy will be able to do to enable you to avoid punishment.

Europe and some U.S. states have increasingly relaxed laws when it comes to possession of small amounts of marijuana. Although the general attitude of the Thai population toward it is very relaxed, and you'll probably meet plenty of people who smoke it or couldn't care less if you did, the law does not reflect this attitude. The search-and-seizure protections you are accustomed to at home do not exist in Thailand. You can be stopped at random on the street and searched; you can be pulled over at any time for no reason and have your person and the car or taxi you are riding in searched. Anything found by the police is fair game, and even a small joint will land you in jail.

EMERGENCIES

In major urban areas and popular tourist destinations on the coast, you'll find easy access to medical treatment and other emergency services, but in more rural areas, services can vary widely. Currently there is no nationwide EMS system in Thailand. If you are involved in an accident in Bangkok, the **Narenthorn Center,** a division of the Ministry of Public Health, has a hotline, **1699,** connected to a network of hospitals and ambulances that can dispatch emergency medical services quickly. For nonurgent care, ask to be taken to a hospital, called a *rung paya ban.*

EMPLOYMENT

Thailand is an emerging economy and has grown, in real terms, around 5 percent each year for the past decade. Much of the country's GDP is dependent on the agriculture sector (which also employs the most people), but manufacturing, technology, oil and gas, and tourism are all important drivers of the economy. Though sometimes it seems like every Westerner working in Thailand is a teacher, in fact there are many opportunities for skilled professionals in these fields and others.

Because of the country's convenient location, good infrastructure, and relatively inexpensive costs, many American, European, and Asian multinational companies use Thailand as a base for their Southeast Asian operations. Many consumer products companies, advertising agencies, car companies, to name just a few sectors, are based in Thailand and employ foreign workers. The country is also a regional base for many NGOs doing work in Southeast Asia. Bangkok, and to a lesser extent Chiang Mai, host a variety organizations and agencies working on issues from child labor to the environment.

© SUZANNE NAM

This doesn't mean that employers are bending over backward to hire foreigners. If you're not coming with an assignment, it may be hard to find a job here unless you have skills and experience. Gone are the days when just speaking English and having a college degree opened doors. Nowadays, you'll be competing with local hires who often have advanced degrees from American or European universities and are willing to work for less than you are.

Think carefully about what you can do before coming to Thailand without a job. If you're not prepared to become an English teacher or don't have a specialized skill, such as hotel management, that's in high demand, it won't be easy to find work. If you don't speak any Thai, you'll be very limited in the types of jobs you can do here.

Self-Employment

STARTING A BUSINESS

In a fast-growing dynamic economy, being an entrepreneur is an adventurous and potentially very profitable endeavor. Foreigners in Thailand are doing everything from exporting to running photo studios to opening bars and hotels. In fact, one of the country's richest men, William Heinecke, is an American who came here with his diplomat family when he was a child and now owns numerous food chains and hotels.

Thailand has a relatively easy process for starting an official business, and

Some intrepid foreigners choose to open bars in Thailand.

Thai government policy is to welcome foreign investment. Under the Treaty of Amity and Friendship, Americans can own 100 percent of a Thai business without running afoul of any regulations (although there are certain types of specific businesses, such as telecommunications, that cannot be 100 percent foreign-owned, and 100 percent for- eign-owned businesses cannot own real estate), so there's no need to find a local partner. Some people run small consulting businesses without going through all the bureaucratic hoops, but if you will be bringing in substantial income, need a work permit, or want to employ others,

Business opportunities are everywhere but are not necessarily profitable.

you'll need to register your business with the government. The specifics of the process are beyond the scope of this book, but it can take a couple of months and cost a few thousand dollars once you factor in registration costs, paid-in capital and work permit fees. The Board of Investment website (www.boi. go.th/english/how/typical_costs_of_starting_and_operating_a_business.asp) has good examples of typical costs to open a business in Thailand.

Types of Businesses

Many foreigners open businesses that target the expat population, perhaps because they know the market intimately and can easily see needs that they can fulfill. You'll find plenty of foreign-owned bars, restaurants, and hotels throughout the country. These businesses are somewhat easy to start since little expertise is required, but they can be tough to run. Travel and tourism endeavors can get mired down in petty corruption, local hostility, and em- ployee relations fiascos, especially if they are small and self-managed. That doesn't mean people aren't successful, but it does mean they take greater risks. It's also hard to make money, since there are so many bars, restaurants, and hotels in competition.

Thailand's economy is growing, and there are plenty of other industries that any serious entrepreneur should look at if they are committed to opening a business here. Food processing, technology manufacturing, and exporting are just a few potentially lucrative industries. There are many others, but the main point is that you should consider the large and increasingly affluent local market and the international market as well as the somewhat limited expat market.

Business Practices

Opening a business in Thailand requires a solid understanding of both the law and the unwritten rules of business. The law is straightforward, and though you may have to deal with some bureaucracy, you can hire a good adviser and rest assured that you've checked all the right boxes, filled out the right forms, and paid the proper fees. The unwritten rules are much tougher to nail, and many foreigners run into problems because they don't understand the work culture, send confusing messages to their employees, and can't navigate business deals with Thais. Whole books have been dedicated to this topic, and anyone considering opening their own business here or buying an existing one should spend time doing research before jumping in.

The Job Hunt

If you don't already have a job in Thailand, it's worthwhile to spend some time researching the job market before you arrive. Read listings in online newspaper websites, check out trade magazines, and look at websites of companies doing business in Thailand. There is no central repository in English for professional job listings in Thailand, but higher-level jobs with multinational companies are listed on Monster.com; Thaivisa.com and Craigslist's Thailand site also have some Thailand jobs listed.

If you are looking for a teaching job, start contacting international schools, universities, and private English schools before you arrive. The International Schools Association of Thailand has a list of all of the accredited international schools in the country (at www.isat.or.th), with links to their websites and contact information. All of the major universities listed in the Resources section have English-language websites with contact information. Many of the larger private English schools also have websites with contact information.

Arrange to meet with people once you are here, even if there are no current job openings. When something comes up, you'll be more likely to be considered for it if you've already met your potential employer.

Many foreigners work at multinational companies.

INTERNATIONAL EMPLOYERS

International companies are doing everything in Thailand from selling soft drinks and shampoo to manufacturing computer components and exploring for oil and gas. Some have staffs of hundreds of foreigners on their payrolls.

Expatriates who work for multinational companies are well compensated by both Thai and U.S. standards (unless they are considered "local hires," in which case they are paid local wages). Most large companies offer to pay relocation expenses, pay a housing allowance, and offer tuition reimbursement for school-age children.

THAILAND'S 10 LARGEST COMPANIES

Thailand's 10 largest public companies by market capitalization are in the oil and gas, construction materials, and financial services industries.

1. PTT
2. PTT Aromatics and Refining
3. Kasikorn Bank
4. PTT Chemical
5. PTT Exploration and Production

6. Siam Commercial Bank
7. Siam Cement
8. Banpu
9. Bangkok Bank
10. Indorama Ventures

Source: Stock Exchange of Thailand

Positions with international companies that do business in Thailand can be very competitive, and many companies recruit for them globally and internally instead of looking locally. Most expat positions are filled by people living outside Thailand who are then relocated. If they are looking locally, they will often be looking for candidates who are bilingual.

NGOS

Nongovernmental organizations such as the United Nations, the World Food Program, the World Health Organization, and others have large offices in Bangkok that serve as regional hubs for operations across Southeast Asia. While landing a full-time job with one of these organizations off the bat is nearly impossible, most frequently hire contract workers on a temporary basis. Communications professionals are the most likely to find project work, although there are also content-based positions available on occasion. These jobs are not always posted, and there is not always a centralized office in each of the agencies through which hiring is done, so it is important to make connections with potential employers and ask to be notified of any openings. You'll have to make connections any way you can. Start with people you know, but don't be afraid to send out unsolicited emails and make phone calls. If you are in communications, contact each organization's press officer (which you can easily find by entering "press officer," the name of the organization, and "Bangkok" in your favorite search engine).

INTERVIEWS

No matter what country you are in when you are looking for a job, there are general rules that apply to doing interviews. Arrive promptly or early, dress professionally and conservatively, and be prepared. Know the company you are interviewing with, the industry you want to work in, and as much about Thailand as you can.

Whether you are interviewing for a position at a Thai company, a multinational company, or an American company, your interview may be a little different from what you've experienced back home. You'll be asked all the usual questions, may be required to take an exam, and may meet different people. You may also be asked questions that would be illegal in the United States: how old you are, whether you are married or have any children, and even your religion. Take these questions in stride as they are considered acceptable here.

VOLUNTEERING IN THAILAND

If you're in Thailand with your spouse or partner and can't find a job or don't want to work full time, consider volunteering at one of the many organizations here. Volunteering at an NGO or charity organization will give you an opportunity to meet Thai people, keep yourself busy, and hopefully do something good in the process.

There are some groups on the Internet that will put together volunteer experiences, but they often charge a fee and only offer positions at well-known organizations. Don't just rely on these or on listed positions; instead approach it as though you were looking for a job and a network. If there is a particular group you want to work with, or a particular issue you are interested in, take the first step and let it be known that you're willing to work for free. Though people with technical or professional skills (such as computer programming or accounting) are often welcomed with open arms, some organizations, especially in Bangkok, can be very picky about who they accept as volunteers. They'll ask for a minimum per-week time commitment, do a background and reference check, and want to know that you'll approach the responsibility as you would any paid job.

Organizations such as the American Women's Club of Thailand (http://awcthailand.org), the British Women's Group Bangkok (www.bwgbangkok.com), the International Women's Club of Thailand (www.iwcthailand.org), and the Dusit Chapter of the Soroptimist International Club (http://sid.in.th/) are heavily involved in philanthropic work in Thailand and have a variety of different types of programs to choose from.

TEACHING ENGLISH

Demand for English teachers is high all over the country, and some people view teaching English as an easy way to make a decent living and get a visa. It can be that, but be careful, as there are plenty of employers who will take advantage of that attitude by offering low wages and treating their teachers poorly and without much respect. Teachers who view their jobs as just a means to stay in Thailand tend to be the ones that get treated the worst. Professional TEFL-certified teachers who appear dedicated to their profession and aren't just doing it because it was their only option get better jobs with better pay and better treatment.

At the low end, English teachers can earn as little as 25,000 baht per month. Is that enough to live on in Thailand? It can be, depending on what part of the country you are in and what type of lifestyle you want. If you are living in Bangkok, earning 25,000 baht per month will make life tough. Decent apartments in convenient areas, even shared ones, are hard to find for under

© SUZANNE NAM

There are thousands of English schools in Thailand, all looking for native-speaking teachers.

10,000 baht per month, and though you'll be able to take advantage of good inexpensive meals, you'll have little money left over at the end of the month to travel or go out. If you're living in Isan, 25,000 baht per month should be sufficient to have a decent roof over your head, get around, and go out, but you probably won't be able to save anything.

Qualified professional teachers can earn substantially more, and they are also provided health benefits and some relocation expenses. If you are interested in becoming qualified, you can even take teaching courses in Thailand. There are numerous schools offering TEFL and CELTA certification courses for around 48,000 baht.

BENEFITS

If you are moving to Thailand for your company, make sure that, at the very least, the package you get includes relocation costs and education costs for your children. These expenses will be substantial, and paying for them yourself will eat away at even the most generous salary. Many companies offer some sort of health insurance, but whether you're given Thailand-only insurance that requires you go to hospitals of the insurer's choice or international health insurance that will cover you no matter where you are depends on the company. Some companies, including many private English-language schools, don't offer any health insurance at all.

Many Thai and foreign companies participate in a voluntary provident fund (similar to a retirement fund) and will match employee contributions anywhere from 3 percent to 15 percent of an employee's annual salary. In some specific industries, and for government employees, there are separate systems. Contributions and any interest earned on them are tax-free and are paid out on retirement. In some circumstances, employees can withdraw funds when they resign, although there are some tax consequences for doing so. Currently employers are restricted in the types of investments they can make with provident fund contributions, and employees do not have any say in how the money is invested.

Labor Laws

Thailand has numerous labor laws in place to protect employees, and these apply both to local and foreign workers. Enforcement is not perfect, however, and there are plenty of horror stories about employers stiffing employees or otherwise abusing them.

WORKERS' RIGHTS

Many rights granted to workers will not apply to foreigners working in Thailand in upper level positions, since they are meant to protect hourly wage-earners. If you happen to fall into that category or if you are an employer, know the following rules.

Workers can only be required to work a maximum of eight hours a day and 48 hours a week unless they are paid overtime wages (1.5 to 3 times the normal hourly wage), and they must be given an hour's break after five hours of work. There are 13 statutory public holidays in Thailand, and if an employee would normally work on one, he or she must be paid for that day. Employees who have worked for more than a year are entitled to at least six days of paid vacation per year. Employees are also granted an additional 30 days of sick leave, although employers can require a doctor's note if an employee is out for more than two consecutive days. Expectant mothers are granted 90 days of maternity leave, at least 45 days of which must be paid.

TERMINATION

Under Thai law, if you have been working for a company for more than four months, you are entitled to automatic severance if you are terminated without cause. The amount of severance depends on the amount of time the employee has been working and ranges from one month's salary to 10 months' salary.

FINANCE

Whatever lifestyle you have, you'll run into some obstacles when setting up your finances in Thailand. You can avoid it altogether by keeping all of your money at home and relying on your ATM card to get money as you need it, and many people do that, but you'll be far better off opening a bank account here.

Cost of Living

You can live very cheaply in Thailand, or you can live a far more lavish life than you could back at home with the same salary. Most Thai professionals earn much less than their American counterparts; entry-level civil servants and administrative assistants, for example, typically earn under 16,000 baht per month. Expenses can also be much lower. Inexpensive apartments can be found for under 5,000 baht per month (and much less in the countryside),

© SUZANNE NAM

HOW MUCH WAS THAT?

One of the benefits of living in Thailand is that everyday expenses can be significantly cheaper. Here's a list of common items and expenses and their cost in Thailand:

Item	Cost in Thailand
Big Mac value meal	US$3.75
Bottle of Singha Beer at 7-Eleven	US$1
Bus fare	US$0.20
Doctor's visit without insurance at high-end hospital	US$15
Five-kilometer (three-mile) taxi ride	US$1.50
Hair blow-out at a local salon	US$3
Haircut at a barber	US$4
Half a pineapple from a street vendor	US$0.40
Noodle soup at street stall	US$1
Pack of cigarettes	US$2
Pirated DVD	US$3
Room in a five-star hotel	US$140
Room in a guest house	US$10
Starbucks coffee	US$3

and food in Thailand is plentiful, good, and inexpensive. You could easily live off shophouse and street-vendor fare for just a few dollars a day. So if you choose to live the way millions of middle-class Thais do, the cost of living here can be very low.

If you choose a lifestyle similar to or better than the one you're leaving behind, you'll still save some money. Housing costs may not be cheaper if you move from an inexpensive American city to a luxury apartment in Bangkok, but it will certainly be cheaper if you're used to paying New York or San Francisco prices. If you shop at local markets, you'll save at least 50 percent on fruit, vegetables, meat, and fish. Even higher-priced supermarkets catering to foreigners and wealthy Thais are cheaper than supermarkets back home, unless you are buying lots of imported foods.

GROCERIES

Local fruits and vegetables are very inexpensive, as are local meat and fish. Fresh fruit is available on the street for 10 baht for a bag of about half a pineapple or a whole guava. Greens, cucumbers, tomatoes, and herbs are also cheap and often sold in 10-baht increments. Ten baht will get you a few tomatoes, a bunch of cilantro, or two cucumbers. A kilo (2 pounds) of large shrimp in Thailand will run less than 150 baht; 450 grams (a pound) of pork around 70 baht. If you buy only local products, you can easy keep your grocery bill under 4,800 baht per month for two people. If you stick with local ingredients, you can keep costs even lower, especially if you have a Thai maid who can cook for you.

When you begin adding in "foreign" and processed food, things get more expensive. Beef imported from Australia can cost much

Customer loyalty cards, popular in Thailand, will save you money.

© SUZANNE NAM

as 1,200 baht per kilo (550 baht per pound). Imported organic peanut butter can cost nearly 300 baht for a jar. Luckily some foreign products are not insanely overpriced. Bread products are popular enough that a loaf of French bread costs about 40 baht (though it can be hard to find outside of international supermarkets and hypermarkets such as Carrefour and Tesco). A box of spaghetti costs just 40 baht.

EATING OUT

If you just go to casual local shophouses, two people can easily enjoy dinner out for under 300 baht. You'll spend as little as 50 baht on enough food to satisfy you for dinner, plus perhaps 40 or 50 baht per beer. If you go to restaurants with air-conditioning, non-Thai cuisine, or special atmosphere, it's easy to spend 3,000 baht on dinner for two, more if you buy wine. Though the prices may seem expensive compared to local restaurants, there are some amazing Italian, Japanese, and French restaurants in Thailand, and when you compare the cost to that of a similar meal back at home, you're actually paying less.

SAVING MONEY IN THAILAND

The cost of living in Thailand is much cheaper than in the West, but it's still easy to spend a lot of money on daily necessities if you're not careful.

- Shop at local markets for produce. The price difference between local "wet" markets and international supermarkets is huge. You may pay three times more for your fruits and vegetables if you shop at a supermarket catering to foreigners and wealthy locals. Some markets in Bangkok and Chiang Mai even carry locally produced organic vegetables. There are markets all over the city, though they are sometimes tucked into small *sois* or not immediately noticeable. Ask your neighbors or building management for the nearest one.

- If you are in Bangkok or Pattaya, shop at Foodland (www.foodland.co.th). Though it's a supermarket chain with lots of imported products, it tends to have better prices than more upscale supermarkets.

- Eat local food often. Everyone craves familiar food, and there are plenty of restaurants across the country serving burgers and pizza and pasta. Don't cut them out entirely, but take advantage of the amazing and inexpensive food sold out of street stalls in shophouse restaurants. A typical meal at a humble establishment or on the street will run you less than 65 baht.

- Think carefully about whether you really need a car. If you're in a rural part of the country, a car may be inevitable, but if you are in Bangkok, there's reliable, fast public transportation that serves the city center, and it's almost always easy to grab a taxi, which will rarely cost you more than a few dollars. Chiang Mai and the islands also have reliable transport systems, though they may consist of *song thaew* and buses.

- Speak some Thai. People will consider you a resident instead of a tourist when you speak even a little Thai, and they will almost always give you a better deal when prices are negotiable.

- Get Skype or another similar service to keep in touch with folks back home. Skype is free and has video, so it beats a regular phone conversation.

- Ask for Thai resident prices when booking hotels. Many hotels and resorts offer discounts for residents, especially in the low season. Call and ask, as they aren't usually listed on their websites.

© SUZANNE NAM

Shop in local markets instead of supermarkets to save money.

DAILY LIFE

© SUZANNE NAM

Streetside cobblers and clothing menders cost a fraction of the price of similar services at home.

GOING OUT

If you live in an urban area, especially Bangkok, what you spend on going out at night may be more than what you spend on groceries. If you stick with taxis (where available), buses, or other public transportation, you can keep the cost of getting wherever you're going to less than 100 baht. Movies are as little as 120 baht for new releases; bowling and karaoke halls are similarly inexpensive. You'll start racking up expenses if you go to bars and clubs that cater to foreigners. A small bottle of Chang beer at a high-end bar in Bangkok can cost as much as 250 baht. At a local watering hole you may pay 40 baht. Big international nightclubs almost always charge an admission fee of as much as 500 baht.

HOUSING

Rental costs vary widely depending on where you live and what you want. If you're living in a rural part of the country, you can spend just a few thousand baht on housing. In Bangkok, Phuket, and Samui, you can easily spend 10 times as much.

Banking

CURRENCY

The Thai currency is the **baht.** Bills come in denominations of 1,000, 500, 100, 50, and 20 baht, and occasionally you'll see an old 10-baht note, although these are no longer printed. Common coins are 10, 5, 2, and 1 baht. The baht is divided into 100 **satang.** There are no small satang coins in circulation, and in fact the only ones you'll see are 25 and 50 satang. Most prices are ex-

one baht

pressed in baht, although in the supermarket you will come across items (often the ones on sale, for some reason) with baht and satang pricing, and this is expressed as, for example, ฿25.50."

DAILY LIFE

Exchange Rates

As of early 2010, the Thai baht was running about 32 to the U.S. dollar and 43 to the euro, but it has been strengthening against both currencies for a couple of years. It's difficult to predict currency trends, but the baht may continue to get stronger, so check the exchange rate when you are planning your trip and be aware of it when you are here, especially if you are paid in a foreign currency. Most bank websites have currency conversion charts, and converters can be found at www.oanda.com and www.xe.com. Note that these will give you interbank rates, not the amount you'll get as an ordinary consumer; that rate will most definitely be less favorable regardless of whether you are buying or selling.

THAILAND'S LARGEST BANKS

There are more than a dozen domestic banks in Thailand along with international banks. Here are the six largest, which have offices and ATMs all over the country:

- Bangkok Bank
- Bank of Ayudhya
- Kasikorn Bank
- Krungthai Bank
- Siam Commercial Bank
- TMB Bank

OPENING AN ACCOUNT

In order to open a bank account with a Thai bank, you'll need to have your work permit (unless your company has a good relationship with a particular branch and can have them bend the rules a little), so you must wait until your documents are in order before beginning the process. You'll need to visit a branch in person, with your passport and work permit, to open your account. Not all bank branches have English-speaking staff, so you'll need to call ahead to find the best branch, unless you can bring someone with you to translate. Student visa holders can also open bank accounts in Thailand.

Think carefully about how much money you want to keep in a Thai account. Foreigners earn lower interest on savings accounts than Thai nationals, so having a lot of cash here isn't necessary a wise investment decision. Under the recently passed Report of Foreign Bank and Financial Accounts Act, American citizens must report their foreign accounts to the IRS if the balance of all accounts combined exceeds US$10,000 at any time during the year, which is an administrative hassle.

Since most transactions are settled by cash (including rent in many cases), you will need a supply of Thai baht on a monthly basis. The biggest problem with not having a Thai bank account is that you will have to pay hefty bank fees (currently 250 baht per transaction) every time you withdraw money from an ATM machine.

Unfortunately, it's also a hassle to transfer money out of Thailand. There are no prohibitions on the amount of money you can transfer out, but you will need to go into a branch in person, with your passport and work permit, to wire money to a foreign bank account. If you are transferring more than US$20,000, you must document how you obtained the money and where you are sending it.

Foreigners typically do not earn interest on bank deposits.

CREDIT CARDS AND DEBIT CARDS

Many places in Thailand now accept credit and debit cards for payment. Most hotels, higher-end restaurants, supermarkets, clothing stores, and drug stores accept plastic with no hassles. Some shops, including high-end jewelers, will charge you a fee to use a credit card. The practice violates the agreement the vendor has with their bank, but there's no way around it. Shophouse restaurants and markets only accept cash.

Taxes

THAI TAXES

If you are living in Thailand and earning money here, you'll be liable for income taxes. Thailand has a progressive tax rate, and the first 150,000 baht of your earnings will be exempt. After that, you pay 10 percent on the next 350,000 baht, 20 percent on the next 500,000 baht, 30 percent on the next 3,000,000 baht, and 37 percent on any income over that amount. Most employers will take care of setting up your tax identification number and withholding, and will even file your taxes for you. If you need to get a tax identification number or pay your taxes, you can do so at the nearest District Revenue Office.

U.S. TAXES

Americans are liable for U.S. taxes no matter where they live in the world. In general, you can exclude up to US$82,000 of your foreign-earned income from federal taxation, but there are many requirements you must fulfill in order to do so. Check the Internal Revenue Service website (www.irs.gov) for more information about who can take the Foreign Earned Income Exclusion. If you happen to be paid as a contractor by a U.S. company, you will not be able to avoid paying self-employment (social security) tax, and you cannot apply the Foreign Earned Income Exclusion to self-employment tax regardless of whether you are paying into the Thai system or not.

Investing

Like any other stable but emerging economy, Thailand presents excellent investment opportunities for those with extra capital who are willing to bear the additional risks that go with higher returns. If you are considering investing in the Thai stock market, consider that overall, Thailand's market, like many other emerging markets, has performed well in the past decade but presents more risk than the markets of more stable and established economies. Although the average price-to-earnings ratio of Thai public companies was somewhere around 14 as of the writing of this book, it's still considered by many stock researchers to be an undervalued market. Obviously it wouldn't be wise to sink your life savings into the Thai market, or any other single market. Calculate your risk profile, and then determine how much money you want to put into emerging markets in general, and Thailand in particular.

HOW TO INVEST

If you are investing in the Thai market, you'll need a local brokerage account. There are numerous banks that can set this up for you. You will typically need to bring in your passport and work permit and set up a cash account to begin trading. Foreigners are generally not granted margin accounts, but some banks may offer the service, depending on the circumstances.

PRIVATE INVESTMENTS

There are a number of mid- to large-sized private equity companies investing primarily or partially in Thailand. Minimum investments are high at these companies, but the good ones offer competitive returns and are professionally run by people from all over the world. If you don't already know the private equity industry well, it can be hard to find the right fund to invest in, but larger international banks also have private investment funds and are easier to locate.

DIRECT INVESTMENT

In 2009, nearly US$10 billion in foreign direct investments came into Thailand. While the majority of that money comes from existing multinational corporations, hundreds of millions of those dollars came from individual entrepreneurs who invested in agriculture, textiles, chemicals, electronics, and the service industry. Buying a factory or starting a Greenfield project might not be a wise idea for someone who doesn't have investment or industry experience, but it can present excellent opportunities for those who do. The Board of Investment offers some general information, including an explanation of tax and other incentives, on their website (www.boi.go.th).

COMMUNICATIONS

Telephone Service

Thailand has an excellent telecommunications infrastructure in major cities and other populated areas, and service prices are typically less expensive than the costs you would incur back home. It's also very easy to set up phone service, whether you're using a landline or a mobile phone.

Thailand's country code is 66, and within the country regional area codes begin with a 0 and have one additional digit, followed by the seven-digit local number. Mobile phone numbers begin with 08. You always have to dial the area code, so if you're in Bangkok and you're calling another Bangkok telephone, you must dial 02 first. If you are calling Thailand from outside the country, dial the international access number, the 66 country code, and drop the leading 0 from the area code. This applies whether you are calling a landline or a mobile phone.

© SUZANNE NAM

To make international calls from Thailand, you must dial 001, 006, 007, 008, or 009 first, then the country code and phone number. Why so many choices? The official number is 001, but the other numbers are other providers that offer cheaper rates. Just know that you'll almost always get routed over a VOIP line, and there may be a noticeable time lag.

PHONE COMPANIES

In Bangkok there are two major companies providing landline services, TOT and True. TOT, the Telephone Organization of Thailand, is the former government phone company, your only option in many other parts of the country. If you are in Bangkok and need to decide which phone company to use, it's really a toss-up; the rates are essentially the same. True tends to be more foreigner-friendly in that it's easy to get an English-speaking customer service representative on the phone, but some people say TOT has better service.

If your apartment building already has phone service, they will typically have everything set up for you and give you the phone bills or incorporate them into your monthly bill, so you don't need to do anything. To set up landline service on your own, whether your home is already wired or not, you'll need to call the phone company (see the *Resources* chapter) and either have them activate the line or come in and install one. Anytime you need to open a new account, you'll need to provide copies of your passport and work permit.

LANDLINES

Mobile phones are so common in Thailand that many people don't even have landlines, but the rates are marginally cheaper, and you'll need one if you want broadband Internet service, so it's wise to get one anyway. Most apartments and houses are already wired for telephone service, so you will only pay a modest activation fee and monthly charges. Typically it costs about 210 baht per month to have a phone line, plus the cost of any calls you make.

MOBILE PHONES

Almost everyone in Thailand uses a mobile phone, both to talk and to text-message. If you don't have one, you'll quickly feel out of place or out of touch.

Mobile phone calls are cheap in Thailand, and they get even cheaper when the three largest providers, **AIS, DTAC,** and **True,** get into price wars, sometimes an annual occurrence. When that happens, calls can drop below 1 baht per minute. Like most parts of the world, except the United States, you do not pay for incoming calls or text messages. If you have a tri-band or quad-band mobile phone and can remove the SIM card, bring it with you and buy a prepaid SIM card when you arrive. This is the cheapest and easiest way to communicate when you are here. You can also pick up a new or used phone in Thailand, often for a lot less than you'd find at home. All cities have mobile phone stores that sell unlocked phones, and there are many secondhand phones available if you want to save some cash. Remember to have the seller test the phone for you so you know it works before you walk away with it. Renting a phone before you leave home or at the airport is generally far more expensive than buying a new phone of your own and should be considered only if you cannot go a few hours without mobile communication or do not have time to pick up a phone on your own.

SIM cards can be found in any convenience store, as are the prepaid cards for the three largest mobile service providers. Note that they sometimes sell their SIM cards under promotional names, such as "Happy" for DTAC or "One Two Call" for AIS. If you just ask for a SIM from one of the three, however, you should get what you want.

All mobile providers have data services, and if you have a newer-model phone or a smart phone, it's very easy and comparatively inexpensive to set up Internet and email access.

If you have a work permit, you can switch from a prepaid calling plan to a plan where you're sent a bill every month without changing your existing phone number. You can keep a prepaid plan as long as you want, but it's a little cheaper to have a regular billed account. It's also easier to set up international roaming for when you travel outside Thailand, and if you need to itemize your phone calls to get reimbursed by your employer, you will need a billed account, as you don't get any documentation when you use prepaid cards. You can either take a very basic package for a few hundred baht per month or sign up for one of the myriad choices that each mobile company offers. Some include text-messaging, minutes, and data, but the variety can be a little confusing. Since you often need to commit for at least six months with any package, make sure you understand what you are getting and what you need before you do so.

Domestic and International Rates

Calls within Thailand are usually cheaper than a few baht per minute, and sometimes much lower, whether you are using prepaid cards or a billed account. SMS messages usually cost 1 baht per message, and data is charged by the minute. Depending on your usage habits, the best deals are the bundled packages of voice, message, and data that all the major companies offer. A typical package will cost around 600 baht per month and include a few hundred minutes of calls within Thailand, a few hundred text messages, and unlimited data. Less expensive packages are available for those who do not use their phones for Internet and email.

International calling rates are surprisingly reasonable when using your mobile phone in Thailand. Standard rates to the United States are around 6 baht per minute and can be less if you use one of the VOIP prefixes.

Mobile Phone Companies

There are three major mobile phone companies, **AIS, DTAC,** and **True,** and all have competitive rates and generally good coverage in populated areas. Each of these companies sells SIM cards in 7-Elevens, shopping malls, and their own shops all over the country. If you'll be living in a more remote area, ask colleagues and neighbors which company they use. Coverage can vary, and some companies have better service in different parts of the country.

Internet and Postal Service

INTERNET ACCESS

The Internet has penetrated into even the smallest urban areas in Thailand, and even in very rural areas it's possible to have satellite Internet set up. If you want home Internet service, TOT and True both provide broadband Internet. Set up fees run around 2,000 baht, not including a router, and monthly fees for speeds sufficient for home use are approximately 1,200 baht.

Any city or tourist area will have plenty of Internet cafés where you can use the service by the hour, or if you have your laptop with you, many hotels and coffee shops also have wireless access. Generally, Internet cafés in Thailand are either packed full of tourists on month-long sojourns or packed full of

Even shopping malls are wired.

© SUZANNE NAM

© SUZANNE NAM

Internet cafés are easy to find in major areas.

local teenagers playing computer games.

In Bangkok, Chiang Mai, Phuket, and Samui, Wi-Fi access is very common and continues to spread. Some places, including hotels and international coffee chains, still charge for the service, but in many places it's free, including any **Coffee World** coffee shop, nearly all of the English and Irish pubs in the cities, and the **Bug & Bee** in Bangkok. Look for "Wi-Fi hotspot" signs, and ask the server if you need a password. If you need to be wired at all times, you can sign up for mobile wireless through your mobile phone service provider. You'll get a USB dongle and installation software so you can browse away for under 1,000 baht per month.

Many people in the country also have telephones with some Web browsing functionality and the ability to send and receive emails. Mobile service providers offer data packages that cost anywhere from 200 baht per month to about 600 baht per month for unlimited usage. If your phone doesn't have a built-in Web browser, consider upgrading it when you arrive. Mobile phones are inexpensive here and do not require contracts with phone companies. Although a Web-enabled smart phone with advanced functionality may cost thousands of baht, you can pick up a basic phone with email and Web browsing for around 3,200 baht.

POST OFFICES AND COURIERS
Mail

Thailand Post (www.thailandpost.com) has locations across the country. Though there are no guarantees you'll find someone who can speak English if you need to ask questions and cannot communicate in Thai, postal workers are generally helpful and will try to figure out what you need and how to give it to you. Mailboxes are painted red and usually have two slots, one for local mail and one for everything else. If you are sending something within Thailand, service is generally quick, inexpensive, and reliable. If you are sending heavy or bulky items from Thailand abroad, postage can be very expensive,

DAILY LIFE

and packages can take weeks to arrive. It is better to plan on taking everything back with you. If you need to send something express, there are **Fedex** (www.fedex.com) and **DHL** offices in Bangkok that do express worldwide shipping. **EMS** also has international express shipping, which is available at any Thai post office.

For incoming mail, don't worry if it's addressed to you in English or Thai, as long as the address and postal code are correct. Postal workers will generally get your mail to you regardless. If you are moving to a rural part of the country where there happen to be few English speakers, your mail carrier will probably hear about the foreigner in advance of any mail that may come to you and already know where you live.

Thai post is reliable and efficient.

Media

NEWSPAPERS AND MAGAZINES
English Language Press

Thailand has a thriving English-language press, so you'll be able to find local and international news quite easily. In addition to the *International Herald Tribune,* widely available in major cities, Thailand has two daily English-language newspapers, the *Bangkok Post* (www.bangkokpost.net) and the *Nation* (www.nationmultimedia.com). Although you won't find them in remote or rural areas, you can buy them or have them delivered to your home virtually everywhere else. You can also check them out on line while you are preparing for your move. If you're curious about what's making headlines in Thailand, what the economy looks like, and even job openings, check their websites before you arrive.

Take any news you read in the English-language press with a grain of salt. Both the *Bangkok Post* and the *Nation* have been known to deliver not-so-objective news, especially as it relates to the political situation in Thailand. The editorial views also do not necessarily reflect the thinking of the majority of people in the country, and foreigners who rely on them to get a handle on the country's pulse will often be steered wrong.

The Thai government's official news agency, Thai News Agency (http://enews.mcot.net/), is another good source for general economic, political, and cultural information. Since it's a government news source, it's also not entirely objective, but at least you'll get a sense of the message the government wants to send.

In every place where large numbers of English speakers live, there are small and not-so-small weekly and monthly publications catering to them or the advertisers who want their attention. At any hotel you'll find a stack of these publications, but you may not find them all that useful. Content is often dictated by the advertisers, so it's hard to trust their food and hotel reviews.

Websites

More and more content about Thailand is available on the Web every day, including tourist guides, expat forums where long-term foreign residents gripe about the difficulties of living in a foreign country, and personal travelogues. Spend some time surfing when you're planning your trip, and at the very least make sure to look at the **Tourism Authority of Thailand** website (www.tourismthailand.org) for specific information about the destinations you're planning to visit.

© SUZANNE NAM

Thailand has two national English-language newspapers.

TELEVISION AND RADIO
Television
In Thailand there are both for-profit television networks and a public television network. They broadcast a mix of local and international news, documentaries, slapstick comedy series, soap operas, and sports. In short, it's just like the television you watch at home, except everything is in Thai.

There are no English-language terrestrial television stations, but if you have cable television, you will have access to the typical international news networks, including CNN and BBC, movie channels such as HBO and Cinemax, and some pan-Asian sports and entertainment networks broadcast in English. UBC is the only cable-television company in Thailand, and it offers both traditional cable television and satellite television, which may be your only option if you live anywhere other than a highly populated area. If you need to have cable or satellite installed in your home or apartment, you will pay 3,200–6,400 baht for installation and equipment. Monthly fees vary depending on the type of package you select, but they start at around 1,200 baht per month for basic service. Serviced apartments offer basic cable for no additional cost.

Out in the countryside, there are some black-market cable companies that aren't licensed but nonetheless provide basic movie and news channels.

Radio
Thai radio stations cover everything from international pop music to political discussions, although very little of it (except for some of the music) is in English. In some areas where many foreigners live or visit, there are some radio stations that cater to English-speaking listeners and broadcast local news in English. Wave 88 FM in Bangkok and 91.5 FM in Phuket broadcast 24 hours a day in English.

Podcasts are a very convenient way to stay in touch with news from around the world and back home. National Public Radio, ABC, CBS, NBC, and many other news providers have hours of free podcasts every day; all you need to access them is a computer and an Internet connection.

TRAVEL AND TRANSPORTATION

Getting Around ·

BY AIR

If you need to travel around this part of the world, Bangkok is an excellent base, as there are frequent flights to Singapore, Malaysia, Indonesia, Vietnam, China, and India. Thailand also has many regional airports served by domestic airlines and competing low-cost carriers. **Thai Airways** (www.thaiair.com), the country's flagship carrier, has flights all over the world as well as to the Andaman coast, Isan, and the north. **Bangkok Airways** (www.bangkokair. com) serves Samui, Sukhothai, Krabi, and other tourist destinations. Don't forget the budget airlines; small ones seem to pop up all the time, but two are reliable and popular. **Nok Air** (www.nokair.com) is partially owned by Thai Airways, and **Air Asia** (www.airasia.com) is one of the largest budget carriers

in Asia. Air Asia continues to expand in the region and has direct flights to many nearby countries. Both also have extensive schedules to popular tourist destinations such as Phuket (between the two, there are more than a dozen daily flights) and limited flights to less popular places. None of the budget airlines show up on any of the travel websites; you have to book through their websites, by phone, or at the airport. Luckily both have very user-friendly websites. Nok Air even lets you book by phone (tel. 1318 or 02/900-9955) and then pay for and pick up your ticket at a 7-Eleven. This will only work more than 24 hours in advance of a flight, but it will really come in handy if you are having trouble using a credit card over the Internet.

BY TRAIN

Thailand has an extensive railway system serving all parts of the country. The train system is run by the **State Railway of Thailand** (www.railway.co.th/english) and you'll find schedules and fares on the website. Seats are available in first through third class, depending on the route, and range anywhere from plush, comfortable air-conditioned cars with snacks and beverages served at your seat to wooden benches, open windows, and café cars serving local beer and inexpensive Thai dishes. Sleepers come in a similar range, but even the second-class sleepers are quite comfortable (you'll even get freshly laundered sheets and blankets). This is a great way to get to see the country and meet people, but it's definitely not the fastest way to travel (buses are usually faster).

You cannot book train tickets on the Internet. You'll either need to go to the train station in person or stop in at any travel agent (you pay a small fee

The State Railway of Thailand has limited routes but hits most popular areas.

WHERE YOU CAN GO IN FIVE HOURS OR LESS

Thailand has plenty to discover within its borders, but it's also a great place to live because of all the other countries you can easily visit while you're there. With so many interesting places just a few hours away, it's possible to do some serious international travel, even on your weekends.

Budget regional airlines Air Asia, Jet Star, and Tiger Airways make international travel not only convenient but relatively inexpensive. If you plan ahead and purchase tickets well in advance, round-trip travel to most destinations will cost 6,500 baht or less.

Here's a list of the top destinations you can fly to from Bangkok in five hours or less:

- Rangoon, Burma
- Hanoi, Vietnam
- Saigon, Vietnam
- Luang Prabang, Laos
- Vientiane, Laos
- Phnom Penh, Cambodia
- Siem Reap, Cambodia
- Kuala Lumpur, Malaysia
- Singapore
- Manila, Philippines
- Bali, Indonesia
- Jakarta, Indonesia
- Delhi, India
- Kolkata, India
- Mumbai, India
- Indonesian and Malaysian Borneo
- Hong Kong, China
- Kunming, China
- Taipei, Taiwan

for this service). If you are planning on traveling on a weekend or around a national holiday, book well in advance, especially if you are taking an overnight train and want a sleeper. Tickets will often sell out days or even weeks in advance of popular travel dates.

Thailand also has a little-known **Rail Pass for Foreigners,** which is a great deal if you are here for at least a couple of weeks and plan on seeing as much of the country as you can. The pass costs 3,000 baht and entitles you to unlimited train travel on any train in any level of service up to second class (this includes second-class air-conditioned sleeping berths on overnight trips). You can only buy the pass if you are a not a resident of Thailand, and you can only buy it at Hua Lumpong Station in Bangkok. You have to show your passport to purchase the pass and to book tickets, and so far no travel agents offer this service. Check the website at www.railway.co.th/English/ asp for details.

BY BUS

Thailand is covered by an extensive network of interregional, regional, and local buses, and it is possible to get almost anywhere in the country by bus if you are willing to spend the time navigating the system. From Bangkok and other major cities, there are frequent air-conditioned buses (sometimes referred to as **VIP buses**) on which you'll be guaranteed a comfortable reclining seat on an express route. If you are traveling to a popular destination, it may be as easy as that. To get to more far-flung areas, you'll generally need to take a bus to the closest big city and then switch to a local or interregional bus for the rest of your journey. A ticket on a standard bus, which may be the only option, depending on where you are going, does not guarantee you a seat, and they can get packed. You may find yourself standing for hours or smashed up against the windshield as the bus you're on speeds along a highway.

Unfortunately, there is no central repository for bus schedules and routes, and they can change. Although there is plenty of information available on the Internet, the best bet is to contact someone at your final destination who will be able to advise you on the best route possible.

The main bus company, with routes from Bangkok to all parts of the country and back, is **The Transport Co.** (www.transport.co.th/Eng/HomeEnglish.htm). The website lists all of the routes, fares, and schedules to and from Bangkok.

Buses will take you anywhere you want to go, if you have the time to wait.

DAILY LIFE

© SUZANNE NAM

BY BOAT

Whether you're commuting to work in Bangkok or island-hopping on weekends off, you're very likely to end up moving from one place to another by boat while you are in Thailand. In Bangkok the river ferry and canal boats are used as regular daily transportation, and for certain routes they are the quickest and most reliable way to go. In the southern islands, boats are often the only way to get from one place to another.

Boat safety is less stringent in Thailand than you might be used to back home, where piers and walkways are secure and everyone has access to a life preserver if necessary. In Thailand, you'll often be expected to jump from a pier to a ferry that has barely stopped, or to wade into the ocean to board a wooden longtail boat to get from one island to another.

Longtail Boats

Longtail boats are basic wooden-hulled boats with long outboard motors. They're the boats you most often see with colorful flags and streamers wrapped around their bows. They are very simple, and some are so small that they can only seat a few people. They are probably the most popular watercraft in the country, used for everything from traveling from one side of the Chao Phraya River in areas the standard ferries don't travel to hopping from one island to another in Phang Nga Bay.

Ferry Boats

In Bangkok, large ferry boats ply the river, and the city's canals and are used almost exclusively by commuters and tourists. Larger ferry boats are used to transport people and things to the islands in the Gulf of Siam and off the Andaman Coast. Most ferry boats are privately operated either under contract with local governments or as for-profit enterprises. Very popular routes, such as from Phuket to Ko Phi Phi or Surat Thani to Ko Samui and Ko Tao, run year-round. Other routes change depending on the season, and it can

Ferries are a necessity if you're living on the islands.

be difficult to find reliable scheduling information. If you are planning a trip involving a ferry, make sure to call the operator to confirm any scheduling information you may find on the Internet.

BY TAXI

You will find taxis in most of the major cities and popular destinations in the country, though you most likely will not find them in rural areas or less affluent places. In Bangkok, taxis are generally reasonable and easy to find. A trip anywhere in the city should run you less than 150 baht (sometimes significantly less, as the meter starts at 35 baht). In places such as Phuket, finding a meter taxi is nearly impossible, and local taxis charge exorbitant rates to take you from one part of the island to another. While tourists are sometimes targets for unscrupulous taxi drivers, you'll find that once you speak a little bit of Thai, drivers will rarely try to rip you off.

BY *SONG THAEW*

For short trips between neighboring villages (or even neighborhoods in Bangkok), these vehicles, which are essentially pickup trucks with seats in the back and roofs overhead, are a common and easy option. These vehicles usually run specific routes and will stop to pick up and discharge passengers along the way for fares starting at 5 baht. Schedules aren't posted, nor are prices, routes, or even stops. They may seem totally inaccessible, but any local person will know the route and be able to direct you. When in doubt, you can just say *Song thaew bai* and the name of your destination, and after a couple of tries, someone will point you in the right direction.

BY CAR

Thailand's major road system is exceptionally well-maintained and relatively easy to navigate. Although driving in Bangkok is probably not recommended unless you're really comfortable navigating confusing streets, dealing with informal rules that often seem completely at odds with what you learned in driving school, and sitting in traffic for hours, once you are outside the city, driving is perhaps the best way to cover a lot of ground and see the country at the same time; you'll also beat the buses and the trains. If you are traveling with small children, it is also the only way to guarantee that you are going to get a seat belt. For very small children, bring a car seat with you or buy one at one of the high-end department stores before you hit the road. The larger Central Department Stores will have them in stock, as will the department stores in Siam Paragon, Central World Plaza, and Emporium in Bangkok.

Outside Bangkok you may not be able to find one easily, and their availability at car rental agencies is limited. If you are coming from the United States, remember that in Thailand, the steering wheel is on the right and you must drive on the left.

Car Rental Agencies

All of the major U.S. agencies, including Avis (www.avis.com), National (www.nationalcar.com), and Hertz (www.hertz.com), have locations in Thailand, although usually in heavily visited places like Phuket and Bangkok. Prices are generally 1,600–3,200 baht per day, with a slight discount if you rent by the week. Most international agencies will require that you are at least 25 years old. There are also local rental car companies with prices that may be significantly cheaper. Make sure you understand the insurance you are getting, however, as you may be liable for any damage to the vehicle.

Legal Requirements

You can use a valid driver's license from your home country to drive in Thailand for the first three months you are here. After that, you'll need an international driver's license or a Thai drivers license. If you are going to be driving frequently or renting cars here, you should have a Thai driver's license, as many car rental agencies will not give you full insurance coverage without one.

To get a Thai driver's license (if you already have a license from your home country), you must be at least 18 years old and possess a valid visa (those here on tourist visas cannot apply). Before you visit your local motor vehicle office, visit your local immigration office and request a certificate of residency; you can also do this at your country's consulate or embassy, but you'll be charged a fee. Once you have the certificate, go to the motor vehicle office with the certificate, copies of the first page of your passport, your visa, and your work permit. If you do not speak Thai, you need to bring a translator along, as the application and some of the testing material will be in Thai. At the motor vehicle office, you will have to watch some instructional material in Thai, take a written test, and have your vision and reflexes tested. If you pass all the tests, you'll be granted a one-year driver's license. Even if you have been driving for years, you may be thrown off by the written exam. Everything is in meters and kilometers, and some rules of the road are different than in other countries. People often fail the test, so it's in your best interest to pick up a copy of the rules and study them before you take the test.

Road Rules

Speed limits are expressed in kilometers, as are car speedometers. On the highway the speed limit is generally 80 km/h (just under 50 mph) to 120 km/h (about 75 mph). On nonhighway roads outside of cities and towns it drops to 80 km/h. Within cities and towns it is usually 60 km/h (35 mph). Seat belts are required for both the driver and the front-seat passenger. Although this law is routinely broken, it's best to stay within the bounds of the law if you are driving in a foreign country (not to mention the safety issues). Drunk driving is a serious offense in Thailand, and a blood alcohol level of 0.05 percent is all that is required to land you in jail. Remember that local beer is significantly stronger than the average North American brew. At 6.4 percent, one Chang Beer, especially if it's a large one, is probably enough to keep you off the road for at least an hour or two.

Remember that you pass on the right, and slower vehicles stay in the left lane.

Most of the road signs and traffic laws are technically the same as in the rest of the world, but the informal rules of the road are probably very different from what you are used to, and they might not make sense if you didn't grow up driving in Thailand. Suffice it to say that other drivers will do things you are not expecting, such as changing into your lane with just a few feet to spare, or turning without signaling. In the United States it's generally not acceptable to make any maneuver that requires the person behind you to hit the brakes. In Thailand, that's not the case; you can move into traffic or make a turn even if it causes the person behind you or to the side to have to slow down. This doesn't mean that you can proceed with impunity or cause other drivers to slam on their brakes, but don't be shy about cutting in, and don't be surprised or angry when someone does it to you. The best way to handle this is to drive cautiously, watch out for other drivers, and keep a *sabai* attitude.

Gas Stations

On major roads and highways there are plenty of gas stations, some open 24 hours (especially on the highway). In smaller village areas, gas stations may close as early as 7 P.M., so keep an eye on your tank if you are driving in more remote areas. You can get diesel as well as leaded and unleaded gasoline, but most newer cars run on unleaded. If you are in doubt, the gas station attendant will know which fuel is right. Gas is relatively inexpensive in Thailand; it is sold by the liter and recently has been priced around 33 baht per liter, which is about US$3.90 per gallon.

Parking

Street parking in Bangkok is nearly impossible and not advised unless you can read the infrequent street signs in Thai to discern the rules, but it is relatively easy to find an inexpensive parking lot wherever you are headed. All major malls, hospitals, hotels, and many larger restaurants offer parking, often with valet service. If you are parking your car in a lot, do not be surprised to see other cars lining the lanes and blocking each other. This is normal, and drivers are expected to leave their cars in neutral without engaging the emergency brake (obviously this does not apply on any sort of slope) so they can be pushed out of the way if necessary.

In less densely populated areas, parking is considerably easier, and there are generally parking lots at larger hotels and restaurants if street parking is unavailable.

Motorcycles

Motorcycles are very common in Thailand, whether you are driving a car and looking to avoid hitting one or riding on one yourself. If you are driving or even a passenger in a car, it is your responsibility to watch out for them. Motorcycle drivers will often straddle lanes, pass between cars, cross highways, and do all sorts of unexpected things. Be aware that there are always motorcycles on the road, and sometimes they are difficult to see in your side and rearview mirrors. If you are on a major highway, it is not unheard of to see someone on a bike attempting to cross the road in front of you (and there are plenty of motorcycle fatalities caused by this every year). If you are opening the door of a car or a taxi, look behind you beforehand. Motorcycles have been known to snake in and out of parked cars, and a quickly opened door can result in an accident.

Renting a motorcycle outside Bangkok is probably easier than buying a can of soda. You will need your passport and cash, but it's almost unheard of to be asked for a license. Sometimes rental agencies will hold your passport as collateral; other times they will ask for a deposit of 500–1,000 baht (if you are asked to leave your passport, make sure you keep a copy of it as well as the rental receipt in case you are pulled over). Expect to pay 200–300 baht per day. In more rural areas, rental shops have even been known to lend out a bike without asking for anything in return. You are required by law to wear a helmet, and the police are generally quick to pull over foreigners without them.

The helmets you get with rental bikes are sometimes little more than plastic hats with chin straps. Ask for the best helmet they have, and if no good ones are available, considering heading to the nearest Tesco, Carrefour, or Big C to buy one.

Most of the bikes available are 100–125 cc semiautomatic scooters, which means that you have to shift gears with your foot but do not need to engage a clutch to do so. That part is easy enough, but do not consider riding a bike unless you know what you are doing. Motorcycles are often the cheapest, easiest, and most enjoyable way to get around, but there are accidents and even deaths every year by foreigners who are overconfident and think that just because everyone in the country is doing it, they can too. Yes, it's true that in any small village you'll probably see 12-year-old girls in their school uniforms piled three on a bike sipping sodas, talking on mobile phones, and navigating the machine in their bare feet. That doesn't make it safe or easy. Motorbikes are a part of daily life, especially in rural areas, and the kids you see riding them probably literally grew up doing so. Even they are not immune to accidents, and hundreds of Thais are involved in serious motorbike accidents every year.

If you are planning on driving a motorcycle frequently, you need to get a motorcycle license, and you generally won't be able to convert your existing license from your home country without taking a road test. The procedure is similar to getting a Thai driver's license except that you must come with a motorbike and take a road test. Considering not getting a license? You probably won't be able to get insurance for your bike, and if you get into an accident without one, especially an accident that involves injury to another person, you could be in serious trouble.

BY BICYCLE

In smaller cities and rural areas, a bicycle can be a great way to get around. They are inexpensive, environmentally friendly, and provide some exercise. Even in Bangkok it's possible to ride your bike around as long as you understand the rules of the road and take adequate safety precautions. I routinely ride a bicycle in Bangkok, and although the first few days were a little scary, I actually feel safer in traffic here than I would back home. Because there are so many people on motorbikes, drivers are accustomed to looking out for smaller vehicles. Before you hit the big roads, make sure you understand how traffic flows, and observe the way drivers behave when switching lanes. If you want to buy a bicycle in Thailand, most of what you'll find is either very inexpensive models without gears or expensive imported bicycles. Bangkok has a couple of bike stores that sell inexpensive city bikes with gears; otherwise they are difficult to find.

PRIME LIVING LOCATIONS

OVERVIEW

Once you've decided to move to Thailand, you have another big decision in front of you—what part of the country to live in. For some, the decision has already been made by an employer or for other reasons, but if you can choose where to live, you have a lot of diversity available.

Thailand is just a little larger than California and has hundreds of cities and villages where foreigners could live comfortably. The following chapters focus only on the areas where expatriates are most likely to end up—Bangkok, northern Thailand (the Chiang Mai area), northeast Thailand (Isan), Pattaya, and southern Thailand, which comprises the southern islands and beach areas. Thailand is a relatively easy place for foreigners to live, though, and there are at least a few living in every one of the country's 75 provinces.

If the living location you've selected is not covered specifically in these chapters and it's in a rural part of the country, there are some generalizations that will apply wherever you live (unless it's in a very remote part of the country). You will most likely live in a village, essentially a cluster of homes or homes

© SUZANNE NAM

and farms that may or may not be very spread out from one another but are considered part of the same area for administrative and community purposes. Village living can be very basic. Although most of the country has running water and electricity, there may not be much more than that in terms of creature comforts. Village housing in many of the poorer parts of the country consists of simple wooden or concrete structures, sometimes with an open-air living space attached, and a basic bathroom with a squat toilet.

Finding a house to rent in these areas of the country can be challenging, as there's not a bustling rental market and homes are seldom unoccupied. It is possible to arrange an informal homestay for as little as 2,000 baht per month (and the best way to do this would be to track down the village chief, although you will need a Thai speaker's assistance), but be aware that you will be living just like the villagers and may end up sleeping in a communal room with no privacy.

More affluent rural areas will have better housing options and more houses for rent as well. You may not get a villa with a private pool, but it is possible to find standard two- and three-bedroom bungalows with modern kitchens and bathrooms. Rent for these homes is contingent on the area you choose but can be as little as 5,000 baht per month.

All of Thailand is well-served by a comprehensive highway system, so no matter what part of the country you choose you will be close to good roads connecting to major highways. Small towns, typically at the center of groups of rural villages or towns, may be 10 or 20 minutes by car but will have banks, a couple of shophouse restaurants, convenience stores, and fresh markets. You are also likely to find a hypermarket—a Big C, Tesco Lotus, or Carrefour— within driving distance of any part of the country you live in.

If the area you are considering moving to is not listed, don't write it off; use the general information in this book as a starting point, and get ready for an adventure.

BANGKOK

Thailand's capital, Bangkok offers expatriates everything they could ever want in a big city, and then some—scores of cultural attractions, a great nightlife scene, and amazing shopping. There are dozens of places to send your kids to school, and apartments priced from a few hundred dollars a month to a few thousand. The city is one of the best in the world when it comes to street food and higher-end dining.

Bangkok is a bustling international city that attracts people from all over the world. It's not uncommon to talk to people from Asia, Europe, Africa, and

Latin America in the same day. It's the economic engine of a growing economy, so business opportunities abound for entrepreneurs.

Along with all the great stuff Bangkok has to offer are some less attractive elements. Bangkok is massive and sprawling, and because of the heat it's nearly impossible to walk from one neighborhood to another. It's just not a walking city, and traffic can be horrendous (we're talking two-hour traffic jams), leaving those who need to get across town in a difficult situation. Parts of the city are really dirty and crowded, and the sex trade, though confined to specific areas, isn't a pretty sight.

More and more luxury high-rises go up every year.

NORTHERN THAILAND

If you love Thailand but don't care for congested cities or touristy beach areas, consider a move to northern Thailand. Characterized as much by the milder weather and lush mountains as the friendly, artsy young people in Chiang Mai, the region is probably the most livable in the country.

Viewed from above, northern Thailand's endless mountain ranges and lush greenery make it appear untouched, and indeed the region is replete with places to enjoy the outdoors, from hiking in gorgeous mountains to white-water rafting.

Pair those advantages with a relatively inexpensive cost of living and plenty of culture to explore, and it's easy to see why so many people love this region. The downsides are that outside of Chiang Mai, northern Thailand can feel very remote, and it is difficult to find employment if you aren't teaching or in development work.

SOUTHERN THAILAND

If you've always wanted to live in a tropical paradise, here's your chance. Southern Thailand has some of the most beautiful beaches and islands in the world, it's not too expensive, and in most places it's convenient for foreigners who choose to relocate but don't want to give up too many of the comforts from home.

If you choose to live on the island of Phuket, the largest island in Thailand, you won't have to make too many sacrifices, as it has international schools, international supermarkets, and a good variety of housing options. Samui is a little smaller and a little less cosmopolitan but nonetheless attracts retirees and others from around the globe.

Island living does come with some trade-offs, the biggest of which is that you'll be living in the middle of some of the most heavily touristed areas in the world. Some people thrive in this environment, while others find the constant influx of transient visitors on vacation quickly becomes a major annoyance.

NORTHEAST THAILAND

Although foreigners on vacation seldom visit northeast Thailand, commonly called Isan, it is an increasingly popular place for expats to settle down. It's not so much the relaxed rural way of life, the friendliness of the people, or even the amazing (and amazingly spicy) cuisine but the fact that many foreign men have married women from Isan and have moved there with their families.

That's not to say that Isan wouldn't be a wonderful place to live without those specific personal circumstances. It is a scenic rural region with a handful of smaller, more livable cities, none with populations over 150,000, along with farms, water buffalo, and more farms.

It is also the poorest part of the country, with per capita annual income less than 27,000 baht. While that means that living expenses in this part of Thailand are very low, it also means that quality of life suffers, and you may feel a vast divide between you and the people around you (or they may feel it). If you have school-aged children, northeast Thailand is particularly challenging, as there are virtually no schools there for kids who do not speak Thai.

PATTAYA

On the surface, Pattaya may not seem very attractive as a place to live. It's a city best known for prostitution and, occasionally, violent crime. Despite these disadvantages, it's the most popular destination for foreigners in all of Thailand. It's just a 90-minute drive from Bangkok's Suvarnabhumi Airport, the beaches are pretty enough, and it has just about every convenience anyone could possible want, including a good selection of international schools, lots of restaurants, and plenty of golf courses.

PRIME LIVING LOCATIONS

BANGKOK

Bangkok, the geographic heart of Thailand, is located at the mouth of the Chao Phraya River in the Central Plains region and is and home to an estimated 10 million of the country's 60 million residents. By area, Bangkok is one of the smallest provinces in Thailand, but in terms of population density it ranks first and is nearly three times denser than any other province in the country.

Bangkok, or Krung Thep as it's called in Thai, is the country's political capital and also Thailand's economic, cultural, commercial, and educational center. Almost every large company doing business in Thailand, whether local or multinational, is headquartered in Bangkok. The country's most prestigious universities are here. The best art museums are here, as are the Grand Palace and Thailand's most revered Buddhist *wat*. Bangkok also has the biggest concentration of great restaurants, nightclubs, and other diversions that can make life more fun on a daily basis. And, of course, it attracts visitors from all over the country and all over the world, so there are plenty of interesting people to meet.

© MONIKA MURPHY

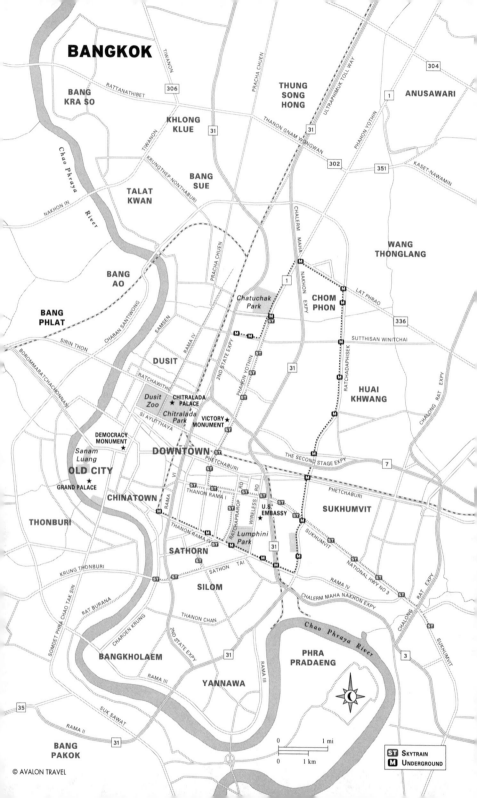

The capital also offers many of the conveniences one would expect in a large city. Public transportation is extensive (although not always rapid), markets are abundant, and you can find just about anything you could need or want in the thousands of shops and restaurants that line Bangkok's streets.

Is Bangkok right for you? Like some of the world's great cities, including New York, London, and Tokyo, one of Bangkok's many lures is that it's impossible to pin down. As Thailand's largest city and one of the largest cities in Southeast Asia, it's big, busy, and full of...everything. To some, the city is modern, cosmopolitan, and replete with conveniences and excess. To others, it's messy, chaotic, and poor. Your experience will depend on your lifestyle, location, cash flow, and perspective.

That's not to say that Bangkok is just a generic big city. Much of the center of the city feels very international, but with so many *wats,* street food hawkers, museums, and the king's anthem broadcast in nearly all public spaces at 8 A.M. and 6 P.M. daily, along with the occasional elephant walking down the street, you won't forget you are living in Thailand.

If you love living in a bustling urban environment with plenty of opportunities for diverse experiences, want to live car-free and enjoy museums, concerts, nightclubs, crowds, noise, and 24-hour conveniences, you will love Bangkok. And if you don't want to invest the time and energy to learn to speak Thai, you'll fare best in Bangkok, where there are plenty of other English speakers and many services available to those who do not speak Thai.

If you're moving to Thailand for work, you might not have a choice, as the capital is where the vast majority of jobs for foreigners are. But if you do have a choice, keep in mind that Bangkok can be a challenging place to live if you are not used to big developing cities. Air quality has gotten much better in recent years, but during the hot season it can be stifling, especially for those with asthma or other respiratory issues. Green space is very limited, and unless you live close to one of the few large parks in the city, you'll have a difficult time finding a place to let your kids (or yourself, for that matter) run around without worrying about them getting hit by one of Bangkok's notorious drivers. And if you really want to immerse yourself in Thai culture and language, the capital may not be the best choice. Unless you are very disciplined, it's too easy to run in expat circles, speak English, and forget you're living in a foreign country.

The Lay of the Land

Bangkok, on the Chao Phraya River basin, is an extraordinarily flat city with few distinguishing geographical features other than the river itself and the numerous canals, built over the past 200 years, that crisscross the land. It is difficult to get a handle on the lay of the land here as organic urban sprawl seems to be the dominant pattern.

The historic city center, Ko Rattanakosin, where the Grand Palace is located, is flanked by the meandering Chao Phraya to the west and has been superseded by the city's modern center a few miles east. In fact, all of Bangkok proper is located to the east of the river, though Greater Bangkok does extend across the river to the west. With few geological impediments to development, Bangkok sprawls out from the center for miles, with plenty of smaller urban areas clustered throughout.

Bangkok is more an organic city than a planned one, with development seeming to follow the will of those with the biggest checkbooks rather than the foresight of city planners with the best interests of the millions of residents in mind. Rapid public transportation is limited to the center of the city, with some service to northern Bangkok on the city's only subway line. Because of the large roads and highways that cut through the city, neighborhoods can feel very disconnected from each other, even if they're just a few hundred feet away.

Street stalls and skyscrapers share space in Bangkok.

Silom and Sathorn, Ratchathewi, Ploenchit, Siam Square, Chitlom, and the Sukhumvit area, all east of the river, are considered part of central Bangkok, and all are served by the city's Skytrain or subway. As you head further north into Dusit, the city becomes less cosmopolitan. With fewer tall buildings and many residential neighborhoods, Dusit feels like what the rest of the city would have looked like had it not been for the amazing economic boom over the past few decades—less international and less convenient, certainly, but much more Thai than modern Bangkok. To the east, branching off of Sukhumvit and Petchaburi Roads, are Huai Kwang, Bangkapi, Phra Khanong, and On Nut, some of which are served by the Skytrain. Though still densely populated with 7-Elevens, high-rises, and restaurants, these areas retain a little more of a neighborhood feeling and have fewer international residents. To the west and south is Thonburi, which, although not a part of Bangkok proper, is part of the city sprawl. Here you'll find fewer high-rises but plenty of restaurants and apartments.

CLIMATE

Bangkok is hot year-round. The average temperature in the city's hottest month, April, is 35°C (95°F). During the coolest month, December, the temperature drops just a few degrees to 31°C (88°F). Average lows aren't much better. In April, the average low is 26°C (79°F), and in December it's 21°C (69°F). While the thermometer doesn't change much throughout the year, humidity and rainfall do. May–October is rainy season in Bangkok, with the most rainfall in September–October. By November, precipitation and humidity drop markedly, making November–March the most pleasant times to be here.

CULTURE

Bangkok offers everything from excellent museums and historical sights to interesting neighborhoods, parks, and other diversions to keep residents and visitors busy and interested for years. The Old City, on Rattanakosin island, is where the country's most important sights, including the Grand Palace and Wat Pho, are located. It's also home to the largest concentration of museums, including the National Museum, the Museum of Siam, the National Gallery, and others. The Old City has some excellent streets for those who love food, and it is worth as much time as you can find to explore.

Chinatown is home to not only some of the best food in the city but also a handful of striking Buddhist *wats* and some of the best market shopping in the city. The neighborhood is often packed full of people, but if you can bear the crowds, take a walk down Yawolat Road, exploring the side streets that connect to the Chao Phraya River. The business center of Bangkok, including Silom and Sathorn, Siam Square, and Sukhumvit, has a little less to offer in terms of traditional cultural sights but has its fair share of galleries, restaurants, parks, and other public spaces, including massive shopping malls and markets. They are also vibrant and interesting parts of the city with plenty of entertainment value.

Daily Life

Bangkok is a major metropolis, a tourist destination, a business center, and a hometown. If you live in Bangkok, you're likely to encounter each of these identities at different times. If you're teaching in a small school on the outskirts of the city and live in a local neighborhood, Bangkok may seem like a simple developing city where the neighbors all know each other's names and kids play outside. If you're working for an international corporation in the city center and live in a high-rise serviced apartment, Bangkok may seem like a wealthy modern city. Your experience here will largely depend on where you work and what you do, where you live, where you go out, and the type of friends you have.

There are hundreds of thousands of foreigners from all over the world living in or visiting Bangkok at any given time, so no matter where you live in the city, you won't feel very isolated. Because there are so many foreigners,

Much of Bangkok is as developed as any major Western city.

The Chao Phraya River is still a major source of commerce.

however, you're also less likely to feel like you're a pioneer, and at times you might not even feel like you're living in a foreign country. If that's important to you, consider moving to another part of Thailand. If not, enjoy the fact that Bangkok is very convenient and very exotic at the same time.

Some foreigners, especially Westerners, like to gripe about the bad treatment they get from locals because they are not Thai. The informal two-tiered pricing system seems to be the biggest complaint. Will you pay more for things in Bangkok because you are an expat? Most likely you will, whether it's an inflated price for a *tuk tuk* ride or a T-shirt at a market. Those who speak more Thai and make an effort to connect to the people around them fare better than those who insist on speaking English, as do those who live in areas of the city that aren't deluged by tourists.

EXPAT SOCIAL SCENE

As a regional hub for big multinational companies doing business in the region, home to one of the largest U.S. embassies in the world, a relatively easy place for ESL teachers to find work, and an inexpensive place for Westerners to retire, Bangkok attracts an interesting and varied group of foreigners. With so many people around, Bangkok has a thriving expat social scene, or rather many different social scenes, depending on the circles you run in and your interests. New moms will find one social scene, foreign journalists another, young singles another, and so on. It's not hard to find others with common interests or backgrounds to spend time with in Bangkok. In fact, the expat social scenes are so compelling that it can be difficult to make Thai friends.

Bangkok has scores of formal and informal expatriate clubs and groups, including those primarily for Americans, Japanese, French, Italians, and Dutch. There are also alumni groups for many large U.S., European, and Australian universities with both Thai and foreign members, parent groups, groups for Thais, and locals with common interests. As for sports, rugby players, Ultimate players, soccer players, tennis players, and hashers will all find groups of other foreigners and Thais to play with.

Nightlife in Bangkok lives up to its reputation, and there are scores of bars and nightclubs across the city where Thais and foreigners go out to drink, dance, and party. Khao San Road, once exclusively a budget-traveler destination, is a hot spot for college-age Thais and foreigners to drink beer with their friends over loud music. Sukhumvit Soi 11 has some swanky nightclubs that attract the young (and not so young) and beautiful from all over the world. RCA has plenty of big nightclubs where the bass is pumping and the kids look like they're barely out of their teens, but also some smaller clubs with live music where a slightly older crowd hangs out. The capital has a handful of live jazz venues that feature local and international musicians and attract a comfortable mix of expats and locals.

RESOURCES

Bangkok has two English-language newspapers, the *Bangkok Post* and the *Nation*. Although neither is all that objective when it comes to covering the country's politics, they both have good local and national news and feature stories as well as good events listings. There are numerous other English-language magazines covering art, food, nightlife, and culture. *BK Magazine* has good food and nightlife listings and is marketed toward both expats and Thais, so it provides a more interesting perspective. It also has a very comprehensive website (http://bkmagazine.com). *Bangkok 101* also has good listings.

HEALTH CARE

Bangkok has some excellent international private hospitals. Three hospitals, Bumrungrad and Samitivej off of Sukhumvit Road and BNH in Silom, are considered the nicest, if only because they have lobbies like five-star hotels, staff members fluent in a multitude of languages, and patient-doctor liaisons to help foreigners. Other hospitals in the city, while not as high-end, are considered to provide excellent medical care, and people from all over the world come to Bangkok specifically to visit them.

SCHOOLS

There are more than 50 international preschools in the Bangkok area that offer instruction in English, and within central Bangkok there are preschools in nearly every neighborhood. Bangkok Mothers and Babies International (BAMBI) lists most of the schools, with contact information, on their website (www.bambiweb.org).

For school-age children, there are dozens of schools in and around Bangkok that are either certified international schools following a U.S., U.K., or International Baccalaureate curriculum or quasi-international schools where instruction is bilingual. There are a myriad of issues to consider when choosing the right school for your child, and the International Schools Association of Thailand has information about academic programs, tuition, and admissions policies on their website (www.isat.or.th), along with a list of their member schools.

Where to Live

Bangkok is a big city and can be tough to get around quickly, so before you decide on where to live, spend some time thinking about how you'll get back and forth to your job, how you'll get your kids to school, and where you'll spend most of your nights out. If you'll be working close to a Skytrain or subway stop, any part of the city is a possibility, as the longest commute on either system is less than an hour. If you'll be working in an area that isn't close to rapid public transportation, test out the bus or taxi commute during rush hour before you commit to an apartment or house, as getting from one part of the city to another can involve multiple buses and can easily take more than an hour.

Once you've narrowed it down, you'll probably still have quite a few neighborhoods available. Spend some time in each one, walking around during different times of the day and evening, to get a feel for them before deciding. In most areas of Bangkok, the farther you get off the main road, the more space you'll have and the quieter your living environment will be. Fortunately, most neighborhoods have a diversity of housing options available in many price ranges, so few neighborhoods will be out of reach, unless you are working with a very tight budget. The type of apartment you'll get for 15,000 baht is going to be a lot smaller and more run-down in Chitlom than what you'll find for that price in Phra Khanong, but at least no neighborhood will be completely off-limits.

Most expats who move to Bangkok end up renting, but there is also a thriving condominium market, and many projects target foreign buyers as well as local ones. Unlike in more developed condominium markets, where size and location dictate price more than anything else, in Bangkok the age of the building, its general appearance, and the amenities available have a far greater impact on pricing than they would back at home. It's quite possible to see two condominiums with the same square footage on the same street that are listed for wildly different prices.

Condominium purchases by foreigners are heavily regulated in Thailand, and there is typically no financing available. Foreigners cannot buy land in any part of Thailand. Although there are some workarounds available (involving either a Thai-domiciled company or a Thai spouse, if you have one) none are airtight.

The following is not a comprehensive list of all of the neighborhoods you could move to in Bangkok, as there are scores of them, but it covers the most popular areas for expats who move to the central part of the city.

CENTRAL BUSINESS DISTRICT

Of all of the areas in central Bangkok, the neighborhoods of Ploenchit, Chitlom, Ratchadamri, and Lang Suan, which make up the central business district, are considered the most sought-after because of their proximity to offices, green spaces, and shopping and because they are all near the Skytrain. The U.S., British, and many other embassies are in these neighborhoods, and

Central Bangkok is desirable because of its proximity to offices, shopping, and parks.

the hundreds of foreign diplomats that staff them are housed here. One of the city's largest public parks, Lumphini Park, is also convenient to the area. If cost is not an issue and you're looking for an area that's well-served by rapid public transportation, has plenty of international supermarkets, high-end shopping malls, and is not overdeveloped, any of these neighborhoods will suit you well. These neighborhoods aren't entirely or even primarily expat, so there are still plenty of opportunities to meet Thais and speak Thai. If you have small children, there are a handful of international preschools in the area. The closest international grade schools and high schools are just east off Sukhumvit Road.

Most of the housing available is apartments or condos, and although there are plenty of larger apartments available in these areas, there are few stand-alone houses. Many buildings cater to affluent locals and expats and have amenities such as swimming pools and gyms. If you look hard, there are also some older buildings, so you can live in the neighborhood and not break the bank on rent.

Rental costs for typical Western-style apartments in these areas run from 25,000 baht for a 93-square-meter (1,000-square-foot) two-bedroom apartment at the low end to 270,000 baht for a 325-square-meter (3,500-square-foot) five-bedroom apartment at the top end. Similarly sized condominiums in these neighborhoods sell for anywhere from 4 million baht up to 30 million baht and more.

SILOM AND SATHORN

Just south of the central business district neighborhoods are the Silom and Sathorn areas, which are also considered prime real estate. Like Ploenchit, Chitlom, Ratchadamri, and Lang Suan, Silom and Sathorn are close to green spaces and shopping and are convenient to Skytrain and subway stations. Although there are plenty of residential enclaves in Silom and Sathorn, they are part of the central business district and are home to many of the city's large office buildings. Silom Road is a bustling busy street filled with office buildings, restaurants, and shops as well as some quieter residential areas on the side streets. With small shopping malls and a couple of international supermarkets, it's a convenient place to get things done, but it can be crowded. In the morning and evening, when office workers are coming and going to work, the sidewalks are packed with people and it's almost impossible to navigate. Sathorn Road to the south is a much wider thoroughfare lined with large office buildings and hotels. It's easier to walk here during rush hour, because the street is so wide and difficult to cross, but it's less pedestrian-friendly, and many who live south of Sathorn Road feel somewhat isolated from the center.

Like other parts of the center, most of the available housing is apartments and condos, although it is not impossible to find a small standalone bungalow. Apartments in these areas vary dramatically, from newly built luxury units with large swimming pools and modern gyms to older less-expensive accommodations, and often you'll find these diverse options on the same block.

Rental costs for typical Western-style apartments in these areas run from 20,000 baht for a 93-square-meter (1,000-square-foot) two-bedroom apartment at the low end to 120,000 baht for a 260-square-meter (2,800-square-foot) four-bedroom apartment at the top end. Similarly sized condominiums in these neighborhoods sell for anywhere from 4 million baht up to 20 million baht.

VICTORY MONUMENT AND VICINITY

If you're looking for more affordable housing but don't want to stray far from the city center, head north up Phaya Thai Road. The stretch of Bangkok between Siam Square and the Ari Skytrain station, which includes Ratchathewi, Pahayothin, Phaya Thai, Victory Monument, and Ari, has some of the best housing for expats who want Western-style apartments in a convenient location but don't need to be right in the center of the business area. There are a few international supermarkets and international preschools as well as one international secondary school, and the neighborhood is right on the Skytrain. Another reason to consider this area is that it still feels very Thai compared to more central areas.

Housing in these areas is mostly apartments and condos, and although there are new buildings going up all the time, the majority of units are in structures built in the 1980s and 1990s, many of which have not undergone significant renovation. As you move farther north (and away from the center of the city) prices get less expensive. Rental costs for typical Western-style apartments in these areas run from 7,000 baht for a 28-square-meter (300-square-foot) studio apartment at the low end to 70,000 baht for a 167-square-meter (1,800-square-foot) three-bedroom apartment at the top end. Small-sized studio condominiums in these neighborhoods sell for anywhere from 2 million baht, and larger units in newer buildings go for as much as 8 million baht.

OLD CITY, CHINATOWN, AND DUSIT

These neighborhoods in the western part of Bangkok offer an opportunity to live in a very different world than central Bangkok. There are very few

© SUZANNE NAM

Apartments in the Old City have their charms, but often lack basics.

Western-style apartments available, especially in Chinatown, and just a handful of intrepid foreigners as neighbors. Foreigners who decide to live in these neighborhoods either adapt to local housing standards or, if they can negotiate a fair deal with their landlords, invest a little money in upgrading facilities.

Dusit, in the northwest part of Bangkok on the east bank of the Chao Phraya, has some of the best street food in Bangkok and feels very local and very Thai. Although it's not a very international area, there are still some conveniences, including supermarkets with some Western products. There are a handful of apartment buildings there catering to UN employees, journalists, and teachers. If you live here and work in central Bangkok, you'll need to commute by river ferry, bus, or taxi to the closest Skytrain station.

It is very difficult to find housing in the Old City. Most apartments are not Western-style and so have small or no kitchens and very basic bathrooms. The upside is that if you do find someone willing to rent to you, you'll most likely be living in an old wooden shophouse apartment and will be able to take advantage of the many bars and restaurants in the area that cater to tourists and local students. There are also a couple of apartment buildings along the river that offer Western-style apartments. The Old City has very little in the way of supermarkets, but there are some local markets to buy meat, fish, and produce. As in Dusit, the best way to commute is via river ferry, or by bus or train to the nearest Skytrain station. Chinatown, referred to as Yawolat after the large street that runs through it, is one of the city's most bustling neighborhoods and has very limited Western-style housing. There are a couple of supermarkets in the neighborhood and one of the largest wet markets in

Bangkok. As in the Old City, most apartments are shophouses, although there are a couple of larger apartment buildings. Chinatown is convenient to the Hua Lumpong subway station.

If you are renting an apartment in one of these neighborhoods, your landlord may be a little old lady, and your lease terms a little more informal than if you were to find an apartment in a typical Western-style building in central Bangkok. Rental costs for local apartments in these areas run from 5,000 baht for a 23-square-meter (250-square-foot) studio apartment in an older apartment building at the low end to 40,000 baht for a 232-square-meter (2,500-square-foot), four-story, three-bedroom shophouse. With the exception of Dusit, it is nearly impossible to buy condominiums in these neighborhoods.

LOWER SUKHUMVIT AREA

The Lower Sukhumvit area, from Sukhumvit Soi 1 to Asoke, is a mishmash of office buildings, hotels, restaurants, and shops. The Skytrain runs along the road, and there are plenty of supermarkets, shopping malls, and even a few international schools in the area, making it one of the most convenient places for expats to live in the city and one of the most highly concentrated expat living areas. The area has one of the most diverse selections of housing in the city, with everything from single-family houses to inexpensive studio apartments. It's not a perfect location, however: On the surface it is severely lacking in charm, although there are some areas off the main road where you might find a tree or two and some nice architecture. Bangkok's seedier side is easily seen in the windows of the many massage parlors and bars that speckle Sukhumvit Road. If that's not something you want to look at or expose your children to every day, choose your housing in this area very carefully. Some streets, such as Sukhumvit Soi 6, have some nice large apartments that are perfect for families, but to get to them you have to walk through Nana, one of the city's well-known red-light districts.

Rental costs for a 28-square-meter (300-square-foot) studio in a smaller Western-style apartment building start at around 7,000 baht per month; older two-bedroom 112-square-meter (1,200-square-foot) units in large apartment buildings with basic kitchens and bathrooms cost about 25,000 baht.

UPPER SUKHUMVIT FROM THONG LOR THROUGH ON NUT

The upper Sukhumvit area, starting east of Asoke, has a variety of different neighborhoods, from young and hip Thong Lor to less-expensive but farther-out On Nut. Each of these neighborhoods has a specific atmosphere, but all share a few things in common—they are convenient to rapid public transportation, thanks to their proximity to the Skytrain, and they have plenty of restaurants and shops nearby. Like Lower Sukhumvit, the neighborhoods that form the Upper Sukhumvit area are all popular enough with expats that it won't be difficult to get by on a daily basis without having to speak or understand too much Thai. Here too you'll find a variety of housing options depending on the neighborhood you pick and what your criteria are. There are still many single-family houses tucked into the side *sois* off Sukhumvit Road for those who don't want to live in an apartment and can afford the higher rents. Apartments run the gamut from older units in smaller buildings that have very basic kitchens and bathrooms and no central air-conditioning to newly built, modern apartments with all the amenities. If you're looking for a single-family home or a multilevel townhouse that might even have a small yard, this area is your best bet.

Rental costs for a very basic Western-style apartment in a more inexpensive area start at around 7,000 baht for a 28-square-meter (300-square-foot) studio apartment. Modern serviced apartments in pricier areas, such as Thong Lor, will cost about 50,000 baht for a 149-square-meter (1,600-square-foot) two-bedroom apartment. Townhouses in Ekkamai can cost as little as 2,500 baht, while a 279-square-meter (3,000-square-foot) five-bedroom house with its own swimming pool and grounds will cost 250,000 baht. There are plenty of condominium developments in this part of Bangkok, and prices range from 3 million baht for a 56-square-meter (600-square-foot) one-bedroom unit and up.

AROUND CENTRAL BANGKOK

There are a number of neighborhoods outside central Bangkok that attract foreigners, either because of their proximity to international schools or jobs or better housing options. Bangna, Bangkapi, Minburi, Nonthaburi, and Pathumthani are some of the more popular suburbs surrounding Bangkok, and all are convenient to the expressway and have large tract-housing developments home to a mix of foreigners and upper-middle-class Thais. Most of these developments offer townhouses and single-family stand-alone homes, and many have swimming pools and fitness centers on the premises, all for what you'd pay for a small condominium in the center of Bangkok. They are also often gated communities, so kids can actually run around the neighborhood and ride bicycles in the street, activities that foreign parents generally prohibit in Bangkok for fear of serious injury.

Within greater Bangkok, it's difficult to find an area that isn't close to a

PRIME LIVING LOCATIONS

wet market, a gas station, a shopping mall, and a hypermarket, and all of these neighborhoods have each of these. With the exception of Nonthaburi and Minburi, all are south and southeast of the city and are thus closer to Suvarnabhumi International Airport. Many housing estates also have their own convenience stores and even noodle stands.

Rental costs for two-bedroom attached townhouses with Western kitchens in developments or buildings with swimming pools start at 12,000 baht per month. Three-bedroom, 279-square-meter (3,000-square-foot) homes in luxury developments rent for as much as 90,000 baht per month.

Getting Around

Traffic in Bangkok can be terrible, and at its worst a trip across town in a taxi can take a couple of hours. To avoid this, you'll need to take advantage of all of the city's transportation options, from the fast but limited Skytrain to the Chao Phraya Express Boat on the river. Plan your travel strategies carefully—try to avoid being on the road during rush hour, and take the subway, Skytrain, ferry boat, or canal boat instead of a taxi whenever you can.

Most commuters in Bangkok, unless they live within walking distance of a Skytrain or subway station, combine two or more forms of public transportation to get where they need to go. With very few exceptions, getting from one part of central Bangkok to another requires very little walking as long as you are willing to take different types of transportation. The formal and informal systems are set up to make this as easy as possible, so, for example, during rush hour there will always be a line of motorcycle taxis or taxis waiting at a particular station to take commuters the final leg of their journey to their office or back home.

SKYTRAIN AND SUBWAY

Bangkok has an elevated train system, referred to as the Skytrain, with two lines, and a single subway line called the MRT. Both are efficient, modern, and inexpensive, and if you ever have a choice between a taxi and the Skytrain or subway, opt for the public transportation.

The Skytrain's Sukhumvit Line runs vaguely west to east along the main artery called Rama I Road, Ploenchit, and Sukhumvit Road. The Silom Line runs north to south from Mo Chit, where the Chatuchak Market and the Northern Bus Terminal are, then hooking west to terminate on the edge of the Chao Phraya at Thaksin Bridge. Trains run every few minutes during rush hour, and even during nonpeak times you will wait less than 10 minutes for a train.

The subway makes a loop that starts at Bang Su in the north, circles the city center, and crosses the Skytrain's Sukhumvit Line at Asok (Sukhumvit Skytrain station connects to Asok subway station) before turning west, crossing the Skytrain's Silom Line at Silom (Sala Daeng Skytrain station) before terminating at Hua Lumpong Station.

The fare is 20–70 baht, depending on the number of stops you travel. You can either buy a prepaid card at the staffed counter of any station or go to one of the automated machines and punch in your destination to buy a one-trip card. Although there are interchanges between the Skytrain and subway, you cannot use the same card for both.

The Skytrain and subway run daily daily 6 A.M.–midnight, and the last train from each station is announced.

RIVERS AND CANALS
Ferries

Given that Bangkok was once a nearly amphibious city, it's no wonder that traveling by boat can sometimes be the best choice for getting around. The Chao Phraya is served by a public ferry system that runs up and down the river, stopping at various piers on either side. If you're taking the Skytrain, you can connect to the ferry at Thaksin Bridge stop, which is Central Pier. Just follow the signs for the pier when you exit the station. There are five different types of commuter boats running along the river, all run by the Chao Phraya Express Boat Company (www.chaophrayaboat.co.th). The company website offers clear schedules and maps for each pier on the river.

The boats run every 10–20 minutes daily 5:45 A.M.–7:30 P.M.

Canal Boats

There are also commuter boats plying some of the major canals in Bangkok, although the service seems to be declining every year. One major convenient route that's still running is along the Saen Saeb Canal, which is right next to Petchaburi Road and goes as far west as the Golden Mount near Democracy Monument and past Sukhumvit Soi 71 to the east. If you are living or working near Petchaburi Road, the canal boats are a very convenient way to get around, but they can be a little more of an adventure than river boats. During rush hour they can be very crowded; they're smaller ,and they move faster. Boats run daily about 6 A.M.–8:30 P.M. and cost between 9–13 baht per ride.

TAXI

Metered taxis come in a variety of crazy colors, bright orange and purple and green, but they are all clearly marked, and you won't be able to miss them. If they're available, you'll see a brightly lit red sign on the passenger side of the windshield; just wave one down. On any major road there are plenty of available taxis, unless it's pouring outside or right around rush hour.

Metered fares start at 35 baht, and getting across town should run you no more than 80 baht unless traffic is really bad (which it often is). Although tipping is not required, most people at least round the fare up. If you're going out of the way,

Bangkok *tuk tuk*

across town, or to the airport, the common etiquette is to ask the driver if he'll take you first, as sometimes they'll turn down a fare if it's too far out of the way or traffic is abominable.

MOTORCYCLE TAXI

Motorcycles are a common mode of transportation in Bangkok and are often the fastest way to get from one point to another, especially if you're going only a few blocks. Motorcycle taxi drivers wear orange vests and can either be flagged down on the street or engaged at one of the many stands in the city. You'll be able to spot them immediately; just look for a bunch of guys on motorbikes wearing orange. Fares are usually fixed and run anywhere from 10 baht for a couple of blocks to 100 baht to get from one neighborhood to another.

TUK TUK

The colorful, ubiquitous three-wheeled half-motorbike, half car is another transportation option. These can be a very convenient and quick way to go short distances, and they are a lifesaver if you are moving lots of stuff from one place to another.

© SUZANNE NAM

Motorcycle taxis have their own informal "stops."

BUSES

In the right circumstances, taking a city bus in Bangkok is convenient and inexpensive. In the wrong circumstances, it's confusing, time-consuming, and a little scary. The city buses, administered by the Bangkok Metropolitan Transporation Authority (www.bmta.co.th/en) cover all of Bangkok and even out into surrounding provinces, so you can get from any place in the city to any other by public bus. In fact, this is the most common form of transportation, as the Skytrain and subway systems are very limited in the areas they cover and are prohibitively expensive for most Bangkok residents.

Public buses come in a variety of colors, depending on the route, the size, and the comfort level involved. The most common are the orange air-conditioned buses, the blue-and-white and red-and-cream open-air buses, and the small green minibuses (these are run by private contractors, not the BMTA). Currently there is no bus map available in English, but there is some limited information available on the BMTA website, including bus routes that pass common tourist sights. Click on the "Travel Guide" link for this information, and be prepared to click through each of the buses listed to determine which one goes from your location to your destination. MapGuideThailand (www.mapguidethailand.com) also has some bus information under the "Bangkok Bus" tab. Although the search function isn't dependable for non-Thai speakers (because spelling varies), if you enter the number of the bus you are considering taking, it will show you the exact route on the map that the bus takes.

Bus stops are marked with signs and often have small benches and covered waiting areas. But even if you are standing at the stop, a bus will not necessarily stop for you unless you wave it down, so make sure to be on the lookout for the bus number, then raise your hand and wave the driver down. Boarding buses is done quickly, and the bus may already be moving before both of your feet are inside. If you find the process intimidating, be heartened by all

PRIME LIVING LOCATIONS

the little old ladies who manage to get on safely. Once you're on, take a seat if one is available, and wait for the fare collector to come to you. Fares are 7–22 baht, depending on the distance and the type of bus. When the fare collector approaches you, tell him or her your destination to find out the fare for your specific route.

Bus schedules for specific routes vary, but nearly all routes run between 5 A.M. and 10 P.M.; some very popular routes run 24 hours. Buses are subject to the same traffic as everyone else on the road, and during rush hour they can move very slowly, making them a good choice only for those with the luxury of time.

NORTHERN THAILAND

Distant mists, birdsong, and a distinct chill greet most mornings in the mountains and valleys of northern Thailand. Among the region's soaring peaks, lush jungles, and fertile plains, you will find a patchwork of lifestyles still largely steeped in tradition. Agriculture, and more recently tourism, are the bread and butter here, and with everyone eventually congregating in the region's string of provincial towns, there is a rich palette of culture and history to be experienced. While modern first-class amenities can usually be found, the pace is relatively slow and the atmosphere relaxed, with the Thai word *sabai* often heard from resident Thais and foreigners.

With the exception of Chiang Mai itself, even the largest towns in northern Thailand are comparatively peaceful places, with smaller crowds and less traffic than other parts of the country. You will find a colorful array of mom-and-pop establishments, ranging from little bars and restaurants to boutique hotels and art shops, dotting the streets and keeping close company with produce markets, traditional medicine shops, and the hawker stands of the hill tribe

© SUZANNE NAM

people who come to sell their art, often dressed in their vibrant and elaborate ancestral costumes. Elegant spas, isolated resorts, sparkling waterfalls, and Buddhist temples spanning seven centuries add to the verdant tranquility. Though you will find the various pit stops in this region woven together with a common thread of lifestyle, cuisine, and history, each locale has managed to retain its own unique character.

If you're considering a move to Thailand but have a limited budget, the region can be a refreshing change from Bangkok and the islands, where the hordes of tourists seem to drive prices for accommodations, food, and transport higher and higher every year. Though the region is extremely popular with both international visitors and Thais on vacation, it remains an exceptional value location.

The hardest part about planning a move to northern Thailand may be finding a job. ESL teachers will fare best, but there are fewer positions than in Bangkok, and on average the pay is lower. Those in other industries may have a harder time, as there are few industries outside of agriculture and tourism, and none are that likely to be looking for foreign employees. But, if you're considering a move to Thailand and have a limited budget, the region can be a refreshing change from Bangkok and the islands.

HISTORY

To live in northern Thailand is to step into the ancient kingdom of Lannathai, whose name means "land of a million rice fields." For centuries the Lanna

© SUZANNE NAM

mountain living

SONGKRAN IN CHIANG MAI

If you are living in Chiang Mai in mid-April, you will find yourself in the best location in Thailand to enjoy the raucous fun of the ancient festival Songkran. Originally a new year's celebration of the Tai people, Songkran is older than Thailand itself and is considered a time to honor your family, community, and religion as well as to show respect for water, the most important element in the agricultural lifestyle of so many people in the region.

Despite such a long history, the festival is probably most famous for its reputation as a three-day no-holds-barred nationwide water fight. Revelers can expect to find themselves in the middle of ritual merrymaking and celebration. The spectacle of people participating in the ancient Songkran rituals is not to be missed, but don't get your hair done in the days leading up to the festival, because simply walking outside guarantees that you are going to get very wet. The water fight is a sort of natural extension of the bathing ceremonies at the heart of the Songkran rituals, and you will see this theme on all three days of festivities.

The first day, **Maha Songkran,** symbolizes the end of the old year and usually falls on April 13. If you sleep late, don't be alarmed by the crack of explosions beginning early in the morning, as it is simply the locals lighting firecrackers in an attempt to chase off the bad luck of the previous year. In Chiang Mai there is a procession of floats and images of Buddha beginning at Nariwat Bridge and winding its way to Wat Phra Singh. People also usually clean their homes, bathe, and wear new clothes on this day.

Wan Nao or **Wan Da** is Preparation Day, the second day of the festival. People will set to work preparing a variety of offerings to honor Lord Buddha. Head to the Ping River in the afternoon to see people gathering sand to be used in the building of sand stupas, which will be richly decorated with colorful flags and flowers and presented to Buddha at the temples later that day.

Day three, **Wan Phaya Wan** or **Wan Taleung Sok,** is the actual first day of the new year. Go to the temples to see offerings of food and other gifts made to the monks, and the **Tan Kan Kao,** the honoring of elders and deceased ancestors with offerings of food and good wishes. This is followed by the unusual ritual of using sticks and branches to prop up Sri Maha Bhodi trees, famous as the tree Buddha was sitting under at the moment he

kingdom was the northern counterpart to the Siamese kingdom of Sukhothai to the south. While a cultural and territorial tug-of-war between Siam and Burma held the kingdom in its crosshairs for centuries, Lannathai eventually became the loyal and integrated part of modern Thailand that you'll see today. However, the northern Thais still see themselves as distinctly different from their southern compatriots, and indeed have a history and ancestry all their own.

became enlightened. Weave your way through the crowds and simply take in the kaleidoscope of activity as people continue to make merry by setting captive birds and fish free and by bathing images of Buddha with sweetly scented water. The young will also bathe the hands of their elders and ask forgiveness for past misdeeds in the **Rot Nam Dam Hua** ritual. There will be a procession of traditional dancers in native costume and beautifully arranged flowers, in which water is poured on respected monks and high-ranking government officials. Unique to the northern provinces, the stupas containing the ashes of ancestors will also be bathed in order to pay respect and receive forgiveness.

The festival is in April because of the Tai people's rich agricultural identity and the importance of the cycles of sowing and harvesting rice in their daily lives, along with the strong astrological associations that Buddhism inherited from Brahman India. The Tais originally placed Songkran in late November, harvest time in southern China, where they lived. As they migrated south into what is now Thailand, these cycles were adapted to the warmer, more tropical climate. There are a handful of rural people who keep with the original tradition and celebrate Songkran in November. As Buddhism captured the hearts of the Tai people, auspicious movements of heavenly bodies that coincided with the April harvest were discovered, and this also played a role in setting the date. In fact the term *Songkran* means "a move in the position of the sun from Aries to Taurus." Even today the position of the sun and the phase of the moon are still the last word on the exact date of Songkran, and it may occur anywhere between April 10 and April 18, although a buzz of excitement precedes the event for days.

If you're in any part of Thailand during this period, stores and shops will be closed, and at the height of the festival it may appear that order has completely broken down. The streets will be teeming with people of all ages toting high-pressure water guns and buckets of water. You'll even see kids piled into pickup trucks functioning as mobile watering units complete with 40-liter (10-gallon) drums of sometimes icy water. And no one will shy away from dousing you just because you are a foreigner. Locals take precautions such as stashing their mobile phones in ziplock baggies, and you probably should too.

THE LAY OF THE LAND

Northern Thailand's topography is characterized by a series of mountain ranges in a vague north-south pattern, with all of the major living areas in the fertile valleys and river basins between the mountains.

Climate

The weather in northern Thailand feels milder compared to the rest of the country, but it is still tropical climate, so expect plenty of heat and humidity in most parts of the region throughout most of the year. During the region's hottest month, April, the average high is 35°C (95°F). During the coolest months, December and January, average highs drop to about 28°C (82°F) but average evening lows drop into the high teens Celsius (60s Fahrenheit), making a sweater or at least long sleeves necessary once in a while. Temperatures vary dramatically depending on elevation, so if you are up in the mountains, lows can drop into the low teens Celsius (50s Fahrenheit). Bear in mind that all of the major cities and towns are actually in the valleys, so you likely won't be living in the coolest parts of the region. May through October is rainy season in northern Thailand, with the most rainfall in September–October.

Chiang Mai

If quiet, rural life is what you're looking for, you'll find it for sure in northern Thailand. But if you decide to live in or around the city of Chiang Mai, you won't have to forgo urban life for all of the benefits the region has to offer. Chiang Mai Province is the second largest in Thailand, and the city of Chiang Mai is the third largest after Greater Bangkok and Hat Yai. With approximately 1 million residents in the Chiang Mai metropolitan area, it's big enough to have good hospitals, an airport with very frequent flights to Bangkok and even some international flights, hypermarkets such as Tesco Lotus and Carrefour, international schools for children, and shops and restaurants to please Western palates, but still small enough to retain the charm and relaxed attitude northern Thailand is known for. Chiang Mai might not be as cosmopolitan as the capital, but as any Thai or foreigner who has relocated there from Bangkok will tell you, it sure is a more livable and civilized place.

LAY OF THE LAND

The city of Chiang Mai, about 675 kilometers (420 miles) from Bangkok, is on the Mae Ping River basin and is surrounded by jungle-covered mountains on all sides. The Mae Ping River flows just to the east of the historic city center and through the center of the metropolitan area.

In the middle of Chiang Mai is the historic city center, a one-square-kilometer (0.4-square-mile) area full of centuries-old Buddhist *wats* and demarcated by the old city walls and protective moat. The city extends out from the historic center in all directions and begins to feel more and more urbanized, industrial, and generic the farther away you travel before development yields

WHO ARE THE HILL TRIBE PEOPLE?

Thailand is home to a number of minority ethnic groups living in the hills and mountains of northern Thailand as well as in Burma and Laos. There are seven major groups – the Karen, Hmong, Yao, Lisu, Lahu, Lawa, and Akha – as well as smaller groups and subgroups.

Although the term *hill tribe* is commonly used, it is somewhat misleading. Individuals within each ethnic group share a common history and language and often a distinct dress and tradition, but there is no real tribal organization within each group, and populations are generally dispersed throughout the region.

Within Thailand, the population of these groups is as large as 500,000, with the Karen making up more than half that number (not counting the many refugees from neighboring countries who come from the same ethnic groups). Many of these people have lived in the region for generations but do not identify strictly with the national boundaries that have been created around them, nor are they always recognized as belonging to the country they live in.

In fact, many hill tribe people are stateless, holding no citizenship, no passport, and no right to vote or receive the basic benefits of citizenship. These ethnic minorities are among the poorest in Thailand, and many continue to live as their parents and grandparents before them – off the land, in basic wooden bungalows in small communities in the mountains. Income sources are generally limited to small-scale agriculture and cottage-industry handicrafts.

These poor minority groups are a major tourist draw in northern Thailand, thanks no doubt to their often colorful traditional dress, craft production, and the desire of travelers to catch a last glimpse of traditional people before they are swept away by modernization. The Kayan, also referred to as "Long-neck Karen" or "Padaung" (mostly in the Me Hong Son area) are particularly sought out by tourists, as the women wear vivid colors and a series of tight brass chokers that elongate their necks, creating a striking visual effect. You can't see these women walking down the street in a typical Thai town; they mostly live in refugee camps that can be visited if you're willing to pay a few hundred baht entrance fee. Where that money goes is a matter of debate. Some goes to the Karenni National Progressive Party, a Burmese Karen separatist group that has been both specifically recognized by the United States as nonterrorist group and criticized by the United Nations for recruiting child soldiers. Some of the money may go to tour operators; little goes to the Padaung themselves.

To learn more about the hill tribe people, check out the **Virtual Hill Tribe Museum** (www.hilltribe.org), a website created by hill tribe people in Thailand to document their culture as they see it.

again to mountain ranges and quieter villages. To the northeast and east are the Nimmenhaemen Road area and Chiang Mai University campus, and finally the base of the large mountain called Doi Suthep, which begins just a couple of kilometers from the historic city center. To the north and south the city extends out to large highways that circle it. East of the historic city center, the city continues to be picturesque and dominated by tourism up to the Ping River.

Local Culture

Northern Thai culture has a distinctly different flavor from the rest of the country. Buddhism is still the prevalent religion, and typical Thai customs and etiquette apply, but things feel a little different. Maybe it's the fact that it was a separate kingdom until the 18th century, or because it's in the mountains, or because, in addition to the predominant cultural group, there are also smaller groups of so-called "hill tribe" people who speak completely different languages and have their own customs and traditions. Maybe it's all of those things, but to the outsider, the distinct cultural differences manifest themselves in everything from the more relaxed, down-to-earth attitude northern Thais seem to have to the quirky artiness of the younger generation.

DAILY LIFE

Chiang Mai is livable, charming, and full of history. As native residents and transplants both like to point out, Chiang Mai is one of the country's largest cities, but it just doesn't feel like one. There are many international schools to choose from, good hospitals, clubs and bars, restaurants, and even shopping malls. Since the city is hugely popular for tourists, there are plenty of services for non-Thai speakers. But much of Chiang Mai doesn't feel like a generic urban area. The atmosphere is far more laid-back than Bangkok, and although tourism is a major moneymaker, things just don't feel quite as commercial as they do on the beaches and islands. Outdoorsy, active people find plenty to do in Chiang Mai, as even from the center of the city it's only a few miles to the nearest mountain.

Because Chiang Mai is a big city, there's plenty of big-city shopping. Though Chiang Mai is known for

© SUZANNE NAM

Share the road.

creative and crafty things to buy in the area, it's also pretty easy to find a blender or a microwave. The Nimmenhaemen Road has excellent designer housewares, but there are also lots of hypermarkets and even a large shopping mall with a Central Department Store.

The larger hypermarkets such as Carrefour and Big C carry some Western food, and there are also Tops Supermarkets in the area's two shopping malls. The Rimping Supermarket chain has four locations around Chiang Mai and carries excellent meats and produce as well as a good selection of Western food items.

As for eating out, there's not much you'll want for in Chiang Mai except maybe really good sushi. Around the city are restaurants serving French, Chinese, Middle Eastern, Mexican, Indian, and Italian cuisine, among others. Of course there are also tons of Thai food and restaurants featuring northern Thai cuisine, central Thai cuisine, and Isan food.

Expat Social Scene

There are thousands of foreigners from Europe, the United States, and other parts of Asia living in and around the city of Chiang Mai. Some are here teaching English, some working for NGOs or other agencies, and many who are either retired or semiretired. There are a few official organizations for expats in Chiang Mai, though none are extremely active, so the best way to meet others is either through work or school. Tuskers and the Writer's Club in Chiang Mai are both well-known expat hangouts and are a good place to start meeting new people.

Resources

The *Chiang Mai Mail* is the region's English-language newspaper and has a website with news and listings (www.chiangmai-mail.com). There are also numerous weekly and monthly magazines that cover food and entertainment in the city and its vicinity. Citylife Chiang Mai has good Web content if you want to get an idea of what the city has to offer before moving in (www.chiangmainews.com). Nancy Chandler's *Map of Chiang Mai* and the accompanying book lay out all of the shopping, restaurants, schools, hospitals, and other resources in the city area, and it is an essential purchase for anyone moving to Chiang Mai.

Health Care

Chiang Mai has many private and public hospitals, including some with multilingual staff. Chiang Mai Ram hospital is considered the best in the area by many expats and is well-equipped for obstetrics, cardiac care, and other routine health care problems. Lanna Hospital likewise has a good reputation and is marginally less expensive for out-of-pocket care than Chiang Mai Ram. There are also scores of smaller clinics and doctor's offices for checkups and routine care.

Schools

Chiang Mai is home to more than half a dozen accredited international schools, some of which enroll students through high school and offer boarding.

HOUSING

The Chiang Mai area offers a huge variety of housing options, from serviced apartments in the middle of the city center to large houses out in the country with acres of land. If you're looking for housing in Chiang Mai, you'll also find prices incredibly affordable compared to Bangkok and most cities in the United States and Europe. As you move farther out of the city center, options will be a little more limited, although prices will get even better. Outside of central Chiang Mai, you won't find any serviced apartments, or even regular apartments, for that matter. Your only option will be a standalone house or, in some more built up areas, a townhouse or shophouse apartment.

WHERE TO LIVE
Central Chiang Mai

If you want to live in an urban environment or have an abundance of Western amenities nearby, your only choice is central Chiang Mai. In fact, most for-eigners who move into the Chiang Mai region choose the city as their home, at least initially. The most sought-after, or at least the most expensive, apartments tend to be right in the center of the city just outside of the old city. Many of these options are serviced apartments and cater to long-term tourists as well as short-term residents. There are also less-expensive apartment buildings in and around the center that run the gamut from very basic units with few bells and whistles to higher-end properties with 24-hour security, swimming pools, and modern furnishings.

The upsides to living in central Chiang Mai are convenience and proxim-ity to all of the restaurants, bars, coffee shops, and cultural sights in the old part of the city. You won't be able to walk everywhere, but the center is small enough that anything you'll need, from hospitals to the airport, will be just a 5–10-minute ride away. If you choose this option, you'll find yourself in

© SUZANNE NAM

Within Chiang Mai, streets are narrow and houses small.

the midst of tourist Chiang Mai, and may end up interacting as often with foreigners as you do with Thai people.

Rental costs for Western-style serviced apartments in the center of the city start at 15,000 baht for a 65-square-meter (700-square-foot) one-bedroom apartment. Local apartments in and near the city center can be rented for as little as 2,000 baht for a 28-square-meter (300-square-foot) studio with no air-conditioning or hot water.

Outside the City Center

Housing options change considerably once you move outside of the center of the city of Chiang Mai, and foreigners who have lived in the region for a while, have some basic Thai, and can navigate living in the country without needing to have English-speakers around all the time find it the best of both worlds. The city is just a short drive, *song thaew,* or bus ride away, prices are extremely reasonable, and the scenery is amazing. There are a number of housing estates 10–15 miles outside the city that are convenient to main roads and necessary amenities such as grocery shopping and international schools. Developments catering to middle-class Thais tend to be smaller and have less-involved kitchens, but are reasonably priced. A two-bedroom, 84-square-meter (900-square-foot) townhouse in one of these neighborhoods can be rented for less than 10,000 baht. More spacious homes with higher end fittings will rent for 15,000–30,000 baht per month.

GETTING AROUND

Within central Chiang Mai, getting around is a fairly convenient affair, and you won't necessarily need your own wheels unless you want them. If you aren't going to be driving a car, motorbike, or bicycle, there are a number of formal and informal public transportation systems—buses, *song thaew, tuk tuks,* taxis, and *samlor*—that are reliable and easy to use once you get the hang of them. None are comprehensive, so depending on your starting point and destination, you may need to use more than one for any given trip. If you will be relying on public transportation, study the different routes carefully before you decide where you'll live.

Buses

The Chiang Mai metropolitan area is served by a limited public bus system that was launched in 2006 in response to increasing traffic in the city. There are currently less than 10 different bus routes that cover the historic city and about a two-mile radius surrounding it. Though they aren't comprehensive, the bus routes do cover most of the main markets, shopping areas, and hospitals as well as Chiang Mai University and the airport. If you happen to be on one of the bus routes, they are a convenient way to get around. At 10–15 baht per ride, the cost is comparable to taking a ubiquitous *song thaew* and a lot more comfortable.

Song Thaew

Song thaew, the colorful pickup trucks that ply the streets, are the most popular way to get around in Chiang Mai. Like public buses, *song thaew* have set routes from one point another and make set stops along the way. In some cases, the route is indicated by the color of the *song thaew,* although *song thaew* of the same color will often travel divergent routes. In high-traffic areas, such as along Huai Kaew Road, the red trucks will be lined up waiting for passengers. Most rides cost just 10–20 baht. To grab one, just flag it down, and to get off, just press the buzzer inside the truck and the driver will stop at the next intersection. Though *song thaew* serve the city and its residents well, they can get very crowded, and in the heat of summer can be very hot inside. There is no published *song thaew* schedule in Chiang Mai, but nearly every resident knows which trucks go where and when.

Tuk Tuks

Though *tuk tuks* are often used by tourists because of their novelty appeal, they also serve a public transport function and are convenient for short trips or

© SUZANNE NAM

Bicycle rickshaws are a common form of transportation in Chiang Mai.

if you have packages. Fares are entirely negotiable between the driver and the passenger. If you speak some Thai and know where you're going, most *tuk tuk* drivers won't overcharge you even though you are a foreigner.

Taxis

Metered taxis in Chiang Mai are used less for short routes and more for longer trips or trips to or from the airport, but they are available. It is possible to flag one down on the street, but there just aren't that many cruising for passengers, so if you need a taxi, the best bet is to call for one. A short taxi ride in the center of the city should run less than 60 baht, but most drivers would rather negotiate a price and don't want to use the meter. Make sure you're up for some haggling, and know what the fair price should be, before beginning negotiations.

Driving in Chiang Mai

If you're used to driving in a major city and have (or are ready to learn) a good understanding of the formal and informal rules of the road in Thailand, driving in Chiang Mai is a feasible option for getting around, especially if you live in an area not well served by public transportation or need to transport kids to and from school and activities. If you need to commute into the center of the city, you'll face predictable driving woes—traffic and lack of parking—but they'll be nothing compared to what you'd deal with driving in Bangkok. The city layout is reasonably straightforward. The old city is ringed by a small road with larger streets radiating off it, and a couple of miles farther out is a larger ring, part of which is one of the region's major highway routes. Still, unless you know your routes well and speak enough Thai to read the road signs and ask for directions, invest in a GPS for your car.

Motorbikes are very popular in Chiang Mai and all over Thailand, and they are another possibility for getting around. It's possible to pick up a used 100 to 125 cc scooter for a few thousand baht, and you won't spend much on gasoline. The challenge even for very seasoned bikers is not just learning to navigate traffic but learning how to drive safely on the mountain roads that connect Chiang Mai to other areas in the region. Steep inclines and dramatic switchbacks are challenging enough. Torrential rains and a lack lighting can make driving a motorbike a near-death experience. If you have the skills and the constitution, though, there's no better way to enjoy the scenery and get around conveniently at the same time.

Chiang Rai

Chiang Rai is the country's northernmost province, reaching slightly farther north than Chiang Mai. It is a generally mountainous area bordered on the north by Burma on one side and Laos on another. This border region was once notoriously known for its drug trade but nowadays is better known for its cooler mountain weather, hill tribes, and beautifully crafted goods as well as good regional agricultural products such as coffee and tea. It is a region that has a lot of appeal for those who like the outdoors and are curious about the different ethnic groups living in the region.

Though the little city of Chiang Rai offers some urban conveniences and amenities and even has an airport with daily flights to Bangkok, the region is remote and rural, and living here requires giving up some of the creature comforts you may take for granted back home. There are no big international supermarkets or even shopping malls in the area, although there are at least some hypermarkets where you'll be able to find all of your necessities.

The most beautiful thing about Chiang Rai is the surrounding area. The city is small, and it's easy to use it as a base for exploring the rest of the province. The handful of foreigners who live in Chiang Rai full-time are generally an intrepid bunch who enjoy exploring the area on two wheels, so if you haven't yet learned how to drive a motorcycle, start learning now, as it's the best, and sometimes only, way to get from one place to another in the mountains.

THE LAY OF THE LAND

The city of Chiang Rai is in the green valley in the mountains of Chiang Rai Province and is a picturesque, verdant little city with Buddhist temples, lots of trees, and a great view of the surrounding landscape. The original city center is less than three square kilometers (a square mile), but the greater Chiang Rai metropolitan area has since spread out to just beyond the highway ring road that partially encircles it. The Kok River flows north to south, just to the east of the center of the city.

Chiang Rai City

Less developed than its sister to the south, Chiang Rai is smaller and more intimate than Chiang Mai, and if you were disappointed to find so much traffic and commotion in Chiang Mai, you may find Chiang Rai more to your liking. Most of the town can be covered on foot, and there are many fresh little sidewalk cafés to fortify you as you stroll its pleasant streets and explore its curious *sois*. Though the atmosphere is distinctly Thai, and even exotic with the addition of minority hill-tribe groups in the region, travelers, tour agencies, guest houses, and a handful of international restaurants and watering holes are still easy to find.

DAILY LIFE

Although there are sufficient places to eat and drink and enough tourist attractions to occupy a weekend, as you might expect, there's not a lot going on in the center of Chiang Rai, and most people who move to this part of Thailand aren't urbanites.

Finding high-end things such as imported wine will be challenging in Chiang Rai, but there are sufficient markets and hypermarkets in the area to provide almost all of your food needs, and there's even a Rimping Supermarket just outside of town for imported foods.

For clothing shopping, you may find it necessary to stock up when you're in Chiang Mai or Bangkok. There are some shops in the area, including Big C and Tesco Lotus, but they may not have the selection you desire.

WHERE TO LIVE

If you're moving to Chiang Rai, you'll most likely be living around the city or within a few kilometers of it, although there are some adventurous foreigners who move out into the mountains. The real estate market in Chiang Rai, especially for renters, is not fully developed, and you'll find it much easier if you get to the area first before looking for a permanent home.

If you're looking to settle in the center of Chiang Rai Town, you won't have much choice of where to live, as the city is so small. Housing options are likewise limited, as the vast majority of rentals available are studios without kitchens. It's possible for long-term visitors to rent rooms in tourist guest houses, and there are some Thai-style apartment buildings that offer small units for rent on a monthly basis as well as one high-rise apartment building with a swimming pool. There are also some bungalow-style houses within central Chiang Rai available for rent.

Rental costs for small Thai-style apartments in the center of the city run from 2,000 baht for a 23-square-meter (250-square-foot) studio with hot water and air-conditioning but no kitchen facilities. Apartments in buildings with more amenities run from 4,000 baht for a 28-square-meter (300-square-foot) studio. Bungalows are usually located just outside the center of the city, and rents start at 10,000 baht for a three-bedroom, 186-square-meter (2,000-square-foot) house with a full kitchen.

If you move out of the center of the city, even by a kilometer or two, it's possible to rent a bungalow or larger house with some land at a relatively reasonable price. This is really the only viable option for families, but so long as you have some means of transport and enjoy peace and quiet, it can be a wonderful option.

Fully furnished, two-bedroom, 93-square-meter (1,000-square-foot) bungalows a few kilometers outside the city limits can be rented for as little as 12,000 baht per month. A little farther out of the city, rentals for modern fully-furnished 232-square-meter (2,500-square-foot) three-bedroom houses with good views cost, at the high end, 25,000 baht.

Other Parts of Northern Thailand

Northern Thailand is vast, and although Chiang Mai and Chiang Rai tend to attract the most foreigners, there are many other places to settle down. Pai, Mae Hong Son, and Sukhothai are just a handful of other areas foreigners have typically moved. If you do decide to venture out into these parts of northern Thailand, understand that the majority of foreigners who settle in these popular areas outside of Chiang Mai and Chiang Rai tend to be travelers who came to visit and never left, and many of these expatriates have either married locals, opened tourism-related businesses, or both. In fact, the biggest challenge to living outside a major city is finding some sort of work to keep the (albeit modest) bills paid. Finding a job will be tough, as aside from teaching English and working in the tourism industry, there aren't many opportunities for non-Thais, and those that do exist will undoubtedly pay little.

If you're retiring in Thailand, have some means of supporting yourself, or find a teaching job in one of the smaller schools in the region, living in, say, a small village in the mountains of northern Thailand could be a tremendously adventurous and rewarding experience. Yes, housing will not be up to the standards you're accustomed to, there will be very few if any other English speakers, and you may have to drive a few hours just to get to the nearest city.

In smaller urban areas, it's possible to find longer-term housing in a guest house or to rent a dormitory-style studio. If neither of those options is available, arranging an informal homestay with a local family is another option. For the most part, there won't be real estate agents or listings to aid in the housing search. Instead, you'll have to rely on word-of-mouth or spend a few days driving around the area you want to live in looking for "For Rent" signs and asking residents if there are any houses or apartments available.

PRIME LIVING LOCATIONS

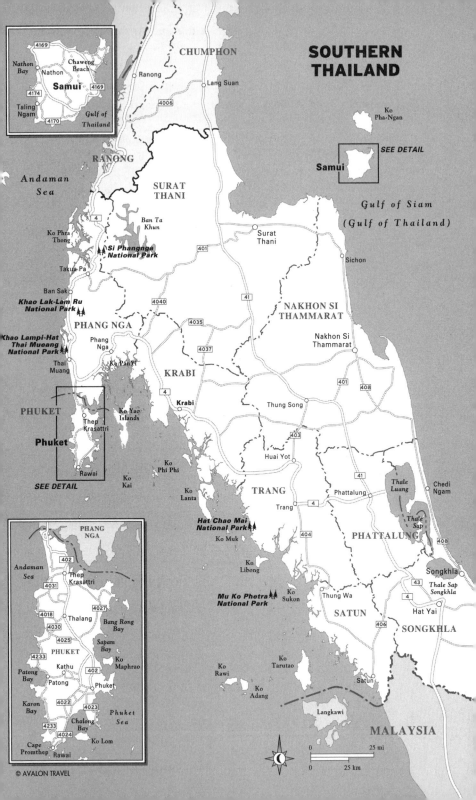

SOUTHERN THAILAND

Lifestyle and employment are the two main reasons foreigners choose to live in the parts of southern Thailand covered in this chapter. The broader region of southern Thailand covers 14 separate provinces on the Malay Peninsula, including well-known and well-visited Phuket, Krabi, and Surat Thani (home to Ko Samui) and also the less-visited provinces closer to Malaysia. Southern Thailand is an ethnically and culturally diverse part of the country where Buddhism and Islam coexist and where it becomes much harder for outsiders to define what exactly "Thainess" really is.

Against that somewhat complicated backdrop is the southern Thailand most foreigners end up living in, the part with the scores of gorgeous beaches and islands and the bustling tourism trade. It's this part of the country that is addressed in this chapter, both because of space constraints and because few foreigners venture too far from there.

Unfortunately, the days of the simple hut right on the beach are over, unless you're living in a bungalow that you're renting by the night and surrounded

by people on vacation, or you move much farther south. If the constant construction and influx of tourists are any indication, the beaches and islands in southern Thailand are booming, and desert-island living is a thing of the past. While that dream may not be attainable, the good news is that lots of commerce means more amenities, better infrastructure, and if you're looking for employment, more chances you'll find something to do.

Phuket

Of all of the areas foreigners choose to live in the region, Phuket is the most popular, with upward of 10,000 non-Thais estimated to be living on the island at any given time. If that sounds like a lot, it is, considering that the official population of the island is just over 300,000 people.

Thailand's largest island feels as much like a small city as a beach-resort town, most likely due to the fact that much of the development you see on the island today occurred over the past few decades. Before Phuket became an international tourist destination, it was best-known for the rich tin deposits found in the country's interior. While the tin industry built the antecedents of the island's main roads and left some amazing Sino-Portuguese architecture, it wasn't until the tourists started arriving that Phuket began to develop into what it is today. In fact, it wasn't until the 1970s that intrepid foreign travelers "discovered" Phuket's beauty and began to visit the island to enjoy

charming Sino-Portuguese architecture in Phuket

AFTER THE TSUNAMI

On December 26, 2004, shockwaves from an earthquake in the Indonesian archipelago triggered a tsunami that swept over much of the Andaman Coast region as well as neighboring countries. The series of giant waves, some as high as nine meters (30 feet), devastated some coastal areas and killed more than 6,000 people in Thailand.

Survivors told harrowing tales of running for their lives to reach higher ground, trying to save family, friends, and strangers, and watching people literally get washed away.

The economic toll on the region was high – tourism virtually stopped in the months after the tsunami as hotels, guesthouses, restaurants, and bungalows that had been hit by the wave struggled to rebuild. The emotional toll on residents was even higher. Children were left orphaned, families homeless, livelihoods destroyed – and many feared the waves would return.

Tsunamis of the scale seen in 2004 are rare but unavoidable. The last one to occur in recorded history was over 50 years ago. The bigger tragedy of the 2004 tsunami is that if people had been warned in time, most lives would have been saved. The earthquake that triggered the waves happened more than an hour before the tsunami, which would have given nearly everyone enough time to get to higher ground, had they only known.

Since 2004 the international community has worked to create a tsunami warning system capable of sending out warnings within minutes of an earthquake that could trigger a tsunami. There is currently a technologically complex warning system employing buoys far out in the ocean that detect suspicious wave patterns and transmit the data via satellite to the National Oceanic and Atmospheric Administration (NOAA) in the United States, which then evaluates the information and if necessary sends alerts out to potentially affected countries.

In Thailand, the meteorological agency has set up a high-tech monitoring office where scientists evaluate information from NOAA and other monitoring agencies and then trigger alarms, which are broadcast on television and radio and also via SMS through the major phone carriers and to warning towers set up along the Andaman Coast.

The system is capable of getting an alarm out within minutes of a potentially tsunami-triggering quake, and the warning towers broadcast alarms that can be heard for miles, warning people in multiple languages to get to higher ground immediately. There are also signs all along the coast directing people to the highest ground in the vicinity.

Many parts of the region physically recovered very quickly from the tsunami. Resorts were rebuilt within months in places such as Patong and Karon. In other regions, such as Khao Lak in Phang Nga, which was the hardest-hit part of the country (more Thais were killed in Phang Nga than any other part of Thailand), recovery was slower, but within a year most of the infrastructure was rebuilt, and to the great surprise of many skeptics, tourists returned in record numbers.

the mountain jungles and pristine beaches. Starting with some small bungalow developments on Patong Beach, the island has boomed into a world-class tourist destination over the past three decades. Bangkok Thais in their 50s and 60s will often laugh and reminisce about what the Andaman Coast used to be like before travelers and developers realized it was a natural tourist destination, when they'd head down on motorbikes for some adventure to the largely untouched beaches. Fast-forward 30 years, and the dirt roads and simple local folks have been replaced by an exceptionally sophisticated infrastructure system with easily navigable roads, hospitals, shopping malls, and an international airport.

Nowadays Phuket's "local" population is not just the descendants of the seafaring people who have been in the region for centuries—fishers and Thai-Chinese who migrated here when the island was filled with tin mines—but thousands of Thais from all over the country who've moved here to open or work in hotels, restaurants, and other tourism-related businesses. The island's identity is tourism, attracting millions of visitors every year and accounting for the majority of the island's revenues.

THE LAY OF THE LAND

Phuket, Thailand's largest island, is about 50 kilometers (30 miles) long and 16 kilometers (10 miles) across. Imagine an elongated star with some extra points on it and you'll have a rough idea of what Phuket looks like from above. The points are promontories, rock formations jutting out into the ocean and separating the island into numerous individual beaches with curving coasts. The central part of the interior of the island is mountainous jungle, but the north and southeast interior are relatively flat and developed with villages and towns.

The most developed beach area on the island is Patong, on the west side of the island, just south of the middle. Above and below are other beach areas and towns and the villages that surround them. In the northern interior is Thalang, and to the east of the southern tip of the island is Phuket Town, the island's capital.

The road system on the island is very well maintained, and there is both a coastal road that encircles nearly the whole island and large multilane inland roads as well. Off the main island, small islands dot the Andaman Sea, and elegant rock formations jut above the water's surface.

Phuket and the surrounding areas rebuilt quickly after the 2004 tsunami, and the momentum from the redevelopment seems not to have slowed once all of the damage was repaired. There are new resorts and villas popping up

NATIONAL PARKS ON THE ANDAMAN COAST

The Andaman region has more than its share of national parks, many of which cover not only mainland nature areas but also swaths of the Andaman Sea and some of the islands off the coast and in Phang Nga Bay.

You may find that the mainland parks lack many well-marked hiking trails, and when they are marked they are often only a couple of miles long. Since there are so few trails, it's also seemingly impossible to get around the parks without wheels of your own, which is unfortunate, as many parks have large main roads cutting through them.

But once you're away from the roads, you'll find the parks peppered with amazing waterfalls, beautiful scenery, and wildlife. In many of the parks right on the coast or on the islands, there are camping and bungalow facilities. The campsites often offer tent rental, bathrooms with cold showers, and even small canteen restaurants serving up more than decent local Thai food at reasonable prices.

The national parks also rent out simple bungalows with bathrooms with cold showers, and some of them even have air-conditioning. Beds are provided but generally not linens, so you'll have to bring your own sheets.

If your priorities are exploring the natural wonders of Thailand or you want to enjoy a beautiful beach or island without the feeling of too much development around you, staying in one of the parks is an excellent option. It's also very budget-friendly: Pitching a tent will cost around 100 baht per night, and renting one of the bungalows often costs less than 1,000 baht per night.

During low season, it's possible to walk into one of the park stations and ask if there are bungalows available, although even then there are times when the bungalows are booked solid for weeks. If you're interested in staying at one of the national parks, make sure to book a bungalow as far in advance as possible. You can book up to 60 days ahead, and in order to reserve a spot, the national parks administrators require that you pay in full before you arrive. To do that from abroad, you'll have to make a wire transfer to the National Park, Wildlife, and Plant Conservation Department. Although the process can seem a little daunting, they've laid out the bank codes you'll need to use at www.dnp.go.th Once you've confirmed that there's a bungalow available and transferred the funds, you must email reserve@dnp.go.th and dnp_tourist@yahoo.com with the confirmation information.

in every corner, and more and more tourists come every year to stay in those new places.

Climate

Phuket and the rest of the region have a tropical rain forest climate, and average temperatures tend to remain around 30°C (85°F) throughout the year. Like the rest of the country, temperatures and humidity drop a few degrees November–February. December–May are the region's driest months, with little or no rainfall. Beginning in April, rainfall picks up, and the wet weather continues through November. May, September, and October are the wettest months of the year, characterized by short bouts of intense downpours.

Culture

Phuket is primarily a tourist town and although there are plenty of people living here and going about their daily lives who don't work in the industry, have no doubt that life in Phuket centers around the foreign visitors who come for vacation. While the island is by no means cosmopolitan, because of the influx of foreigners, it does have an international feeling to it. There are also plenty of outdoor activities and water sports to engage in, including snorkeling, diving, sailing, and golfing.

Some foreign residents complain that with all the focus on tourism, the island is lacking in cultural attractions, as there are few art galleries that aren't overtly commercial and very little in the way of theater, dance, and live music. That complaint isn't inaccurate, but if you're looking for a place to live with a thriving art scene, chances are you won't find one on any tropical island.

Phuket has an increasingly interesting and diverse restaurant scene, especially on the coast, with everything from upscale Italian to cheeseburgers. With so many Europeans visiting the area, there tends to be more European fare than food from other regions, but it's still quite easy to find decent sushi, Indian restaurants, and others in popular parts of the island.

WHERE TO LIVE

Expats in Phuket are scattered across the island, and where you live on Phuket is to a large extent dictated by what you're doing here. If the beaches are the main attraction, you don't need to commute to a job, and you don't mind paying a premium for the area, you'll probably end up living on the west coast near one of the many beaches on that side. If you are coming to Phuket for work, consider traffic routes when picking your new home. Phuket is a big island, and while it's relatively easy to get from one beach to the adjacent one, driving (or riding) in traffic from the beaches in the northwest part of the island to Phuket Town can easily take an hour each way. Those looking for a more normal lifestyle away from all of the tourists should consider living away from the beaches and the areas that surround them. Phuket Town, Kathu, and Thalang are all inland but have a good variety of housing options and plenty of conveniences nearby.

Northern Phuket

This area includes some of the beaches in the northern part of the island, the towns surrounding them, and the areas inland. Despite the coastal location and proximity to the airport, northern Phuket has had much less tourism development than the southern part of the island, and it is much less crowded and bustling than beach areas to the south. Instead, you'll find long stretches of quiet beach (some protected national park land), a few resorts, and a small but increasing number of high-end property developments interspersed between the beach to the west, the green jungle interior, and Phang Nga Bay to the east. The beaches on this part of the island are a little less desirable than those to the south, as the sand is coarser and the tides and drop-off make them less safe for swimming year-round, but they are still quite beautiful. Thalang, in northern central Phuket, has much less of a resort feeling to it and is very convenient because of its location on the main road that crosses the island.

Traditional high-rise condominiums and apartments are difficult to find in this part of the island, as most of the developments are houses and low-rise apartments in luxury developments, although there are a handful of developments that feature apartments and a few new ones that will be completed by 2014. Two-bedroom condominiums within walking distance of the beach with about 75 square meters (800 square feet) of space and sea views are selling for 8 million baht and up, and if you can find one available for a long-term tenant, they can be rented for about 30,000 baht per month. Renting a modern three-bedroom 186-square-meter (2,000-square-foot) house with a yard a short drive to the beach will cost around 25,000 baht per month. More opulent homes in villa developments with private swimming pools and luxury fittings will cost upward of 40,000 baht per month for a similarly sized home. Villas for sale in the area range widely, and prices for properties of the same size can vary tremendously depending on proximity to the water, view, and design. A newly built, three-bedroom, two-story villa with a shared swimming pool less than 1.6 kilometers (one mile) from the beach costs at least 6 million baht, but in some of the most exclusive high-end developments, villas are listed for as much as 100 million baht.

Thalang offers the best values in northern Phuket, and it is possible to get a modern three-bedroom house with 111 square meters (1,200 square feet) of space for 13,000 baht per month. Homes of this size in the area sell for 3 million baht and up.

PRIME LIVING LOCATIONS

Kathu

Kathu, in southern central Phuket, is east of Patong Beach and northwest of Phuket Town. It's a convenient area and an easy commute to the beaches, shopping malls, and international schools. Since it's not on the beach, it has a more residential feeling to it, and because it's a more established area than other parts of Phuket, there's also a wider variety of housing options available. Kathu has a good selection of high-rise condominiums, some adjacent to the area's golf courses, as well as stand-alone homes and villas in new developments. Two-bedroom condominiums with 111 square meters (1,200 square feet) of space in newer buildings can be purchased for 5 million baht and up. Rentals for similar units start at 25,000 baht per month. Three-bedroom 111-square-meter (1,200-square-foot) houses can be purchased for as little as 3 million baht and rented for 20,000 baht or less per month. These homes usually have Western-style bathrooms and kitchens but aren't part of subdivisions with swimming pools and other facilities. For those, expect to pay more than twice as much.

Phuket Town and Chalong

The island's administrative center is also Phuket's most historic and established community. If you're looking for an island feeling, you won't find much of it here. Instead, Phuket Town has a very urban vibe to it (in fact, it was recently upgraded from a town to a city, but is still referred to by most people as "Phuket Town"). Alongside the gorgeous Sino-Portuguese architecture

Phuket Town, now a city, feels miles away from the beach.

JBREMER57/WIKIMEDIA COMMONS.COM

Patong Beach

left from Phuket Town's tin-mining heyday are plenty of generic low-rise concrete buildings. Just south of Phuket is Chalong, which spreads almost to the southern tip of the island and includes some coastal areas (though no swimmable beaches). Chalong is a popular area with foreigners and has good housing options across price ranges. Chalong Bay, an active bay with plenty of boat traffic, is home to a high concentration of expats, many of whom work in the tourism industry. Although it's not on the beach, there are also a handful of bars and restaurants that target the foreign market.

In Phuket Town proper, it is possible to find a small, 28-square-meter (300-square-foot) one-bedroom apartment in a complex with a swimming pool for 7,000 baht per month. Multistory townhouses with 186 square meters (2,000 square feet) of space and three bedrooms in established neighborhoods can be rented for as little as 30,000 baht per month. As you head south towards Chalong, two-bedroom 130-square-meter (1,400-square-foot) houses in older housing estates sell for 4 million baht and up. Villas with private pools and good views in luxury developments can fetch 30 million baht or more.

Central and Southern West Coast Beaches

The beaches along the west coast, especially Patong Beach, have traditionally been the heart and engine of Phuket's tourism industry. Patong, the island's most popular beach, is also one of the biggest, and there are literally hundreds of guesthouses, resorts, hotels, restaurants, and bars spreading out from the beach eastward that cater to visiting tourists. With all the people coming in and out, the Patong area can feel overrun at times, or at least very touristy.

Patong is also very convenient, though, and has a selection of good supermarkets and the best general shopping on the island. Kamala, just north of Patong, has a similarly beautiful beach but doesn't have nearly the same level of hotel and restaurant development. It also has more housing options, including freestanding homes across price points, and is close to everything in Patong. South of Patong are Karon then Kata Beaches and surrounding villages, which are also less built-up than Patong but are still considered prime tourist locations. Nai Harn Beach, at the bottom of Phuket, is quiet and relaxed and has one of the island's prettiest beaches, which opens out onto a sloping bay and is fringed with pine trees.

Since the west coast beaches from Kamala south are so popular for tourists, real estate prices are generally at a premium compared to those in other parts of Phuket, and there are fewer places to choose from since it has been developed as a tourist area and not a residential area. Many of the housing options cater to investors who rent their homes and apartments to long-term visitors, although there are more and more houses and apartments marketed toward retirees and others who choose to put down roots on the island. In Patong, most of the housing close to the beach is condominiums and apartments; as you move out farther into the hills, there are stand-alone houses and villas. A two-bedroom 93-square-meter (1,000-square-foot) condominium in a modern building with a swimming pool about 1.6 kilometers (one mile) from the beach will cost from 22,000 baht per month. Listings of similar units for sale start at 5 million baht. Two-story three-bedroom 93-square-meter (1,000-square-foot) houses in housing developments just outside Patong start at 8 million baht. The same house can be rented for 35,000 baht per month.

In Kamala, a three-bedroom 102-square-meter (1,100-square-foot) apartment about 1.6 kilometers (one mile) from the beach will cost 28,000 baht per month to rent. A two-bedroom 93-square-meter (1,000-square-foot) unit in one of the area's newer condominium developments will sell from 6 million baht. A two-story 102-square-meter (1,100-square-foot) house with three bedrooms in the suburbs of Kamala just outside the main beach area will rent for as little as 20,000 baht. Newly built three-bedroom luxury villas with small private swimming pools will fetch 12 million baht or more.

In Karon and Kata, a small 65-square-meter (700-square-foot) one-bedroom apartment in a modern development with a shared swimming pool in the hills to the east of the beach will cost 20,000 baht per month. Condominiums in newer developments currently start at 5 million baht for a 56-square-meter (600-square-foot) one-bedroom unit. Three-bedroom 121-square-meter

(1,300-square-foot) townhouses about 1.6 kilometers (one mile) from the beach sell for 4 million baht and up. To rent a similar home would cost 20,000 baht per month.

Detached three-bedroom houses in Nai Harn with 111 square meters (1,200 square feet) of space start at 20,000 per month to rent. Older houses of this size sell for 6 million baht and up. Newer houses in luxury developments begin at about 10 million baht.

DAILY LIFE
Expat Social Scene

Phuket has thousands of expats, and when you first arrive you'll see a scene dominated by the stereotypical older white foreign man who's dating or married to a younger Thai woman, and you think that most of the socializing done by expats in Phuket happens in English-style pubs. The majority of Western expats in Phuket are men, and it is harder to find expat networks on the island that appeal to families or to women. That's not to say that there aren't small networks of other types of expats around, but there are fewer of them, and it's harder to get connected. New expats in Phuket, particularly those with families, don't find a social network ready and waiting when they arrive; rather they build it over time through their children's schools, their neighbors, or even their golf buddies.

Resources

Phuket has a handful of English-language newspapers and magazines that publish local news, classifies, and events listings. Both the *Phuket Gazette* and the *Phuket Post* also have up-to-date website portals with access to most stories they print along with breaking local news. The Phuket International Womens Club (www.phuketiwc.com) has frequent meetings and activities and is open to everyone. There is also a fairly active Facebook group, Phuket Thailand Expat Group, where new and old residents can connect and share information.

Health Care

Although Phuket doesn't match the capital when it comes to access to affordable world-class health care, there are some large international private hospitals on the island that are equipped to handle everything from basic checkups to births. Bangkok Phuket Hospital and Phuket International Hospital, both in or next to Phuket Town, are the largest private hospitals and have doctors and other staff who speak English and other foreign languages. There

PRIME LIVING LOCATIONS

© SUZANNE NAM

Much of Phuket is characterized by concrete and traffic.

are also scores of smaller hospitals and clinics in most parts of the island for routine health care.

Schools

Phuket has dozens of schools calling themselves international, but most only have nursery programs or programs for primary school students, or bilingual programs designed primarily for native Thai speakers. Parents of children in primary grades will find adequate school options on the island, but parents with high school–age children have much more limited options. Right now there are just a couple of accredited international schools offering programs for older children, using either a British curriculum or a U.S.-based English curriculum.

GETTING AROUND

Phuket has a public transportation system that consists mostly of *song thaew* (covered pickup trucks with seats in the back) connecting the beaches to each other and to other parts of the island. There are also public buses that run routes from and around Phuket Town, but neither the buses nor the *song thaew* are comprehensive, nor do they run reliably after dark. If you do not have your own means of transport, you'll have to rely on *tuk tuks* and taxis to get around when *song thaew* and buses are not available. It may be much less expensive to have your own car or scooter.

Krabi

Krabi, the mainland province across Phang Nga Bay from Phuket, shares much in common with its island brother. The beaches are beautiful, much of the coastline is characterized by dramatic limestone cliffs, and it is also home to some of the most beautiful small islands in the bay (including world-famous Ko Phi Phi). Since greater Krabi Province isn't an island and hasn't yet become completely overrun by tourism, it also offers residents a more ordinary life and more opportunities to get to know Thai culture. It also offers more conveniences, since supermarkets, shopping malls, and the like are easier to get to, and prices don't have an island markup factored in. The Krabi airport, which has frequent flights to Bangkok, Singapore, Hong Kong, and some European cities during high season, is easily accessible from most parts of the province.

Climate

Krabi, like Phuket, has a tropical rain forest climate, and average temperatures tend to remain around 30°C (85°F) throughout the year. Temperatures and humidity drop a few degrees November–February, and along the coast evening temperatures are often mild enough that air-conditioning isn't necessary, even during the hot season. December–May are the region's driest months, with little or no rainfall. Beginning in April, rainfall picks up, and the wet weather

© SUZANNE NAM

the view from Ko Phi Phi

PRIME LIVING LOCATIONS

continues through November. May, September, and October are the wettest months of the year, characterized by short bouts of intense downpours.

Culture

Krabi is a predominantly Muslim province, and besides tourism, fishing and agriculture are a significant part of the economy. Although there has been a sometimes-violent Muslim insurgency in the far south of Thailand, there have never been incidents in Krabi, and the Buddhist and Muslim people of the province live together without any apparent friction.

The Western expat community in Krabi is small, at well under 1,000, and many foreigners who live here are either involved in the tourism industry as hotel managers, chefs, or diving instructors or are teachers and retirees. There are fewer opportunities to socialize with other foreign residents in Krabi than there would be on Phuket, though if you live or work in Ao Nong you won't have any problem meeting other expats.

WHERE TO LIVE

If you aren't looking for an expensive vacation home and would rather live in a Thai community, finding a home in Krabi will be challenging. It's not that the local people wouldn't welcome you into their neighborhoods; rather, most real estate rentals and even sales are done informally through word of mouth or simple posted signs. If you will be living here long-term, it really is best to arrange temporary housing from abroad, and once you arrive, spend some time driving around, meeting with local real estate agents, and asking people in the community you want to live in about houses or apartments available for rent. Condominiums in Krabi are virtually nonexistent, and although there are a few villa developments that appear to have been set up to comply with legal requirements for foreign ownership, most of the land and house sales in the area are done using proxy Thai corporations, a practice that appears to be legal but has never been tested in the Thai courts.

Krabi Town

Krabi Town is just a few kilometers inland from the coast but feels worlds apart from the touristy beach areas that most people think of when they think of Krabi. The town, with a population of about 25,000, has a very comfortable, friendly feeling to it. Although parts of it are charming and picturesque, es- pecially around the Krabi River, it also has some very generic, urban concrete areas where two- and three-story concrete buildings dominate.

Much of the stuff going on in town is in Thai, and there are very few places to go out that cater to Western tourists. For those looking to immerse themselves in Thai language but want to be close to the beach, Krabi Town may be the best option available.

There are virtually no long-term housing options that are marketed toward Westerners in Krabi Town, but while it may be difficult to find a home here, prices are reasonable and the quality of the homes is typically decent. A basic 28-square-meter (300-square-foot) studio apartment with no kitchen in Krabi Town will cost about 3,000 baht per month. Two-story concrete shophouses can be rented for 15,000 baht per month.

Ao Nang Beach Area

Ao Nang is Krabi's most popular beach, and although it is built up enough to have a McDonald's and a handful of other international chains, it is still small enough to feel like a quiet resort town, especially during low season. Most of the tourist development is centered on the main street that runs parallel to the beach, but there are some housing developments farther inland that cater to wealthy Thais and expats. Newly built, modern three-bedroom 186-square-meter (2,000-square-foot) villas a couple of kilometers from the main beach cost as little as 4 million baht, and similar properties can be rented for 30,000 baht per month.

Ao Nang

DAILY LIFE

Krabi is a relaxed, friendly province where residents largely follow their tradi-tional ways but are open to foreigners and accepting of their differences. Because there are so few other expats around, living in a place like Krabi, especially if you choose to live away from the beach areas, can be somewhat alienating and lonely if you don't make an effort to connect to the people around you. Learn to speak some Thai (although the dialect and accent here are different from standard spoken Thai, you will be able to communicate sufficiently), as you'll most likely spend a lot of time getting to know the Thais that live here. Make an effort to engage neighbors, colleagues, and even people you meet on the street in conversation, and you'll be surprised at how warm the reception will be.

Resources

There are no local English-language newspapers in Krabi, but both the *Bang-kok Post* and the *Nation* are readily available.

Health Care

There are many smaller clinics and some public hospitals in and around Krabi that are considered adequate for routine visits, but most foreign residents travel to Phuket for any serious medical treatment.

Schools

There is currently only one international school in Krabi; it follows the British system and has kindergarten through primary school. There are also a couple of bilingual schools in Krabi, and some expats choose to send their kids to these programs, although if your child does not speak any Thai at home, it will be a very challenging environment. Because of the dearth of educational facilities for foreign students, parents in Krabi have recently begun collective homeschooling programs, where small groups of similarly aged kids are grouped together, and instruction is either by parents or hired teachers.

GETTING AROUND

There are public buses that follow routes from Krabi Town to Ao Nang and around the province, but unless you have a lot of time to get from one place to another, it's best to have personal transportation, a car or a scooter, for transport.

Samui

Once just a quiet island happily going about its business farming coconuts, Ko Samui is now one of the most popular vacation spots in Thailand. Filled with palm trees and rimmed by white sandy beaches, the island is a lovely oasis in the Gulf of Siam. If you're arriving by plane, the moment you step off the airplane and onto the tarmac you'll understand what the island is all about. There's no steel or glass at the international airport. Instead, it's a group of thatch-roofed huts where you check in and pick up your luggage. To get to and from planes, passengers are taken by open-air buses akin to large golf carts.

© HANSANDRE/WIKIMEDIA COMMONS.COM

secluded laguna in the north of Ko Samui

The island is not all huts and palm trees, but up until a few decades ago, the main trade on Samui was coconuts and rubber, and it wasn't until the 1970s that the island even got a main road. Like Phuket, the island's identity is now largely that of an international tourist destination. Thanks to a ring road that now circles the entire island, and infrastructure put in place to support the tourism industry, you'll have easy access to basic necessities such as medical care and shopping if you decide to live here.

Compared with the larger and more developed island of Phuket, finding housing on Samui can be a real bargain, and while there are multimillion-dollar developments, there are also many apartments, condominiums, and houses that can be rented for less than 15,000 baht per month or purchased for just a few million baht. The downside is that Samui is quite small, comparatively, and because it's more than 80 kilometers (50 miles) off the coast, it's not that easy to get back to the mainland.

THE LAY OF THE LAND

Samui is a somewhat circular island just under 24 kilometers (15 miles) across at its widest point. The beaches are fringed with coconut trees, and the interior is characterized by mountains and rolling hills covered in lush jungle growth. Because most of the interior of the island is mountainous, most development has occurred around the beaches that ring the island. The northeast part of the island is where two of Samui's most popular beaches, Chaweng and Bophut, are located, as well as the small Samui International Airport. The most heavily touristed and most attractive beaches on Samui are on the island's east and north coasts. Along the west coast, the beaches are less impressive, mostly due to the long gentle sloping of the shore that makes it nearly impossible to get into water above your knees during low tide on some of the beaches, and the "all business" feeling from the main port at Taling Ngam. This part of Samui is much less densely populated than the east side, and arguably more convenient if you're traveling from the mainland by ferry instead of by plane.

Climate

Samui has similar weather patterns to the rest of the region, with one important difference—the rainy season is much shorter, lasting just a couple of months, mid-October–mid-December, but overlapping with the beginning of the North American winter holidays. Samui also tends to be a little hotter than some of the other popular regions in the country, and historic average temperatures are in the low 30s Celsius (high 80s Fahrenheit) throughout most of the year. The temperature drops a few degrees November–February.

Culture

Samui is a tourist island, and because of its size, it's difficult to find activities that aren't geared toward short-term visitors or people in the tourism industry. Many of the island's foreign residents who are not involved in tourism don't live on Ko Samui year-round but rather come for part of the year and rent their homes out to visitors for the rest.

For art and culture fixes, you'll need to head to Bangkok, as the art, music, and performance scene is limited to live music in beach bars (the island has only one movie theater), but if you're into sailing, diving, or other ocean sports, Samui is heaven. The island does have a surprisingly diverse and high-quality restaurant scene, with European, Asian, and even Latin American cuisine available.

WHERE TO LIVE

Given the size of Samui, different areas on the island don't offer dramatically different environments, neighborhoods, or pricing. The biggest distinction in Samui is whether the property is near a popular beach area on the east coast or in the less-developed west coast area. Homes a little farther inland tend to be much more luxurious than those very close to the beaches or villages surrounding the beaches. This is because inland areas were largely untouched before people began to think of Samui as a residential area, so developers could start from scratch and had more space to work with.

Long-term renters will have a tougher time finding suitable housing and negotiating with landlords, since much of the renting on the island is for vacationers coming for a month or less, and prices are accordingly higher. Landlords will often require a few months' deposit in advance for those wishing to stay a year or more but will often give a discount on monthly rates.

Chaweng and Lamai

The most expensive and most sought-after real estate tends to be found around these two beach areas on the east coast, mostly because they are the most popular places in Samui for tourists, which drives land prices up. Chaweng is the most famous beach in Samui, and it always draws lots of tourists, especially those traveling from other countries. The beach itself is a beautiful long strip of soft light sand backed by palm trees, and the water is warm, clear, and generally calm. There's a reef just offshore that serves to break most incoming waves. During high season, you will feel a little hustle and bustle here, and visitors flock to the numerous resorts that line the beach. It's the most built-up area on the island, and in addition to the bungalows you'll find fronting the shore, there are also lots of restaurants and vendors. On the main street

PRIME LIVING LOCATIONS

© TOEFFIE/WIKIMEDIA COMMONS.COM

street in Lamai Beach

SAMUI REAL ESTATE

Harry Bonning visited Samui for the first time in 2000 and liked it so much that he decided to relocate to the island a year later. He's now the managing director of Ko Samui Properties (www.kosamuiproperties.com) and offers advice here to foreigners looking to rent or purchase homes.

Why is Samui a great place for foreigners?

The climate and cost of living, I would suggest, are the principal factors. It does get quite hot during hot season, but for most of the year it is very comfortable. If you eat Thai food, you can live here for next to nothing, but even foreign food is not that expensive, and you have an amazing range to choose from. Name a country and there is almost certainly a restaurant from that country in Samui!

What, if any, are the big frustrations about living on an island?

Very few, as far as I am concerned, although the cost of flying to Bangkok is one. Apart from that I suppose the slow pace of improvement in infrastructure and the poor supply chain to shops can be a little galling, but are far outweighed by simply living and working on a tropical island.

What are some of the best areas on the island for families with children?

International schooling is very limited on the island, and there are only two private schools teaching an international curriculum in English. Both are in Chaweng, and therefore for convenience, the northeast of the island is preferable. There are no facilities for higher education on the island that would be suitable for foreigners. For families with smaller children, there are a number of play groups, but again mainly in the northeast.

What are some of the best areas on the island for retirees?

It depends on the lifestyle they want. They southwest and west of the island are much quieter than the busy areas of Chaweng and Lamai and to some extent Bo Phut and Mae Nam. However, there are fewer facilities in that part of the island with very limited restaurant choice and only small supermarkets. The islands roads, while slowly improving, are not for the timid, particularly at night between Chaweng, through Lamai, and to Taling Ngam. A number of retirees live in the south and perhaps venture out once a week for shopping at Tesco in Chaweng or Lamai and probably less often for a visit to a restaurant in those areas.

Retirees with a more active lifestyle would almost certainly choose the northeast, anywhere between Maenam and Chaweng, with many in the Bo Phut area where there is a large selection of bars, restaurants, and shopping facilities. Few will live in the immediate Chaweng Beach area but will be spread around the Bo Phut Hills and either side of the ring road through Bo Phut and Mae Nam and to Big Buddha, Plai Laem, and Chengmon.

Where are the most popular locations on Samui?

The northeast — anywhere from Mae Nam, through Bo Phut and Plai Laem, to Chongmon and parts of north Chaweng. Why? There are a number of reasons. Proximity to the airport is a prime one, but also the availability of facilities such as restaurants, shops, and hospitals, and of course this becomes self-priming. This is also born out by property prices being higher in these areas and the proliferation of new developments there rather than in the south.

How long does it typically take to close on a property and move in?

Three months would not be unusual, but without complications and with goodwill all around, it can be done within a month. Delays tend to be due to legal issues, particularly due diligence and the transfer of funds. It can, however, take very much longer for many reasons, and I currently have one case that has still not completed after 10 months.

The issues around buying property in Thailand would merit a dissertation by themselves, as foreigners cannot own land, and various devices have been established to get around this – not all of which are legal and subject to challenge. These are important and very relevant issues to consider.

For buyers who will only live in Samui for a few years and plan to rent their homes or sell them afterward, how realistic is that? Is it very difficult to manage renting a property from abroad?

There are quite a lot of people who do this, and it is generally better to own a property on a managed development, although quite a number of people do this with stand-alone properties managed by specialist management companies.

The Thai real estate market is in essence no different from any other real estate market – it goes up and down over a period of time, and if you look at most scenarios around the world, this tends to be roughly on a 10-year cycle. Real estate is not a short-term investment.

Is there anything to watch out for when buying property on Samui that most foreign buyers wouldn't think of?

Pay for a good lawyer, and make sure they do the due diligence on the land title, and in particular the access rights. Access should include rights for vehicular access, water supply, and three-phase electricity supply.

Construction here is basic, mostly reinforced concrete frames with tiled roofs. With older properties in particular, check the electrical installation, drainage, and water supply, which will rarely be up to Western standards. New properties tend not to have these issues, but still, buyers should be wary.

Make sure the land boundaries are clearly marked out and defined. If the title is *Chanot*, they should be. It may not be very clear with your neighbors where they lie, and if there is any doubt, pay the Land Office to mark them out for you. Coconut palms on a boundary can be the source of major disputes as to ownership, especially with long-term local residents.

Any other tips for those who want to move here?

If you intend buying here, rent somewhere for as long as you can before making that decision. This will allow you to get to understand island life, the good and the bad, and to know better exactly where you want to be based.

that runs parallel to the beach, it feels more like a little city than a quiet beach town. Here you'll see familiar brands such as McDonald's, Pizza Hut, and Starbucks. In fact, it might be hard to notice you're in Thailand at all, as most of the signs are in English.

Lamai is second to Chaweng in terms of development, and for lots of residents, it represents a happy medium between development and seclusion. There is a good selection of amenities and ample places to eat, but it's also less developed than its neighbor to the north. The beach itself is typical of Samui—a gently curving bay, bathwater water temperatures, and lots of surrounding coconut trees swaying in the wind. Lamai Beach has rougher water, as there's no reef to break the waves as they come in.

In both Lamai and Chaweng there is virtually no long-term housing available right on the beach. Most developments and stand-alone homes are at least a couple of blocks away, and most of the larger developments have good ocean views but are a long walk to the water. Chaweng also has an increasing number of housing developments overlooking Chaweng Lake, just a short walk inland from the beach area.

It's still possible to rent a simple townhouse a few blocks from Chaweng Beach for a comparatively reasonable price. A very basic two-bedroom attached townhouse with 74 square meters (800 square feet) of space in Chaweng rents for 10,000 baht per month. The same units can be purchased for 2 million baht. Modest two-bedroom 74-square-meter (800-square-foot) homes in Lamai can be rented for 15,000 baht per month. Similar homes are listed for sale at 3.5 million baht. There are a few serviced apartments in the area that rent to long-term guests; for a one-bedroom 46-square-meter (500-square-foot) unit with modern facilities and daily maid service, expect to pay about 25,000 baht per month. At the highest end there are three-bedroom 186-square-meter (2,000-square-foot) villas with ocean views and resort amenities in Lamai and Chaweng selling for 25 million baht.

Northern Coast

Mae Nam, Bo Phut Beach, and Big Buddha Beach are all adjacent to each other on the northern coast and are the second most popular area for visitors to Samui. Each of the beaches is in a softly curving cove, and although there's no view of either sunset or sunrise, the beach, the water, and the surrounding greenery are quite beautiful. There are a handful of inexpensive backpacker bungalows here, some of the nicest resorts on the island, some trendy upscale places to eat, and not much else. Mae Nam Beach is the quietest of the three, and it is a great choice if you want to live in a quiet area but also have easy access to amenities and entertainment. Bo Phut Beach is particularly charming, especially due to the adjacent fishing village with its charming wooden shophouses, although there is no long-term housing available in the village itself. Big Buddha Beach, named after the large golden Buddha that sits on a nearby hill overlooking the island near the airport, is the most bustling beach in the area.

The northern coast has a wide variety of housing available for buyers, from small and basic two-bedroom, 56-square-meter (600-square-foot) attached bungalows within walking distance of the beach for just over 1 million baht to ultramodern 743-square-meter (8,000-square-foot) four-bedroom homes with private swimming pools in the hills overlooking the gulf. Renters will likewise find a wide variety of options in the area. In Mae Nam it's possible to rent a 37-square-meter (400-square-foot) studio bungalow for 14,000 baht per month. Basic three-bedroom houses up to 1.6 kilometers (one mile) from the beach rent for as little as 25,000 baht per month.

West Coast

The west coast of Samui, including Taling Ngam and Lipa Noi, is less touristed and less built-up than the east coast, and it also has fewer large housing developments. Although it's slightly less convenient to shopping and other necessities, it is quieter and more relaxed than other parts of the island and is convenient to the ferry to the mainland. Because fewer people choose this side of Samui to live, housing options are more limited, and it can be difficult to find inexpensive long-term rentals without visiting the island first. A modern three-bedroom home with 130 square meters (1,400 square feet) of space and a private swimming pool can be rented for 30,000 baht per month. Similar properties for sale are priced from 7 million baht.

DAILY LIFE

The best part of living on an island that's an international tourist destination is that it's very easy to get by in English, and there are plenty of shops, restaurants, and services that cater to foreigners. Large hypermarkets on the island carry a decent selection of Western foods, and among them and the smaller department stores, one can find almost everything necessary to set up a home.

Resources

Samui has one English-language newspaper, the *Samui Express,* which is a small tabloid-style publication reporting on local and international news. There are also numerous websites with information about Samui, many posting local news and classifieds. These websites tend to have lots of property and hotel advertisements but do offer some useful information as well. Thai Visa (www.thaivisa.com) has an excellent forum on living on Samui, and anyone looking for specific information about buying or renting property, shopping, child care, and schooling should search the Thai Visa forums. There are a limited number of clubs on Ko Samui where expats come together over common interests. Sisters on Samui (www.sos.onsamui.info) meet on a monthly basis for social networking, friendship, and charity

pumping gas in Samui

activities, and they welcome foreign and Thai women who are on the island to join them.

Health Care

Samui has three large, private international hospitals that offer routine and emergency treatment. Bangkok Hospital Samui in the southern part of Chaweng Beach is considered by many to be the best, although it is also more expensive. Samui International Hospital, in the northern part of Chaweng, as well as the Thai International Hospital, in Bophut, have English-speaking staff and a good reputation for competent treatment and lower prices.

Schools

Samui has limited schooling options for parents wishing to enroll their children in programs that use English as the language of instruction. Children who speak Thai at home fare slightly better, as there are public Thai schools on the island and private schools that use both Thai and English for instruction. There is currently only one accredited English-language high school on Samui, and because of that, some parents choose to send their children to Bangkok for boarding school. "A work in progress" is a good way to describe the international school scene on Samui. While there are some schools with good reputations, recent history has been a little rocky, with quick expansions, unexpected closures, and very upset parents.

GETTING AROUND

Ko Samui's ring road is serviced by frequent *song thaew* that just drive around in a circle all day, picking up and dropping off passengers for 10–60 baht, depending on the length of your journey. The service only runs during the day; at night the *song thaew* are still making the loop, but they charge extra for it. If you're going somewhere that is not right on the loop, you'll need to hire a taxi or else consider getting a scooter or car to get around.

NORTHEAST THAILAND

Isan, the common name for the northeast region of Thailand, is the country's agricultural heart and where you'll find sweeping green plains, rice fields, dirt roads, and water buffalo as well as impressive mountain ranges and the meandering Mekong River. Aside from some beautiful landscapes, Isan is also home to scores of impressive ruins from the Khmer empire and some of the most important archeological sites in the country.

Unlike Bangkok, the Andaman Coast, and Chiang Mai, few foreigners pass through Isan, so those who choose to move to this part of the country, even if they are based in one of the region's small cities, will find themselves quickly immersed in Thai culture, or rather Isan Thai culture. Isan shares as much of its lineage with neighboring Laos as it does with the other dominant cultures that came together to form modern-day Thailand, and the language spoken in the region (referred to as Thai Isan or Isan) shares much in common with Laotian.

According to the Thailand National Statistics Office, more than 80 percent

of Isan's residents make some or all of their income from farming, and most everyone in the region who does not live in the city lives on a farm or has family members who do. Outside major urban areas, it's not uncommon to see rice drying on the roads, water buffalo in the streets, and even an occasional elephant. Much of the farming in Isan is backbreaking manual labor: Little of it is mechanized, and there are few large commercial farms.

Most people in Isan who work the land own or lease small plots of land as subsistence farmers, and Isan is the poorest and least developed region in the country. Another significant source of income in Isan is remittances from family members who have moved to Bangkok or other big cities where there are more opportunities for work. In fact, many of the people in service industries in Bangkok have spouses and even small children that they support back home in the country.

Because of the poverty and rural nature of the region, Isan is often looked at by city folks as a backwater, and there is apparently a growing divide between the people of this part of the country and those in Bangkok, most recently evidenced by the region's continuing support of deposed prime minister Thaksin Shinawatra, who was seen as a champion of rural workers. It's true that life on the plateaus of northeast Thailand is a lot slower, but the people generally have an open friendliness not always seen in the more international parts of the country, and visitors often like to refer to it as the "real" or "authentic" Thailand because of this. And none of the common gripes about the rest of the country apply here—there's no overcrowding, very little sex tourism (except in major cities), and no sense that everything around you has been created to cater to tourists. Those looking for high-end accommodations may find options lacking, but those looking to live in more modest homes and apartments will find Isan very inexpensive by Western standards.

Some of the foreigners who do choose to live in Isan are typically teachers, the majority of whom come to schools in urban areas and stay for a short period of time. The vast majority of foreigners who live in Isan are *koey farang,* foreign husbands of local women who have settled in the area either to raise families or to retire. While some of these families live in central urban areas, most live in smaller towns and villages near other family members. There are, of course, exceptions to these generalizations, but they are few and far between. Those who move to Isan for personal or family reasons and live out in the country will face additional social, cultural, and relationship challenges not addressed in this chapter.

The Lay of the Land

Northeast Thailand is essentially one large plateau bordered by Laos and the Mekong River to the north and east and Cambodia to the south. The region, the largest in Thailand, is shaped like an irregular circle with a number of small cities making a loose loop around it and scattered across it. Geographically, the city of Khon Kaen is in the center, with Udon Thani to the north, Ubon Ratchathani in the southeast corner, and Surin and Nakhon Ratchasima to the south.

Though Isan is a rural province, even outside the major cities you will find decent infrastructure and very good highways that connect virtually all of the region's smaller towns and villages. If you live in a remote village, you may have to do some dirt-road driving, but typically you can get around easily and, at least vis-à-vis the road system, won't feel like you are in the middle of nowhere.

Other things that can make life easier or more enjoyable are lacking, at least from the perspective of those who are accustomed to them. In general, Isan is a much simpler, poorer part of Thailand than Bangkok, Pattaya, or Phuket, so air-conditioning in most homes is limited, as are Western-style bathrooms. Across the region, it is very difficult to find a variety of English-language print media. The *Bangkok Post* and the *Nation* newspapers are available in major urban areas and some larger towns, but the *International Herald*

PRIME LIVING LOCATIONS

© SUZANNE NAM

plenty of buffalo in Isan

Tribune is nearly impossible to find in most parts of Isan. The availability of Western food is limited to items that the local population consumes. You'll find popular items such as peanut butter and spaghetti in larger supermarkets and hypermarkets but probably won't be able to find nonlocal produce such as avocados or bell peppers.

CLIMATE

The northeast region experiences a three-season weather pattern similar to the rest of the country. The most comfortable time of year is during the cool, dry season from November to February. Evenings and early mornings can be cool, especially if you are in the northern part of the country or in the mountains, though the average high temperatures will be in the high 20s Celsius (80s Fahrenheit), and there will be little if any rain. During the hot season, March–May, high temperatures are often over 35°C (95°F) and sometimes break 38°C (100°F). It's generally pretty dry during this season, causing frequent droughts that make life even tougher for the farmers, although by May there can be significant rainfall. From June to October it's hot and humid and can be very wet.

Nakhon Ratchasima

Nakhon Ratchasima, also referred to as Khorat, is on the western edge of the Khorat Plateau and is just three hours by car from Bangkok. Though most of northeast Isan is flat plains, Nakhon Ratchasima is home to some of the only mountain ranges in the region and the country's largest national park, Khao Yai, surrounding them. Because Khorat is so close to Bangkok and has a relative diversity of terrain, it's one of Isan's most pleasant and easiest to provinces to live in.

WHERE TO LIVE
Nakhon Ratchasima (Khorat) City

Despite being the administrative capital of such a nice province, this small, relatively quiet city isn't particularly scenic or reflective of Isan's distinct identity or long history. Rather it's a testament to the generic, concrete urbanization that is so widespread across the country, and most people will probably find it less interesting and aesthetically appealing than the smaller villages and rural areas that surround it. As a place to live, Khorat City is convenient and has just about everything you will need in terms of necessities for daily life, including health care, movie theaters, shopping, and even some nightlife. With a population of around 145,000, it is still quite small and easy to navigate.

If you can't bear living far from "civilization," less than 30 kilometers (20 miles) outside the city are a handful smaller quasi-suburbs that are very popular with foreigners who live in the area as they offer more stand-alone houses and space but are still convenient to the city. Housing prices drop off substantially outside the city, but it's much more difficult to get around without your own transport if you choose to live outside an urban area.

Phimai, about 56 kilometers (35 miles) northeast of Khorat City, is another popular place for foreigners, if only because they are familiar with it from touring the city's ancient temples. The town has a population of only about 14,000, but because of the temples it is much livelier than its numbers (though by no means is it a bustling city). Like anywhere else in Isan, outside the city there are scores of smaller towns and villages worth considering that are too numerous to cover in depth here.

In Khorat City, Thai-style studios with no kitchen facilities can be rented for 4,500 baht. Typical Thai-style townhouses with two floors and 74 square meters (800 square feet) of space can be bought for under 2 million baht and rented for 6,000 baht per month. Newly built, three-bedroom stand-alone houses with 139 square meters (1,500 square feet) of space and a small yard a few minutes outside the city in the Joho area can be rented for well under 10,000 baht per month, and they list for as little as 1.5 million baht.

Khao Yai Area

The area around Khao Yai National Park in the southwest part of Nakhon Ratchasima is a mix of both rural farmland areas and more expensive and upscale enclaves due to its proximity to Bangkok and the protected park areas. What makes this part of the country so special is that it has a stunning physical landscape, fresh country air, and even cool temperatures during cool season, yet it's just a few hours' drive from a city of 10 million people.

Most of the country's small wineries are located here, in and around the Pak Chong area, along with some very expensive and exclusive resorts. In addition, there are a handful of farms and ranches that attract mostly local ecotourists for touring, camping, and horseback riding. While there are still reasonably priced homes to be bought or rented here, there are also some very expensive mountain retreats available, which are mostly being purchased by wealthy Bankokians, and some housing developments have sprung up over the past few years marketed toward Europeans.

Those who decide to move to the Khao Yai area will find enough basic

KHORAT RESIDENT DEREK LEVITT

Derek Levitt moved to Nakhon Ratchasima Province eight years ago from the United Kingdom. Since then, he has married, built a house, and retired from full-time work. He and his wife are currently raising their five-year-old son in Thailand.

Why did you move to Khorat? Was it an easy decision?

We built our home in my wife's village, so the decision was simple. For a very long time it had been my intention to take early retirement and live outside of the United Kingdom. In the mid-'80s I spent a year on a friend's cotton farm near Monteria in Northern Colombia, and that is where I thought I would live out the latter years of my life. I met my wife about nine years ago, and after we decided to get married, there was never a doubt that we would live in Thailand, so Khorat was the natural choice. We live on a family compound in a village about 45 kilometers (28 miles) northwest of Khorat near the town of Non Thai.

How do you support yourself here in Thailand?

I am not working here and have recently retired. We live off my savings, and in a couple of years my pensions will kick in too. We are currently building a mini-mart to keep my wife busy and hopefully bring in extra income. We also own several plots of farmland that bring in some income, but most years there is little profit, as it either rains too much or too little. It is not called "subsistence farming" for nothing.

How long do you expect to remain here?

I have every intention of staying in Thailand for the rest of my life; it is now where I call home. After my wife's first visit to London, I asked her if she would like to live there. She said it would not be a problem for her but that I would miss Thailand more than she would. She is right.

What is the most challenging part of raising kids in Thailand if both parents are not Thai?

Cultural differences relating to discipline of the child. Rural Thais tend to give their kids free reign to do what they want until someone gets hurt or something gets broken, and then it's straight to the nearest tree to break off a large twig and beat the child with it. I do not believe in corporal punishment, but do believe that children need to have boundaries and to live within them. Don't get me wrong; I am not saying this is what my wife does, well, certainly not when I am around, but it goes on all time within the village.

As my son's entire life apart from home is Thai-oriented, we speak only English at home. I feel a very strong obligation to give him some Western background, as who knows what the future holds here in my adopted country, and possibly his future will be in the United Kingdom.

Was it difficult to figure out where to send your child to school?

This is the biggest problem in my life. Isan has a very poor standard of education compared to Bangkok and places more popular with foreign expats, like Pattaya and Phuket.

When Matthew reached school age, we moved into the city of Khorat so he could get a bilingual education. The school was great, and I would very strongly recommend it, but my son didn't like living in Khorat and being away from his cousins and friends. So we returned to the village, and he is now edu-

© DEREK LEVITT

the house Derek Levitt and his family built in Isan

cated at a very nice school in Non Thai, which probably will be where he stays for the next few years.

When he gets into upper grades we will start him in school in Khorat again. So I have a few years before I must decide where, and hopefully with the influx of foreigners, better schools will open, or the established ones will improve.

Is it easy to make friends, both Thai and foreign, where you live?
I have made many very good friends here, and I do go into Khorat a couple of times a week to meet up with them. I have a few Thai friends, mainly from my wife's extended family.

Is there a strong community of foreigners where you are?
When I first moved here, there were very few in the Khorat area, but now there is a larger population. There is not a sense of community here, though, probably because the majority of foreigners live out in the sticks, so distance and having other things to do are major obstacles.

What do you miss about living in a big Western city that you didn't think you would miss?
The only thing I miss is Indian curry.

What are some of the unexpected rewards of living in Khorat?
I have the best of both worlds, as I have a lovely life in the country and I get my couple of days in [the city of] Khorat. Every day has its unexpected rewards, whether it is passing a herd of water buffalo wallowing in our local lake or bumping into a long-lost friend in Khorat and having a drink or three with them.

Any advice you would give to folks planning to move to the region?
You have to be happy with yourself to live up here. It is not a tourist hot spot with all that entails. Before you decide to move here, especially those who will be building in their wife's or girlfriend's village, stay a month or two before deciding. Village life is not for everyone. And if you have kids, be aware of the problems you'll have finding a good education up here.

amenities, such as a big Tesco Lotus superstore, to get by, but you will need to travel to either Bangkok or Khorat City for health care, shopping, and Western groceries. There are a handful of bars and restaurants in the area that have been opened by expats and serve the foreign community.

Newly-built, modern, Western-style three-bedroom houses with 111 square meters (1,200 square feet) of space in the Pak Chong area, within driving distance of the national park, can be rented for 20,000 baht per month or less. Similar homes can be purchased for 3 million baht. Less opulent two-bedroom 93-square-meter (1,000-square-foot) homes in tract developments can be rented for 5,000 baht per month. At the high end, houses in the Pak Chong area are selling for as much as 25 million baht for four-bedroom 186-square-meter (2,000-square-foot) newly built resort-style ranch houses.

DAILY LIFE

Daily life in Khorat will differ dramatically depending on whether you live in the city itself, near Khao Yai National Park, in one of the smaller towns in the province, or out in the country. If you are living in the city, you'll easily be able to find all of your basic necessities, but unless you want to forsake familiar comforts and diversions entirely, you will need to head to Bangkok at least once in a while to stock up on food, books, and other things you'll miss. If you are out in the countryside, you'll at least still likely be close to a large hypermarket (a Tesco Lotus, Carrefour, or Big C) where you can find some Western groceries.

Expat Social Scene

While the majority of expats living in Khorat are Western men who have married Thai women and have chosen to raise their families in Isan, or have come back to retire there, there are also some ESL teachers and, increasingly, retirees and others with enough means to be able to live all or part of the year in the Khao Yai area. If you don't fall into one of these groups, it will be very challenging to find other foreigners to hang out with or talk to. Immersing yourself in Isan culture will no doubt be a wonderful experience, but it can be isolating to live anywhere in this part of the country if you do not have a connection to the community through family or work or don't speak enough Thai to make friends.

Resources

There are no English-language newspapers, magazines, or even frequently updated websites in the Khorat area. Korat Farang (www.koratfarang.com)

ISAN FACTS

- Agriculture as a percentage of GDP: 22 percent
- Households with Internet access: 1 in 75
- Per capita annual income: 26,317 baht
- Percentage of GDP: 8.9 percent
- Percentage of population below the poverty line: 26 percent
- Percentage of population living in urban areas: 6.3 percent
- Percent of population of Thailand: 30 percent

has an online community of foreigners who live in the region and is a good source of information and a way to connect to others in your area.

Health Care

While those with family members who speak Thai can navigate the public and private hospitals with few English-speaking staff members, many foreigners opt for the Bangkok Hospital Ratchasima in Khorat City for their health care needs. It is an international hospital with general practitioners, specialists for routine matters, and an emergency room. For complex health issues, many foreign residents choose to head to Bangkok.

Schools

The Khorat region has very few private schools that conduct all courses in English, and currently only one of those schools, Saint Stephen's International School, enrolls high school students. Saint Stephen's uses a British curriculum and also offers boarding for children of families who do not live in the area. Children who speak some Thai at home will have more options as there are a number of private nursery and primary schools in the Khorat area that offer Thai language instruction along with intensive English-immersion courses.

Small cities in Isan make a big deal out of cultural events.

GETTING AROUND

If you are living exclusively in Khorat City or in one of the close suburbs, you can potentially get by relying on the city's buses and *song thaews* along with the informal motorcycle taxi and *samlor* system. If you are living outside the city, there are buses connecting the province's towns and villages to one another, but realistically you will need to have your own transport if you need to commute from your home to your job or for errands outside the village.

UDON THANI

Udon Thani is in the northern part of the Khorat Plateau, just 80 kilometers (50 miles) from the capital of Laos, Vientiane. The city of Udon Thani, or Udon, as it's known, has a population of just 145,000, and feels like a compact, neat city with just enough amenities and conveniences for most people. Although Udon Thani is a little over 500 kilometers (300 miles) from Bangkok, it does have its own airport with daily flights to the capital, making it one of the most convenient places in the region to live. Outside the city, rural Udon Thani has one of the least-expensive costs of living in Thailand, so housing and food will cost a little less than they might elsewhere. Keep in mind that Isan as a whole is a very inexpensive region to live in, so you may not notice huge savings compared to one of the other areas covered in this chapter.

The region seems to get more and more foreign visitors every year, mostly because Udon Thani is a transit point on the well-beaten backpacker path to Laos. Many travelers stop in Udon Thani on their way to Nong Khai, north of Udon on the Laotian border, where you can cross into Laos and continue north. Like other parts of Isan, there is still a lot of farming going on outside the city center. Around the city, more and more tract home developments are popping up to cater to middle-class locals.

More and more retirees are moving to Nong Khai, just 50 kilometers (30 miles) outside the city of Ubon Thani. The city of Nong Khai (it's also a province) gets significant tourist traffic because of the border crossing between Thailand and Laos, but with a population of just 20,000, it has a very small-town feeling.

Within the Udon Thani city limits, small two-bedroom homes with 84 square meters (900 square feet) of space can be rented for 10,000 baht per month. Just outside the city, newly built, modern three-bedroom homes with 111 square meters (1,200 square feet) of space can be rented for 7,000 baht per month. More opulent five-bedroom, 232-square-meter

(2,500-square-foot) homes with larger land tracts and swimming pools close to the city are listed for as much as 7 million baht. Simple homes with small plots of land in areas outside the city can be purchased for 1.5 million baht.

Ubon Ratchathani

Tucked into a corner of Thailand on the Cambodian and Laotian borders, Ubon Ratchathani Province has had quite a history—it was a prehistoric settlement of people living off the area's fertile plains, part of the Khmer Empire, and later the staging ground for U.S. air strikes. It is the country's largest and most eastern province. Unlike much of the region, which is characterized by flat plains, Ubon Ratchathani has plains, dramatic rivers, and even lush mountains. Because of its distance from the capital, proximity to neighboring countries, and partly mountainous terrain, it feels distinctly different from any other province.

As you move out of the city and into more rural areas, much of Ubon Ratchathani feels like the rest of Isan—farms and farmers as far as the eye can see. At the province's eastern border you'll find Kong Jiam, where the Mun River, which starts in the mountains of Nakhon Ratchasima Province, flows into the Mekhong River, flanked by a valley and surrounded by lush greenery. While the scene may not be as dramatic as the towering mountains and azure waters you'll see in other parts of the country, the calm beauty of the landscape will leave a lasting impression.

Although the province is far from Bangkok, the Ubon Ratchathani airport has multiple flights from the capital every day.

UBON RATCHATHANI CITY

On the surface, Ubon Ratchathani looks like any small modern city, but Ubon, as it's sometimes referred to, has a distinct Isan identity that sets it apart. Perhaps thanks to the two universities in town, Ubon Ratchathani feels much more vibrant than other cities of its size in Isan. There's plenty of hustle and bustle for a city of just over 100,000 residents, albeit on a much smaller scale than in Bangkok. Although Ubon Ratchathani is not without the typical two- and three-story concrete buildings that characterize smaller cities, the addition of the Mun River, which flows just south of the city, makes the environment a little more picturesque than other cities in the region.

PRIME LIVING LOCATIONS

Ubon has a bigger selection of limited-service apartments than most of the region, and if you're relocating here, getting a temporary apartment in the city while you search for a more permanent home is a good strategy. Furnished studios with cable television, Wi-Fi, and biweekly maid service can be rented for 4,000 baht per month. Most of the serviced-apartment units in the city are studios, although there are a few larger units that rent for 7,000 baht or more per month.

DAILY LIFE

Daily life in Ubon Ratchathani City won't be much different from what you'll experience in other larger cities in the region, as it's just a little smaller than Khorat or Udon Thani. You'll find plenty of shopping, restaurants, bars, and cafés to keep you entertained, as long as you don't need to be in an environment where people speak or understand English. Outside of the city, there are very few foreigners living in the province, and as you move closer to the borders, there are fewer amenities, hypermarkets, and signs of development. If you want a simple life in which you shop at the wet market on a daily basis and don't spend much time interacting with other foreigners, the outer parts of the province may be just the answer. If that type of living seems intolerable, live closer to the city.

Expat Social Scene

Ubon Ratchathani has a very limited expat social scene dominated by just a handful of hangouts in the city that are owned by foreigners and attract other non-Thais for conversation and community.

Resources

There are no English-language newspapers, magazines, or even frequently updated websites that cater to foreigners who live in the Ubon Ratchathani area.

Health Care

There are a couple of private hospitals in Ubon Ratchathani that have English-speaking facilities and are used by the small contingent of expats that live in the city and outlying areas. These hospitals have more limited technical facilities than government hospitals in the area, so those requiring anything more than routine preventative care or minor treatment should consider seeking treatment at the city's public hospitals or traveling to Khon Kaen or Bangkok.

Fields and flat earth characterize the region.

Schools

So far, there are no private schools in Ubon Ratchathani that offer instruction primarily in English. Parents with children who do not speak enough Thai to be enrolled in either the public schools or the private schools that offer dual-language instruction can either send their children to board at schools in Bangkok or consider homeschooling options.

GETTING AROUND

Like in the rest of the region, it is possible to get around the province's major city, but once you're out of the urban area, it's really necessary to have your own transportation, unless you want to rely on slow intercity buses and *song thaew.*

Khon Kaen

Khon Kaen, considered the political and economic urban center of Isan, is a small comfortable city with both businesses and universities, making it an attractive place for those who wish to live in the region but need to find employment. The city is more built-up than other Isan cities (there are even a few high-rises), has a variety of different housing options available, and feels more like a small city and less like a large town than other parts of Isan. Although the city of Khon Kaen seems relatively affluent and developed, the province in general is one of the poorest in the country, and as you move farther away from the urban center, the poverty becomes more apparent.

PRIME LIVING LOCATIONS

In Khon Kaen City, high-end two-bedroom 93-square-meter (1,000-square-foot) serviced apartments in high-rise buildings rent for as much as 25,000 baht per month, but if you want simpler accommodations, it is possible to rent a small 28-square-meter (300-square-foot) studio with no kitchen facilities for under 5,000 baht per month. Just outside of the center of the city, it's possible to rent a Thai-style four-bedroom house with air-conditioning in the bedrooms for 5,000 baht per month. Similarly sized homes with Western bathrooms and kitchens and hot water rent for 10,000 baht per month.

DAILY LIFE

If you are living in the city of Khon Kaen, you'll have the option of living a fairly modern, Western lifestyle if you choose, as there are enough cafés, shops, and restaurants around, although everything is on a much smaller scale than in Bangkok, the southern islands, Pattaya, and Chiang Mai. As of early 2010, the city even has metered taxis, the first in the region. The vast majority of people you interact with will not be able to communicate much in English, so unless you want to walk around in a state of confusion, it is essential that you learn at least some Thai. If you decide to live out in the country or in one of the smaller towns in the province, you'll probably find yourself in a very rural environment, where farming skills are essential to survival and where the highlight of the month is the temple fair.

Expat Social Scene

Khon Kaen has a very limited expat social scene, which is limited to a handful of bars and restaurants run by expats.

Health Care

Khon Kaen has a handful of public and private hospitals located in the city, and is generally considered to attract some of the best doctors in the region. Whether this is true or not is hard to gauge, but Srinagarind Hospital, with nearly 1,000 beds and the capacity to treat routine matters, emergencies, and more complicated health problems, is a teaching hospital affiliated with Khon Kaen University.

Schools

There are no schools in Khon Kaen that use English as the primary language of instruction. Parents with children who do not speak enough Thai to be enrolled in either public schools or the private schools that offer dual-language instruction can either send their children to board at schools in Bangkok or consider homeschooling options.

GETTING AROUND

The city of Khon Kaen has a network of *song thaew,* buses, *tuk tuks,* motorcycle taxis, and metered taxis that cover all of the city. If you are living or working outside the city, there are some *song thaew* that ply the streets to the ring road, but if you live or work farther than that, a car or motorbike will make life much more convenient.

Buriram, Surin, and Sisaket

These three provinces in the southern part of Isan along the Cambodian border are all characterized by small towns, villages, and plenty of farming. If you found the major cities in the rest of the region too big, you're in luck here, as the provincial capitals of Surin, Sisaket, and Buriram have populations of only 25,000–40,000. Despite some decent roads and daily train service from Bangkok, these provinces feel very rural, largely because there's no big main urban area but instead development is spread out.

Buriram, which borders Nakhon Ratchasima (Khorat) to the west, is know to outsiders only because of the scattering of Khmer temple ruins found in the province. Surin, which also has the largest city of the three provinces, is known to outsiders because of its annual Elephant Roundup, where people from all over the country come to watch a display of elephant management techniques and celebrations. Sisaket, which borders Ubon Ratchathani on the east, is part of the Mun River valley and is marginally lusher and greener than either Surin or Buriram.

Life in this part of Isan is perhaps even simpler than in other nearby provinces, considering the extent of development. Most residents here still shop at the wet market every day for most of their grocery needs. There are some foreigners, mostly those married to Thais, living in the area, and although there are no precise figures available, some estimate their numbers at as many as 10,000 in the three provinces.

FINDING A HOME

It is difficult even to find a real estate agent in this area, and most land transactions, whether rentals or purchases, are done without an intermediary. The best way to find a home in these provinces is to go and explore the areas you are considering living in. Talk to potential neighbors about vacant houses, and drive around looking for signs. If you are planning on settling down in the area permanently, consider doing a test run first before building or investing a lot of money to see if you will enjoy living in this part of the country.

PATTAYA

Sixty years ago the city of Pattaya, about 160 kilometers (100 miles) southeast of Bangkok on the east coast, was just a nondescript fishing village. Over the past few decades it has become a highly developed vacation and retirement spot, and some would say an endlessly tacky and even dangerous "Sin City" where the sex trade carries on in flagrant violation of the law and local and foreign organized crime rings commit everything from real estate fraud to murder. The latter may be an exaggeration, but be aware that many consider Pattaya a less-than-desirable place to spend quality time with the family.

U.S. servicemen began to popularize Pattaya in the late 1950s when the GIs started flocking to its beaches from U.S. Air Force bases in the region. As troop levels surged throughout the Vietnam War years, Pattaya turned into a red-light city with infamously raucous nightlife. Surprisingly to some, Pattaya is now the most touristed region in all of Thailand. The wars in Southeast Asia are long over, but the strip bars and general seediness of the city remains, at least in the central area. Soldiers have been replaced by (mostly male) foreign

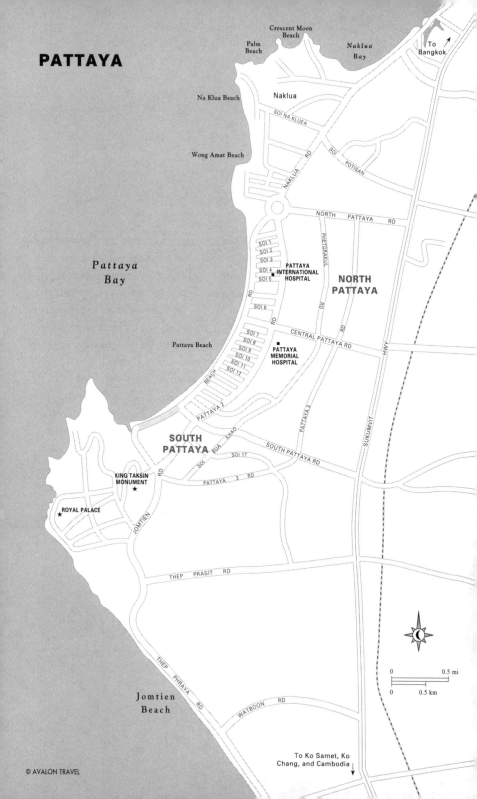

tourists, but otherwise the vibe is probably pretty much like it has always been—lots of drinking, loud music, and scantily clad women.

But government officials have been on a crusade to turn the town's image around, spruce it up, and attract more foreign vacationing families and retirees who are more interested in the fact that Pattaya is just 90 minutes from Bangkok's Suvarnabhumi International Airport and has pleasant scenery and inexpensive rounds of golf than in cheap beer and go-go bars.

At this point, yes, there's still plenty of lurid nightlife that caters to the bachelor set, and that's not likely to change any time soon. But outside of the Walking Street area in central Pattaya there are also plenty of luxe housing developments, some good restaurants, decent shopping, and a variety of popular golf courses. In fact, for foreigners who want to live on the beach in Thailand but don't want to give up any of the creature comforts of home, Pattaya is an exceptionally convenient place to live, and that's probably why thousands of retirees from Europe and the United States spend some or all of their time here.

Pattaya is also significantly cheaper than Samui and Phuket, especially when it comes to buying condominiums. Real estate agents in Pattaya are now trying to pitch it as a sure-fire investment, which it may not be, but nonetheless, Pattaya is booming right now.

Pattaya's beaches don't compare in terms of cleanliness, peacefulness, and scenery to the beaches on the Andaman Coast and in the lower Gulf of Siam, but they are still pleasant enough to attract visitors from all over the world. Those who like to be near the ocean but don't require it to be pristine find the beaches of Pattaya more than sufficient.

Lay of the Land

Pattaya is a relatively small strip of eastern coast in Chonburi Province that faces west toward the Gulf of Siam. The Pattaya Bay area, which curves gently away from the Gulf, is loosely divided into four areas—north Pattaya, which includes the Na Klua area and Wong Amat Beach just to the north of Pattaya Bay; central Pattaya, the main strip of beach on Pattaya Bay and the surrounding city area; Jomtien, the large bay and beach area directly south of Pattaya; and east Pattaya, inland from the beach area.

If you continue traveling south along the irregularly shaped coastline, you'll quickly run into some industrial parks and manufacturing zones along the coast before passing into Rayong Province, home to the little resort island of

Pattaya's main beach is bustling with sunbathers and boats.

Ko Samet. The vast majority of foreigners who relocate to this part of Thailand choose to live in the Pattaya area and not farther east or south.

LANGUAGE

Pattaya is one of the few places in Thailand where it's possible to live for years without having to speak a single word of Thai other than to say hello. Because of the millions of international visitors who come every year, English is Pattaya's de facto lingua franca. Almost every sign, billboard, or posting you come across is in both English and Thai, and people who work in the service industry, such as at hotels, supermarkets, and restaurants, will be able to communicate in basic English.

Daily Life

Depending on what part of Pattaya you're living and hanging out in, Pattaya feels either like a bustling urban area or a pleasant, relaxed coastal city, but either way you'll have plenty of nearby amenities. Because the city has been essentially purpose-built for foreign vacationers and retirees, it has most of the things most foreigners want or need on a daily basis.

The opening of the high-end Central Festival Pattaya Beach Mall on Pattaya Beach in 2009 upgraded the area's shopping choices tremendously. Now, in addition to some low-rent malls and hypermarkets, there's a high-quality department store that carries local and international brands, an electronics store and a home-goods store, and even English-language bookstores in the area. Many of the newer shops in Pattaya cater to high-end customers, but there are still also less-expensive places to shop.

For groceries, Pattaya has a selection of supermarkets as good as any outside Bangkok. Between the hypermarkets such as Carrefour, Tesco, Big C, and Makro and standalone supermarkets that include Tops Supermarket and even Foodland, Pattaya has almost anything a foreigner could possibly want.

Because Pattaya attracts holidaymakers and retirees from all over the world, it's quite easy to find midrange and more expensive restaurants serving cuisine from pizza to Eastern European fare (although quality is not on par with the best restaurants in Bangkok). The largest concentration of foreign-food restaurants are scattered in the streets between Central Pattaya Road and South Pattaya Road, but there are also restaurants farther north and in the Jomtien area.

Those who like outdoor sports will find plenty to do in the Pattaya area, where there are more than 20 different golf courses as well as a handful of family-friendly private country clubs with swimming pools and tennis courts. There are windsailing groups in Pattaya and sailing clubs in Jomtien, where it is possible to rent a sailboat or take sailing lessons.

EXPAT SOCIAL SCENE

The stereotypical expat social scene here is a bunch of overweight middle-aged and older white men hanging out in city's seedy drinking joints, picking up younger women in go-go bars, and complaining about everything that's wrong with Thailand in general and Pattaya specifically. Walking Street is full of go-go bars, strip clubs, and regular bars staffed by "bar girls"; and even outside of that area, most bars (except in high-end hotels) in Pattaya have women hanging out whose profession is unclear. Most of the clientele are short-term visitors, but there are plenty of foreign residents who patronize these places, and the truth is that Pattaya's sex industry is so pervasive and in-your-face that it's hard to avoid. Although prostitution is illegal in Thailand, the whole city of Pattaya, it appears, has a get-out-of-jail free card.

If that's not your scene, it's not a very pretty one to witness, but the good news is that there really is a variety of foreigners living in Pattaya; they're just less immediately visible than the stereotypes. Breaking in to a more ordinary expat social scene is challenging in Pattaya, as there are few clubs and organizations that cater to families and women, but school clubs and sports clubs are a good place to start. The Pattaya International Ladies Club (www.pattaya-pilc.com) is the only formal women's expat group in Pattaya. PILC is an active community-oriented organization with a couple of hundred members in the area and has regular monthly open house–style coffee hours; details are posted on their website.

RESOURCES

Pattaya has a number of English-language news publications and websites with local news, classifieds, and listings: *The Pattaya Mail* (www.pattaya-mail.com), *Pattaya People* (www.pattayapeople.com), *Pattaya Daily News* (www.pattayadailynews.com), and *Pattaya Today* (www.pattayatoday.net). The *Bangkok Post* and the *Nation* also cover bigger news stories in Pattaya and have events listings.

HEALTH CARE

Because of the growing number of medical tourists who visit Pattaya for everything from face lifts to open-heart surgery, Pattaya has five different international hospitals—Bangkok Hospital Pattaya, Pattaya Memorial Hospital, Pattaya International Hospital, and Banglamung Hospital—to choose from for routine health care, emergency treatment, and more complicated health matters. Bangkok Hospital Pattaya is probably considered the best hospital in the Pattaya area, although some long-term foreign residents complain that it is unnecessarily expensive and that you can receive the same quality of care (though not the same bells and whistles) at other hospitals. All of the major hospitals have 24-hour emergency rooms and ambulances on call. As in other parts of the country, ambulances aren't sent from a central dispatcher but rather

Just outside of Pattaya, things calm down significantly.

hired directly from the hospital, so it's essential to have some hospital phone numbers handy in case of a situation requiring immediate attention.

SCHOOLS

There are a number of large international schools in the Pattaya area or within a 30-minute drive that enroll students from nursery school to high school. Many programs offer instruction exclusively in English, some using a British curriculum and some a U.S. curriculum. There are currently four different schools in Pattaya with programs for high school students: Garden International, International School Eastern Seaboard, International School of Pattaya, and Regents School Pattaya. Some of these schools, including Regents School, have hundreds of students enrolled and offer a variety of courses and extracurricular activities on spacious campuses with good facilities. Student body is typically made up of around 25 percent Thai nationals and 75 percent other nationals, and only about one third of the students at these schools are nationals of English-speaking countries. Garden International, Regents, and St. Andrews us a British curriculum; International School Eastern Seaboard uses an American curriculum. The International Schools Association of Thailand website (www.isat.or.th) has basic information about most of the schools in Pattaya and is a good place to start.

Where to Live

The greater Pattaya area isn't that large, and it's fairly easy to get around, so where you decide to live will be based mostly on lifestyle and price.

Foreigners are scattered across all of the Pattaya area, but those with families who still want to be close to the beach tend to end up in north Pattaya and Jomtien. East Pattaya (inland), particularly close to some of the golf courses and country clubs in the south, attracts people with families with young children and also retirees. Most foreigners who live in central Pattaya are singles in apartments, due to the housing and lifestyle issues, but there are some exceptions.

NORTH PATTAYA

This area includes the northern part of Pattaya Beach starting at Pattaya Neua Road (North Pattaya Road) and the Na Klua area and Wong Amat Beach just north of that. North Pattaya tends to attract a more upscale tourist crowd and is home to some of the most expensive resorts in the area. Although there are plenty of restaurants and bars, the flavor of north Pattaya is quite different from central Pattaya, and it's not surprising that it's considered by some to be the best place to live in the area. Some Bangkok-based brand-name building companies are developing swanky high-rise condominium projects in the area, but since parts of it also have well-established residential enclaves, there are also stand-alone homes available for rent or purchase.

A two-bedroom, 111-square-meter (1,200-square-foot) stand-alone home in an established residential area in Naklua can be rented for 24,000 baht per month. You can purchase a three-bedroom, 204-square-meter (2,200-square-foot) home with a private swimming pool and modern kitchen and bathroom in the area for 7 million baht. Those looking for smaller apartments will find prices significantly higher than in central Pattaya. In north Pattaya, the typical 28-square-meter (300-square-foot) studio apartment with kitchenette rents for as much as 12,000 baht per month; expect to pay at least 20,000 baht per month if you want something more spacious that's on the beach. 65-square-meter (700-square-foot) two-bedroom apartments in the newest luxury buildings in north Pattaya are selling for as much as 15 million baht.

CENTRAL PATTAYA

This area includes the main strip of beach on Pattaya Bay and the surrounding city area to the east. Central Pattaya is the heart of the area, and you'll find everything from seedy bars to shopping malls to restaurants, plus the well-known (or notorious) Walking Street.

Some find this part of Pattaya dirty, depressing, and definitely not fit for families, and it is difficult to defend it as a prime location for anyone who does not want to spend a lot of time partying or being surrounded by tourists. Pattaya Beach, especially this stretch, is mediocre, even compared to beaches just north and south, and it's a hustling, busy area with few pockets of peace and quiet.

The housing stock in this part of Pattaya is in general a little more run-down than the rest of the area, mostly because it was the first part to develop, and it is starting to show its age. Newer apartments and condos rent and sell at a premium because of the central location, however. A 33-square-meter (350-square-foot) furnished studio with a kitchenette in a building with modern amenities rents for 15,000 baht per month. A three-bedroom 139-square-meter (1,500-square-foot) unit in one of the new luxury buildings scheduled to be completed by 2012 can be purchased for 10 million baht.

Marketers are pushing Pattaya as a retirement destination.

JOMTIEN

Jomtien, the large bay just south of Pattaya, has always been considered less party-oriented and more family friendly that Pattaya Beach itself, and on average it attracts more Thais, both for vacation homes and short stays. The beach area has numerous high-rise condominium complexes and resorts and can get very crowded with beach umbrellas, touts, and tourists, especially during high season, so it's not really an oasis of peace and quiet. The southern end of Jomtien Beach, called Na Jomtien, is much quieter and less crowded, although it's also less convenient.

At the low end, Jomtien tends to have the best resale condominium pricing, and it's possible to spend 6,000 baht per month for a furnished studio in an older building with a swimming pool and a fitness center. Similar units sell for as little as 700,000 baht. It is possible to rent a modern 111-square-meter (1,200-square-foot) two-bedroom detached home with its own swimming pool 1.6 kilometers (one mile) from the beach for 30,000 baht per month.

EAST PATTAYA

Anything east of Sukhumvit Road, the major thoroughfare that runs roughly perpendicular to the beach about 1.6 kilometers (one mile) inland, is considered east Pattaya. As you move farther away from the beach into the suburban area surrounding Pattaya, the issues that make Pattaya problematic for families recede, although so does the ocean. In exchange, you get a lot more space for your money and might even feel like you're living in Thailand.

In east Pattaya it is possible to rent a two-bedroom 149-square-meter (1,600-square-foot) house with a Western kitchen and bathrooms for 12,000 baht per month. Two-bedroom 70-square-meter (750-square-foot) attached townhomes in newer developments can be purchased for as little as 1 million baht. At the high end, 45 million baht will get you a six-bedroom 557-square-meter (6,000-square-foot) hacienda with a gourmet kitchen, a large private swimming pool, a guesthouse, and a good view.

Getting Around

Pattaya has an decent formal and informal transportation system that covers most of the area. The most visible and most used public transport in the city and environs is the *song thaew,* referred to as the "baht bus" in Pattaya. *Song thaew* follow somewhat fixed routes that are usually denoted by the color of the pickup truck, and there are routes that can take you from north Pattaya to Chonburi and beyond. Intercity buses travel longer routes from one beach to another and on to Bangkok but can also be used to get from, say, Jomtien to Sri Ratcha (north of Pattaya).

There are also probably hundreds of motorcycle taxis in Pattaya, identified by the brightly colored vests the drivers wear. Motorcycle taxis will take you to any destination in Pattaya. Fares are usually set for locals but should be negotiated in advance. To hail a motorcycle taxi, either go to one of the many areas the drivers congregate or flag one down on the street.

There are also limited metered taxis in Pattaya that were introduced a few years ago and are currently fraught with issues: It's nearly impossible to call a taxi in advance, and taxi drivers refuse to use their meters, requiring that you negotiate the fare in advance.

RESOURCES

Embassies and Consulates

ROYAL THAI CONSULATES AND EMBASSIES

United States
ROYAL THAI EMBASSY, WASHINGTON
1024 Wisconsin Ave.
Washington, DC 20007
tel. 202/944-3600
fax 202/944-3611
www.thaiembdc.org

ROYAL THAI CONSULATE-GENERAL, CHICAGO
700 N. Rush St.
Chicago, IL 60611
tel. 312/664-3129 or 312/664-3110
fax 312/664-3230
www.thaichicago.net

ROYAL THAI CONSULATE-GENERAL, LOS ANGELES
611 N. Larchmont Blvd.
Los Angeles, CA 90004
tel. 323/962-9574
fax 323/962-2128
www.thaiconsulatela.org

ROYAL THAI CONSULATE-GENERAL, NEW YORK
351 E. 52nd St.
New York, NY 10022
tel. 212/754-1770 or 212/754-2536
fax 212/754-1907
www.thaiconsulnewyork.com

Canada
ROYAL THAI EMBASSY, OTTAWA
180 Island Park Dr.
Ottawa, ON K1Y OA2
tel. 613/722-4444 or 613/722-5360
fax 613/722-6624
www.magma.ca/~thaiott/mainpage.htm

ROYAL THAI CONSULATE-GENERAL, VANCOUVER
1040 Burrard St.
Vancouver, BC V6Z 2R9
tel. 604/687-1143
fax 604/687-4434
www.thaicongenvancouver.org

United Kingdom
ROYAL THAI EMBASSY, LONDON
29-30 Queens Gate
London SW7 5JB
tel. 020/7589-2944
fax 020/7823-9695
www.thaiembassyuk.org.uk

Australia
ROYAL THAI EMBASSY, CANBERRA
111 Empire Circuit Yarralumla
Canberra, ACT 2600
tel. 02/6206-0100
fax 02/6206-0123

ROYAL THAI CONSULATE-GENERAL, SYDNEY
131 Macquarie St.
Sydney, NSW 2000
tel. 02/9241-2542 or 02/9241-2543
fax 02/9247-8312
http://thaiconsulatesydney.org

ROYAL THAI CONSULATE-GENERAL, BRISBANE
87 Annerley Road
South Brisbane, QLD 4102
tel. 07/3846-7771
Fax 07/3846-7772
www.thaiconsulate.org.au

ROYAL THAI CONSULATE GENERAL, ADELAIDE
Level 1, 72 Flinders St.
Adelaide, SA 5000
tel. 08/8232-7474
Fax 08/8232-7474

ROYAL THAI CONSULATE GENERAL, MELBOURNE
Suite 301, 566 St Kilda Road
Melbourne, Vic 3004
tel. 03/9533-9100
Fax 03/9533-9200

ROYAL THAI CONSULATE GENERAL, PERTH
Level 8, 14 Victoria Ave.

Perth, WA 6000
tel. 08/9221-3237
Fax 08/9221-1635

FOREIGN EMBASSIES AND CONSULATES IN THAILAND

AMERICAN EMBASSY IN BANGKOK
120/22 Wittayu Road
Bangkok 10330
tel. 02/205-4000
http://bangkok.usembassy.gov

AMERICAN CONSULATE IN CHIANG MAI
387 Wichayanond Road
Chiang Mai 50300
Tel: 053/107-700
fax 053/252-633
http://chiangmai.usconsulate.gov

CANADIAN EMBASSY IN BANGKOK
15th Floor, Abdulrahim Place
990 Rama IV Road Bangrak
Bangkok 10500
tel. 02/636-0540
fax 02/636-0566
www.canadainternational.gc.ca/
thailand-thailande/

CANADIAN CONSULATE IN CHIANG MAI
151 Super Highway

Tahsala, Muang
Chiang Mai 50000
tel. 053/850-147 or 053/242-292
fax 053/850-332
www.canadainternational.gc.ca/
thailand-thailande/

BRITISH EMBASSY IN BANGKOK
14 Wittayu Road
Lumpini, Pathumwan
Bangkok 10330
tel. 02/305-8333
fax 02/255-9278
http://ukinthailand.fco.gov.uk/

BRITISH HONORARY CONSULATE IN CHIANG MAI
198 Bumrungraij Road
Muang, Chiang Mai 50000
tel. 053/263-015
fax 053/263-016
http://ukinthailand.fco.gov.uk/en

BRITISH CONSULATE IN PATTAYA
Unit 3, 489/3 Moo 12
Jomtien Soi 5, Nong Prue
Banglamung, Chonburi 20160
fax 038/267-113
http://ukinthailand.fco.gov.uk/

AUSTRALIAN EMBASSY
37 South Sathorn Road
Bangkok 10120
tel. 02/344-6300
fax 02/344-6593
www.thailand.embassy.gov.au

Making the Move

RELOCATION COMPANIES
ALLIED PICKFORDS
50/808 Moo 3 Soi La Salle 34
Sukhumvit 105
Bangna, Bangkok 10260
tel. 02/361-3961
http://th.alliedpickfords.com

ASIAN TIGERS TRANSPO
3388/74-77 Sirinrat Building, 21st Floor,
Rama 4 Road

Klongtoey, Bangkok
tel. 02/687-7888
www.asiantigers-thailand.com

CAREPACK MOVING AND STORAGE
36th Floor, CRC Tower
All Seasons Place, 87/2 Wittayu Road
Bangkok
www.carepakmoving.com

CROWN WORLDWIDE
www.crownworldwide.com

EXPAT MOVERS THAILAND
Suite 1502, TKS Tower
2 Moo 6, Soi Lad Krabang 1, Lad Krabang Road
Bangkok
tel. 65/6259-3327 (Singapore)
www.expatmovers.net

HONG KONG TRANSPACK
59/44 Sukhumvit Soi 26

Klongtoey, Bangkok
tel. 02/259-0088
www.hktranspack.com

RELOCATIONS ASIA PACIFIC
5th Floor Q-House Convent Building
38 Convent Road, Silom Bangkok
tel. 02/632-0228 or 02/632-0229
www.relocations.co.th

Housing Considerations

REAL ESTATE AGENTS

Nationwide
ASIA PROPERTIES GROUP
3rd Floor, 178/1 Sukhumvit Road
Bangkok
tel. 02/252-6290
www.asia-properties.net

CB RICHARD ELLIS
46th Floor, CRC Tower
All Seasons Place, 87/2 Wittayu
(Wittayu) Road
Bangkok
tel. 02/654-1111
www.cbre.co.th

JONES LANG LASALLE
19/F Sathorn City Tower
175 South Sathorn Road, Sathorn
Bangkok 10120
tel. 02/624-6400
www.joneslanglasalle.co.th

KNIGHT FRANK
23rd Floor, Chamnan Phenjata Business
Center
65/192 Rama IX Road
Huay Kwang, Bangkok
tel. 02/643-8223
www.knightfrank.com/Thailand

SIAM REAL ESTATE
36/8 Viset Road
Rawai, Muang, Phuket
tel. 07/6288-908
www.siamrealestate.com

Bangkok
BANGKOK RENTS
tel. 02/662-3828
www.bangkokrents.com

EVE HOUSE
25/5 Sukhumvit Soi 16
Bangkok 10110
tel. 02/663-1134
www.evehouse.com

MR. ROOMFINDER
www.mrroomfinder.com

RIGHT PROPERTIES
22 Sukhumvit Soi 35
Klongton Nua, Wattana
Bangkok 10110
tel. 02/260-4706 or 08/9444-8035
www.right-properties.com

SOHO PROPERTIES
9th Floor, 19/57 Sukhumvit Soi 13
Bangkok 10110
tel. 02/651-3930
www.soho-properties.com

Chiang Mai and Chiang Rai
LANNA REALTY
165/1 Moo 5, Thanon Rimkok
Chiang Rai 57100
tel. 08/9661-5840
www.lannarealty.com

CHIANG MAI LIVING
www.chiangmailiving.com

Northeast Thailand
ISAN PROPERTIES
358 Pho Klang
Nakhon Ratchasima 30000
tel. 04/425-2916
www.isaan-properties.com

ISAAN REAL ESTATE
241/9 Surin Lamchee
Surin 32000
tel. 08/6264-1463
www.isaanrealestate.com

Pattaya
BENCHMARK PROPERTY CONSULTANTS
315/309 Thepprasit Road
Pattaya
tel. 03/830-4133
www.benchmarkthailand.com

EAST COAST REAL ESTATE
485/4 M.10 Pattaya 2nd Road
Nongprue, Banglamung
tel. 03/872-3615 or 03/872-3616
www.thaiproperty.com

PATTAYA PROPERTIES
315/170-171 Thappraya Road
Jomtien Beach, Nongprue, Banglamung

tel. 03/830-3515 or 03/830-3518
www.pattayaproperties.com

Phuket
PHUKET LAND
55/1A, Bandon-Cherngtalay Road
Cherngtalay, Phuket 83150
tel. 07/661-5858
www.phuketland.com

PHUKET.NET REAL ESTATE
177/34 Moo 4, Srisoonthorn Road
Srisoonthorn, Phuket 83110
tel. 07/662-0055
www.phuket.net

Samui
KO SAMUI PROPERTIES
52/5 Moo 3, Bophut
Koh Samui, Surat Thani
tel. 07/7230-606
www.kosamuiproperties.com

SAMUI ESTATE CORPORATION
5/5 Moo 6, Bophut
Koh Samui, Surat Thani
tel. 07/741-4222
www.samuiestate.com

Language and Education

LANGUAGE SCHOOLS

Bangkok
AMERICAN UNIVERSITY ALUMNI (A.U.A.) LANGUAGE CENTER
179 Ratchadamri Road,
Bangkok 1033073
tel. 02/252-8170
www. auathailand.org

WALEN SCHOOL OF THAI
Times Square Building, 3rd Floor
246 Sukhumvit Road
Bangkok 10110
tel. 02/253-9371
www.thaiwalen.com

LANGUAGE EXPRESS
Unit 1, Mahatun Plaza Building,
Ploenchit Road
Bangkok 10330
tel. 02/675-3915
www.languageexpress.co.th

UNION LANGUAGE SCHOOL
328 The Church of Christ in Thailand
Office Building
Phayathai Road
Bangkok 10400
tel. 02/214-6033

UNITY THAI LANGUAGE SCHOOL
Times Square Building, 15th Floor
246 Sukhumvit Road
Bangkok 10110

RESOURCES

tel. 02/653-1538
www.utl-school.com

Chiang Mai
AMERICAN UNIVERSITY ALUMNI (AUA) LANGUAGE CENTER
73 Ratchadamnern Road
Chiang Mai 50200
tel. 05/5327-8407
www.auathailand.org

CHIANG MAI UNIVERSITY LANGUAGE INSTITUTE
Language Institute Building
239 Huay Kaew Road
Chiang Mai 50200
www.teflcmu.com

CHIANG MAI THAI LANGUAGE CENTER
131-133 Rachadamnern Road
Chiang Mai 50200
tel. 05/327-7810
www.chiangmai-adventure-tour.com

Pattaya
AMERICAN UNIVERSITY ALUMNI (AUA) LANGUAGE CENTER
Pattaya Bazaar 1st floor
266/33-38 North Pattaya Road
Banglamung, Chonburi 20260
tel. 03/841-4634
http://aua.buu.ac.th/pattaya/index_en.html

PRO LANGUAGE SCHOOL
116/33 Moo 9 Central Pattaya Road
Nongprue, Chonburi
tel. 03/848-9225 or 03/848-9227
www.prolanguage.co.th

WALEN LANGUAGE SCHOOL
194/74-75 Soi Paniad Chang
Central Pattaya Road
Nongprue, Chonburi
tel. 03/841-0526
www.thaiwalen.com

Phuket
PATONG LANGUAGE SCHOOL
5/19-20 Had Patong Road
Patong Beach, Phuket
tel. 07/634-0373
www.phuket-languageschool.com

PHUKET LANGUAGE SCHOOL
9/1 Moo 6
Wichitsongkram Road
Kathu, Phuket
tel. 08/4008-5673
www.phuket-language-school.com

Samui
MIND YOUR LANGUAGE
142/7 Moo 1
Bophut, Koh Samui
tel. 07/796-2088
www.mindyourlanguagethailand.com

INTERNATIONAL SCHOOLS
International Schools Association of Thailand has a comprehensive list of their member institutions at www.isat.or.th.

Bangkok
BANGKOK PATANA SCHOOL
643 La Salle Road (Sukhumvit 105)
Bangkok 10260
tel. 02/398-0200
fax 02/399-3179
www.patana.ac.th

RASAMI INTERNATIONAL SCHOOL
48/2 Soi Rajavithi 2
Rajavithi Rd. Phayathai
Bangkok 10400
tel. 02/644-5291 or 02/644-5292
fax 02/640-9527
www.rasami.ac.th

HARROW INTERNATIONAL SCHOOL
185/45 Soi Kosumruamjai 7
Sikan, Don Muang
Bangkok 10210
tel. 02/503-7222
fax 02/503-7223
www.harrowschool.ac.th

ST.ANDREWS INTERNATIONAL SCHOOL, BANGKOK
9 Soi Pridi Banomyong 20
Sukhumvit Soi 71, Prakanong
Bangkok 10110
tel. 02/381-2388
fax 02/391-5227
www.standrews.ac.th

SHREWSBURY INTERNATIONAL SCHOOL
1922 Chareon Krung Road
Wat Prayakrai, Bang Kholaem
Bangkok 10120
tel. 02/675-1888
fax 02/675-3606
www.shrewsbury.ac.th

NEW INTERNATIONAL SCHOOL OF THAILAND
36 Sukhumvit Soi 15
Bangkok 10110
tel. 02/651-2065
fax 02/253-3800
www.nist.ac.th

Pattaya
THE REGENT'S SCHOOL, PATTAYA
33/3 Moo 1,Pong, Banglamung
Chonburi 20150
tel. 038/418-777
fax 038/418-778
www.pattaya.regents.ac.th

Phuket
BRITISH INTERNATIONAL SCHOOL, PHUKET
59 Moo 2, Thepkrasattri Road
Koh Kaew, Muang
Phuket 83000
tel. 076/238-711 or 076/238-720
fax 076/238-750
www.bcis.ac.th

Chiang Mai
CHIANG MAI INTERNATIONAL SCHOOL
P.O. Box 38, 13 Chetupon Road
Chiang Mai 50000
tel. 053/306-152 or 053/306-234
fax 053/242-455
www.cmis.ac.th

UNIVERSITIES
CHULALONGKORN UNIVERSITY
254 Phayathai Road, Pathumwan
Bangkok 10330
Tel: 02/215-0871 or 02/215-0873
fax: 02/215-4804
www.chula.ac.th

THAMMASAT UNIVERSITY
2 Prachan Road, Phra Nakorn
Bangkok 10200
tel. 02/613-3333
www.tu.ac.th

KASETSART UNIVERSITY
50 Phahonyothin Road, Chatuchak
Bangkok 10900
tel. 02/579-0133
fax 02/942-8998
www.ku.ac.th

MAHIDOL UNIVERSITY
999 Phuttamonthon4 Road, Salaya
Nakhon Pathom 73170
tel. 02/441-5090
fax 02/441-9745
www.muic.mahidol.ac.th

SILPAKORN UNIVERSITY
22 Borommarachachonani Road
Talingchan, Bangkok 10170
tel. 02/880-8684 or 02/880-8361
fax 02/880-9937
www.suic.org

CHIANG MAI UNIVERSITY
239 Huay Kaew Road, Muang
Chiang Mai 50200
tel. 053/941-000
fax 053/217-143 or 053/943-002
www.chiangmai.ac.th

KHON KAEN UNIVERSITY
123 Mitraphap Road, Muang
Khon Kaen 40002
tel. 043/202-173 or 043/202-424
fax 043/202-424
www.kku.ac.th

ASSUMPTION UNIVERSITY OF THAILAND
592/3 Ramkhamhaeng 24
Hua Mak, Bangkok 10240
tel. 02/300-4553 or 02/300-4562
fax 02/300-4563
www.au.edu

BANGKOK UNIVERSITY
Phahonyothin Road, Klong1
Pathumthani 12120
tel. 02/350-3500
fax 02/249-6274
www.bu.ac.th

SRIPATUM UNIVERSITY
61 Phaholyothin Road, Jatujak
Bangkok 10900

Tel .02/579-1111 or 02/561-2222, ext. 1124 or 1125
fax 02/561-1721
www.spu.ac.th/english/index_eng.html

Health

INTERNATIONAL HOSPITALS

Bangkok
BUMRUNGRAD INTERNATIONAL HOSPITAL
33 Sukhumvit3, Wattana
Bangkok 10110
tel. 02/667-1000
fax 02/667-2525
www.bumrungrad.com

BANGKOK HOSPITAL
2 Soi Soonvijai7, New Petchburi Road
Bangkapi, Huay Khwang
Bangkok 10310
tel. 02/310-3000
fax 02/318-1546 or 02/310-3327
www.bangkokhospital.com

SAMITIVAJ HOSPITAL
133 Sukhumvit Soi 49, Klongtan Nua
Vadhana, Bangkok 10110
tel. 02/711-8000
fax 02/391-1290
www.samitivejhospitals.com

Pattaya
PATTAYA INTERNATIONAL HOSPITAL
255/4 Beach Road Pattaya City
Nongprue, Banglamung, Chonburi 20150
tel. 038/428-374
fax 038/422-773
www.pih-inter.com

BANGKOK HOSPITAL PATTAYA
301 Sukhumvit Road, Km. 143
Banglamung, Chonburi 20150
tel. 038/259-999
www.bangkokpattayahospital.com

Phuket
PHUKET INTERNATIONAL HOSPITAL
44 Chalermprakiat Ror 9 Road
Phuket 83000
tel. 076/249-400
www.phuketinternationalhospital.com

BANGKOK HOSPITAL PHUKET
2/1 Hongyok Utis Road, Muang
Phuket 83000
tel. 076/254-425
fax 076/254-430
www.phukethospital.com

Samui
SAMUI INTERNATIONAL HOSPITAL
90/2 Northern Chaweng Beach
Bophut, Koh Samui, Surat Thani 84320
tel. 077/230-781 or 077/422-272
fax 077/230-049
www.sih.co.th

BANGKOK HOSPITAL SAMUI
57 Thaweerat Phakdee Road
Bophut, Koh Samui, Surat Thani 84320
Tel: 077/429-500
fax: 077/429-540
www.samuihospital.com

Northeast Thailand
RAJAVEJ UBONRATCHATHANI HOSPITAL
999 Chayangrul Road, Muang
Ubonratchathani 34000
tel. 045/280-040
fax 045/283-894

AKE UDON INTERNATIONAL HOSPITAL
555/5 Posri Road, Muang

Udonthani 41000
tel. 042/342-555
fax 042/341-033
www.aekudon.com

BANGKOK HOSPITAL RATCHASIMA
1308/9 Mitrapap Road, Muang
Nakhon Ratchashima 30000
tel: 044/429-999
fax: 044/256-421

Employment

RECRUITING AGENCIES
GRANT THORTNON
18th Floor, Capital Tower
All Seasons Place
87/1 Wittayu Road
Bangkok
tel. 02/205-8222
www.grantthornton.co.th

PR RECRUITMENT AND BUSINESS MANAGEMENT
29th Floor, 2034/82 Ital-Thai Tower
New Petchburi Road
Bangkapi, Bangkok
tel. 02/716-0000
www.prtrexecutive.com

PRICEWATERHOUSECOOPERS EXECUTIVE RECRUITMENT
13th Floor, Bangkok City Tower
179/74-80 Sathorn Tai Road
tel. 02/343-1200
www.pwc.com/Thailand

CHAMBERS OF COMMERCE
AMCHAM THAILAND
7th Floor, GPF Wittayu A
93/1 Wittayu Road
Bangkok
tel. 02/254-1041
www.amchamthailand.com

AUSTRALIAN-THAI CHAMBER OF COMMERCE
Unit 203, 20th Floor
Thai CC Building
889 Sathorn Thai Road
Bangkok
tel. 02/210-0216
www.austchamthailand.com

BRITISH-BCCT
7th Floor, 208 Wittayu Road
Bangkok
tel. 02/651-5350
www.bccthai.com

CANADIAN THAI CHAMBER OF COMMERCE
9th Floor, Sethiwan Tower
139 Pan Road
Bangkok
tel. 02/266-6085
www.tccc.or.th

Communications

INTERNET SERVICE PROVIDERS

CSLOXINFO
tel. 02/263-8222
www.csloxinfo.com

INTERNET THAILAND
tel. 02/257-7111
www.inet.co.th

KSC
tel. 02/979-7000
www.ksc.net

TOT
Hotline tel. 1100
www.tot.co.th

TRUE
tel. 02/900-9000
www.truecorp.co.th

PHONE COMPANIES

TOT
Hotline tel. 1100
www.tot.co.th

TRUE
tel. 02/900-9000
www.truecorp.co.th

ENGLISH-LANGUAGE MEDIA

Newspapers
THE BANGKOK POST
tel. 02/240-3777
www.bangkokpost.com

THE NATION
tel. 02/338-3000
www.nationmultimedia.com

News Websites
ASIA SENTINEL
www.asiasentinel.com

NOT THE NATION
www.notthenation.com

BANGKOK PUNDIT
www.asiancorrespondent.com/bangkok-pundit-blog

Glossary

cha yen iced tea

chedi pagoda

chofa spire-like ornamentations that adorn temple roofs

darma rule of Buddhism

gaeng or kaeng curry

gai chicken

gai yang grilled chicken with smoky, spicy sauce

guay teow traditional noodle soup

hat beach

khai eggs

khan toke the formal northern meal in which various dishes are shared and hands are used

khanom chin thin rice noodles with curry

khanom Thai coconut puddings scented with jasmine and other unexpected flavors

khao mountain

khao phad fried rice

khao soi soft noodles in sweet, savory rich yellow curry, covered with crispy fried noodles and usually served with chicken or beef

khlong canal

ko island

mahout elephant trainer

mai pen rai no worries

mai phet not spicy

mu or moo pork

muay Thai Thai boxing

naga sacred snake

nam phrik spicy dips served with a selection of fresh vegetables

nam tok marinated meat salad with sliced grilled beef or pork

pad thai stir-fried noodles with peanut sauce

ped duck

phra that relic of the Buddha

prang tower

prasat castle

Ramakien the Thai version of the *Ramayana*

roti pancake-like cooked dough, served with either sweet or savory fillings or dishes

sabai to be relaxed or comfortable

sala pavilion or sitting area

samlor rickshaw-like bicycles

satay grilled meat

soi side street

som tam shredded green papaya salad, with fresh long beans, tomatoes, dried shrimp, peanuts, lime juice, fish sauce, garlic, palm sugar, and chilies

song thaew pick-up trucks with benches in the back that essentially serve as a cross between a bus (they usually run on fixed routes) and a taxi (you hail one down and just climb in)

tambon community

tom yam kung spicy, aromatic soup with shrimp

tuk tuk three-wheeled motorcycle taxis

ubosot coronation hall

wai gesture of greeting and a sign of respect where people put their hands together in a prayerlike motion and bow their heads at each other

wat temple

wiharn Buddhist assembly hall

yam som o pomelo salad with shrimp

RESOURCES

Thai Phrasebook

Unless you are living in a serviced apartment and working at a international company you'll notice pretty quickly that most people in the country speak little English. Though English-language studies are compulsory for all students, even most college graduates do not speak English at any level of fluency. That fact, coupled with a different script, makes Thailand a bit of a challenge at best and frustrating at worst. Expect communication problems—you are traveling in a foreign country. Of course, the language barrier is a great opportunity, too. Although it's a travel cliche, it's still a sweet experience when little children come up to you to practice saying *hello,* and students of all ages will usually be happy to try out a little English on willing foreigners, although they may be too shy to engage you first. If you are looking to spend an extended period of time here, there are plenty of places you can teach English, either on a volunteer or paid basis.

The Thai language, with its confusing tones and difficult to decipher script, is too difficult to master before taking a vacation. But learning a few words and phrases will make all the difference, especially words and phrases such as *hello* and *thank you.* No one in the country will expect that you speak the language fluently as a vacationer, so a little bit of Thai will go a long way in terms of breaking the ice. You'll find that people across the country will react positively to any effort you make (even if that positive reaction involves a little bit of laughter).

The Thai alphabet has 44 consonants, more than 20 vowel forms, and four tone marks. The alphabet was invented by King Ramkhamhaeng in the 13th century and was undoubtedly influenced by the Khmer alphabet in use at the time. That may not help too much in understanding what the letters mean; many foreigners find the script difficult. If you're just here on vacation, you won't have the time to do much more than familiarize yourself with the way it looks, but if you want to learn the language, you'll need to master Thai script.

PRONUNCIATION AND TRANSLITERATION

Thai is a tonal language with five tones—low, high, mid, rising, and falling, and a word's meaning will vary depending on how it is pronounced. Say the name "Bob" out loud as if you were yelling at your little brother, then as though you were picking up the phone and wondering if Bob was on the other line. To speakers of non-tonal languages, Bob is Bob, though you've intonated the word differently in different contexts. To speakers of tonal languages, the first pronunciation and the second can mean vastly different things. Tones are identified in Thai script through the use of different consonants, vowels, and tone marks, depending on the tone you wish to express, but, as Thai script is too difficult to really master without months of study, your best bet is to memorize a few basic expressions and try them out when you arrive. Listen carefully to the way native speakers say common phrases (you'll hear plenty of hellos and thank yous) and do your best to imitate them.

A tonal language also presents another challenge for visitors, as tones are impossible to replicate with the paltry 26-letter Roman alphabet. The word *khao* for example, means white, mountain, rice, news, he/she, knee, or to enter, depending on which tone you're using and whether the vowel is long or short. Using the Latin alphabet to transliterate Thai words is just a rough approximation, which is why Thai speakers will often misunderstand you or find your pronunciation of a word incomprehensible despite the fact that you are pronouncing it exactly the way it is spelled in Roman letters. This is also why you'll see Thai words spelled in English in so many different ways—*Petchaburi* and *Petburi* or *ko* and *koh* are just two common examples.

We've used the **Thai Royal Institute** system of transliteration in this book, as it is the official system and the one used to translate place names on road signs and other notices. This system isn't perfect—it ignores tones and vowel length completely—but is the least complicated and doesn't require that you learn a new system of tone marks; an imperfect compromise.

In the case of proper names of sights, restaurants, shops, and lodging, we've used either whatever spelling is approved by the Tourism Authority, what is printed on commonly available maps, what the business goes by, or what is printed on Thai street signs, whether or not it is consistent with the Thai Royal Institute system.

MASCULINE AND FEMININE PARTICLES

Even if you can't make out many Thai words, you will notice that nearly everyone you speak with ends their sentences with either *ka* or *kap*. These are polite particles meant to convey respect, but in truth they are used nearly universally and regardless of whether you are speaking with your boss or the teenage cashier at 7-Eleven. Which one you use depends not on what you are saying or who you are speaking to, but your gender. Women always end their sentences with *ka*, men with *kap*, and you should be particularly careful about making sure you do, too. You'll probably notice that the polite particles are also used on their own, meaning the equivalent in English of *okay, go on*, or *yes*.

BASIC AND COURTEOUS EXPRESSIONS

Remember that everything you say should end with a polite particle. Here we've listed *sawadee* as hello, but you would almost never hear that phrase spoken without a *ka* or *kap* following it.

Hello/Goodbye Sawadee
How are you? Sabai dee mai?
I am well. How are you? Sabai dee. Sabai dee mai?
Okay; good. Dee.
Not okay; bad. Mai sabai.
Thank you. Khopkhun.
You are welcome/no worries. Mai pen rai.
yes chai
no (depending on context) mai chai
I don't know. Mai ru.
Just a moment. Sak khru.
Excuse me. Khothot.
Pleased to meet you. Yindi thi dai ruchak.
What is your name? Chue arai?/Khun chue arai?
Do you speak English? Phut phasa Angkrit dai mai?
I don't speak Thai. Phut phasa Thai mai dai.
I don't understand. Mai khaochai.
How do you say . . . in Thai? Riak . . . wa arai nai phasa Thai?
My name is . . . Chan chue . . . (female)/ Phom chue . . . (male)
Would you like . . . Ao . . . mai.
Let's go to . . . Pai . . . kan thoe.

TERMS OF ADDRESS

I (female) Chan
I (female, very formal) De chan
I (male) Phom
I (male, very formal) Kra phom
you (formal) khun
you (very formal, to show high respect) than
you (familiar) khun
he/him khao
she/her khao
we/us rao
you (plural) phuak khun
they/them phuak khao
Mr./Sir Khun or Khun phu chai (very formal, used to address someone who has a higher position than you)

Mrs./Madam *Khun or Khun phu ying (very formal, used to address someone who has a higher position than you)*
Miss/young lady *Khun or Nong (Nong is translated as younger brother or sister. It is used to address an unknown person who looks younger than you.)*
wife *phan ra ra*
husband *sa mee*
friend *phuean*
sweetheart *wan jai*
boyfriend/girlfriend *fan*
son *luk chai*
daughter *luk sao*
older brother/sister *phee*
older brother *phee chai*
older sister *phee sao*
younger brother/sister *nong*
younger brother *nong chai*
younger sister *nong sao*
father *pho*
mother *mae*
grandfather (on father's side) *khun pu or pu*
grandfather (on mother's side) *khun ta or ta*
grandmother (on father's side) *khun ya or ya*
grandmother (on mother's side) *khun yai or yai*

TRANSPORTATION
Where is . . . *. . . yu thinai.*
How far is it to . . . *Pai . . . ik klai mai.*
from . . . to . . . *chak . . . pai . . .*
Where is the way to . . .? *. . . pai thang nai?*
the bus station *sathani khonsong/khonsong*
the bus stop *pai rotme*
Where is this bus going? *Rotme khan ni pai nai?*
the taxi stand *pai taxi*
the train station *sathani rotfai*
the boat *ruea*
the airport *sanambin*
I'd like a ticket to . . . *Kho tua pai . . .*
first (second) class *chan nueng (song)*
round-trip *pai klap*

reservation *chong*
Stop here please. *Yut thi ni.*
the entrance *thangkhao*
the exit *thang-ok*
the ticket office *thi khai tua*
near *klai (raising voice)*
very near *klai mak*
far *klai*
very far *klai mak*
to; toward *pai*
by; through (as in, I am going by/through Chiang Mai on my way to Pai) *pai thang*
from *chak*
turn right *liao khwa*
turn left *liao sai*
right side *dan khwa*
left side *dan sai*
straight ahead *trong pai*
in front *dan na/khang na*
beside *dan khang/khang*
behind *dan lang/lang*
the corner *hua mum*
the stoplight/traffic light *fai yut/sanyan fai charachon*
right here *thi ni*
somewhere *sak thi*
street; road *thanon*
highway *thangluang*
bridge *saphan*
toll way/toll fee *thangduan/kha phan thang*
address *thiyu*
north *nuea*
south *tai*
east *tawan-ok*
west *tawantok*

ACCOMMODATIONS
hotel *rongraem*
Is there a room avaliable? *Mi hong wang mai?*
May I see it? *Kho du dai mai?*
What is the rate? *Rakha thaorai?*
Is there something cheaper? *Mi rakha thuk kwa ni mai?*
single room *hong diao*
double room *hong khu*
double bed *tiang diao (king size)*
twin bed *tiang khu*

with **private bathroom** *mi hongnam suantua*
hot water *nam un*
shower *fakbua*
towels *phachettua*
soap *sabu*
toilet paper *thit chu*
blanket *pha hom*
sheets *pha pu tiang*
air-conditioned *ae (air)*
fan *phatlom*
key *kunchae*
manager *phuchatkan*

FOOD

I'm hungry. *Chan hio. (female)/Phom hio. (male)*
I'm thirsty. *Chan hio nam. (female)/ Phom hio nam. (male)*
menu *menu*
to order food/order *sang ahan/raikan ahan*
glass *kaeo*
fork *som*
knife *mit*
spoon *chon*
napkin *pha chet pak*
soft drink *nam-atlom*
coffee/hot coffee/iced coffee *kafae/ kafae ron/kafae yen*
tea/hot tea/iced tea *cha/cha ron/ cha yen*
lime juice *nam manao*
bottled water *nam khuat*
beer *bia*
juice *nam phonlamai*
sugar *namtan*
snack *khanom*
breakfast *ahan chao*
lunch *ahan thiang*
dinner *ahan kham*
The check, please. *Chek bin. Or Kep ngoen duai.*
eggs *khai*
fruit *phonlamai*
pineapple *sapparot*
guava *farang*
watermelon *taeng mo*
rose apple *chomphu*
papaya *malako*

coconut *maphrao*
lime *manao*
durian *thurian*
jackfruit *khanun*
mango *mamuang*
fish *pla*
shrimp *kung*
chicken *gai*
beef *nuea*
pork *mu*
fried *thot*
grilled *ping/yang*
barbeque *babikhio*
not spicy *mai phet*
(prepared with) one chili *prik nung met*

SHOPPING

money *ngoen/tang*
bank *thanakhan*
Do you accept credit cards? *Rap bat khredit mai?*
How much does it cost? *Rakha thaorai?/Ki baht?*
expensive *phaeng*
cheap *thuk*
more *mak kwa/mak khuen*
less *noi kwa/noi long*
a little *nitnoi*
too much *mak pai*

HEALTH

Help me please. *Chuai duai.*
I am sick. *Mai sabai.*
Call a doctor. *Tho tam mo./Riak mo.*
Take me to . . . *Pha chan (or phom for male) pai thi*
hospital *rongphayaban*
drug store/pharmacy *ran khai ya*
pain *puat*
fever *khai (raising tone)*
headache *puathua*
stomachache *puatthong*
burn *mai*
cramp *ta khrio*
nausea *khluen sai*
vomiting *achian/uak*
diarrhea *thongsia*
antibiotic *ya patichiwana*
pill; tablet *ya met*

paracetamol/acedomenaphin *ya kae puat*
cream *ya tha*
birth control pills *ya khumkamnoet*
condoms *thung yang anamai*
toothbrush *praengsifan*
toothpaste *yasifan*
dentist *mo fan*
toothache *puat fan*

POST OFFICE AND COMMUNICATIONS

long-distance telephone *thorasap thang klai*
I would like to call . . . *Chan/phom yak tho pai thi . . .*
collect/collect call *kep ngoen plaithang/thorasap riak kep ngoen plaithang*
credit card *bat khredit*
post office *praisani*
by air mail *air mail/chotmai thang akat*
letter *chotmai*
stamp *sataem*
post card *post card/praisaniyabat*
registered/certified *longthabian*
money order *thananat*
box; package *khlong*
tape *tape*

AT THE BORDER

border *chaidaen*
customs *sunlakakon*
immigration *dan truat khon khao mueang*
arrival card *bat khakhao*
inspection *kan truat/chut truat*
passport *passport/nangsuedoenthang*
profession *achip*
insurance *prakanphai*
driver's license *bai khapkhi*

AT THE GAS STATION

gas station *pam nam man*
gasoline *namman*
unleaded *rai san takua*
full *tem thueng*
tire *yang rotyon/yang*
air *air/khrueang prap-akat*
water *nam*

oil change *plian namman*
grease *charabi*
My . . . doesn't work *. . . sia / . . . mai thamngan*
battery *battery*
radiator *monam*
alternator *alternator/dai charge/dai panfai*
generator *generator/khrueang panfai*
tow truck *rot lak*
repair shop *ran som*

VERBS

to buy *sue*
to eat *kin*
to climb *pin*
to make *tham*
to go *pai*
to walk *doen*
to love *rak*
to work *thamngan*
to want *tongkan*
to need *tongkan/champen*
to read *an*
to write *khian*
to repair *som*
to stop *yut*
to get off (the bus) *long (rot me)*
to arrive *ma thueng*
to stay (remain) *yu (thi)*
to stay (sleep) *yu thi*
to leave *ok chak*
to look at *mong thi*
to look for *mong ha*
to give *hai*
to carry *thue/hio*
to have *mi*
to come *ma*

NUMBERS

zero *sun*
one *nueng*
two *song*
three *sam*
four *si*
five *ha*
six *hok*
seven *jed*
eight *paed*
nine *kao*

10 *sip*
11 *sip et*
12 *sip song*
13 *sip sam*
14 *sip si*
15 *sip ha*
16 *sip hok*
17 *sip jed*
18 *sip paed*
19 *sip kao*
20 *yisip*
21 *yisip et*
30 *samsip*
100 *nueng roi*
101 *nueng roi et*
200 *song roi*
1,000 *nueng phan*
10,000 *nueng muen*
100,000 *nueng saen*
1,000,000 *nueng lan*
one-half *khrueng*

TIME

What time is it? *Wela thaorai laeo?/ Ki mong?*
It is one o'clock *Nueng nalika.*
It's four in the afternoon. *Sip hok nalika.*
It is midnight. *Thiang khuen.*
one minute *nueng nathi*
one hour *nueng chuamong*

DAYS, MONTHS, AND SEASONS

Monday *Wan Chan*
Tuesday *Wan Angkhan*
Wednesday *Wan Phut*
Thursday *Wan Pharuehatsabodi/Wan Pharue Hat*
Friday *Wan Suk*
Saturday *Wan Sao*
Sunday *Wan Athit*
January *Mokkarakhom*
February *Kumphaphan*
March *Minakhom*
April *Mesayon*
May *Phruetsaphakhom*
June *Mithunayon*
July *Karakadakhom*
August *Singhakhom*
September *Kanyayon*
October *Tulakhom*
November *Phruetsa Chi Ka Yon*
December *Thanwakhom*
today *wanni*
yesterday *muea wan*
tomorrow *phrungni*
a week *nueng sapda*
a month *nueng duean*
after *lang*
before *kon*
rainy season *ruedu fon*
cool season *ruedu nao*
hot/warm season *ruedu ron*

Suggested Reading

ART AND ARCHITECTURE

Diskul, M. C. Subhadradis. *Art in Thailand: A Brief History.* Bangkok: Krung Siam, 1991. Comprehensive review of Thailand's art epoch's written by a Silpakorn University archeology professor.

Gosling, Betty. *Origins of Thai Art.* Trumbull, CT: Weatherhill, 2004. An accessible early history of Thai art, Gosling's book is full of beautiful photographs of building details and sculptures to illustrate the history she lays out.

Kerlogue, Fiona. *Arts of Southeast Asia.* London: Thames & Hudson, 2004. This small, nicely illustrated, and easy-to-read book offers a basic overview of the history of art across the region. Although not specifically focused on Thailand, the information provided is essential to putting the art and artifacts in the country into a broader context.

Poshyananda, Apinan. *Modern Art in Thailand: Nineteenth and Twentieth Centuries.* Singapore: Oxford University Press, 1992. Though most books on art in Thailand focus on the distant past, Poshyananda explains the different influences on modern art in a comprehensive manner.

Ringis, Rita. *Thai Temples and Thai Murals.* Singapore: Oxford University Press, 1990. For those interested in more than a cursory tour of Thailand's scores of temples, this book offers an excellent overview of temple architecture and mural work. There are also in-depth descriptions of some of the most popular temples in the country.

Woodward, Hiram. *The Art and Architecture of Thailand: From Prehistoric Times through the Thirteenth Century.* Boston: Brill Academic Publishers, 2005. Woodward's book provides the first comprehensive survey of art in Thailand through the 13th century. The book is academic in nature and offers a sociohistoric view of art history. Those with an interest in archaeology will find it very useful.

BUSINESS AND POLITICS

Doyle, Michael. *A Practical Guide to Thailand Business Law.* Bangkok: Seri Manop, 2006. Written by an American lawyer who has been practicing in Thailand for more than a decade, this guide covers the basics of setting up a business in Thailand, including employment and tax consequences.

Wylie, Philip. *How to Establish a Successful Business in Thailand.* Bangkok: Paiboon, 2007. Offers practical tips for those looking to open small businesses in Thailand.

HISTORY

Baker, Christopher, and Pasuk Phongpaichit. *A History of Thailand.* Cambridge, UK: Cambridge University Press, 2005. This is one of the few books that offer a modern history of the kingdom; it tracks the economic, political, and social changes in Thailand over the past 300 years.

Handley, Paul M. *The King Never Smiles.* New Haven, CT: Yale University Press, 2006. Banned in Thailand before it even hit the shelves, Handley's biography of King Bhumipol tells the story of how Thailand's current king came to power and how he has created an important role for the monarchy over the past 60 years. Handley, a former journalist based in Bangkok for over a decade, offers a well-researched, though controversial, look at the king's life and reign.

Higham, Charles. *The Archaeology of Mainland Southeast Asia: From 10,000 B.C. to the fall of Angkor.* Cambridge, UK: Cambridge University Press, 1989. Respected archaeologist Charles Higham takes readers through the region's early social history using archaeological evidence found in Southeast Asia. For those planning to visit any of the major Khmer archaeological sites, such as Phanom Rung or Phimai, this book offers in-depth (albeit dense and academic) information to complement a visit.

Somers Heidhues, Mary. *Southeast Asia: A Concise History.* London: Thames & Hudson, 2001. This is an easy and quick general overview of the history of the region for those looking for an understanding of Southeast Asia without devoting hours of study.

Tarling, Nicholas. *The Cambridge History of Southeast Asia, Vols. I and II.* Cambridge, UK: Cambridge University Press, 2000. These two volumes offer a comprehensive social and political history of the region as a whole, which is essential to adequately understand the history of Thailand.

CULTURE

Ziv, Daniel, Guy Sharett, and Sasa Kralj. *Bangkok Inside Out.* Jakarta: Equinox Publishing, 2004. This thoughtful, irreverent, and honest book explains all of the quirky, seemingly inconsistent pieces of the capital city without relying on clichés or judgmental descriptions. It's full of great photos too.

Index

www.moon.com

DESTINATIONS | ACTIVITIES | BLOGS | MAPS | BOOKS

MOON.COM is ready to help plan your next trip! Filled with fresh trip ideas and strategies, author interviews, informative travel blogs, a detailed map library, and descriptions of all the Moon guidebooks, Moon.com is all you need to get out and explore the world—or even places in your own backyard. While at Moon.com, sign up for our monthly e-newsletter for updates on new releases, travel tips, and expert advice from our on-the-go Moon authors. As always, when you travel with Moon, expect an experience that is uncommon and truly unique.

MOON IS ON FACEBOOK—BECOME A FAN!
JOIN THE MOON PHOTO GROUP ON FLICKR

MAP SYMBOLS

▦▦▦ Expressway	○ City/Town	✗ Airfield
▬▬ Primary Road	◉ State Capital	✈ Airport
▬▬ Secondary Road	✳ National Capital	▲ Mountain
∙∙∙∙∙ Unpaved Road	★ Point of Interest	⚲⚲ Park
∙∙∙∙∙∙∙∙ Ferry	■ Other Location	⛷ Skiing Area
▬∙▬∙▬ Railroad		

▬ Archaeological Site
⚰ Church
⛽ Gas Station
▦ Mangrove
▦ Reef
▦ Swamp

CONVERSION TABLES

$°C = (°F - 32) / 1.8$
$°F = (°C × 1.8) + 32$
1 inch = 2.54 centimeters (cm)
1 foot = 0.304 meters (m)
1 yard = 0.914 meters
1 mile = 1.6093 kilometers (km)
1 km = 0.6214 miles
1 fathom = 1.8288 m
1 chain = 20.1168 m
1 furlong = 201.168 m
1 acre = 0.4047 hectares
1 sq km = 100 hectares
1 sq mile = 2.59 square km
1 ounce = 28.35 grams
1 pound = 0.4536 kilograms
1 short ton = 0.90718 metric ton
1 short ton = 2,000 pounds
1 long ton = 1.016 metric tons
1 long ton = 2,240 pounds
1 metric ton = 1,000 kilograms
1 quart = 0.94635 liters
1 US gallon = 3.7854 liters
1 Imperial gallon = 4.5459 liters
1 nautical mile = 1.852 km

°FAHRENHEIT	°CELSIUS	
230	110	
220	100	WATER BOILS
210		
200	90	
190	80	
180		
170	70	
160		
150	60	
140		
130	50	
120		
110	40	
100		
90	30	
80		
70	20	
60		
50	10	
40		
30	0	WATER FREEZES
20	-10	
10		
0	-20	
-10		
-20	-30	
-30		
-40	-40	

INCH 0 1 2 3 4

CM 0 1 2 3 4 5 6 7 8 9 10

MOON LIVING ABROAD IN THAILAND

Avalon Travel
a member of the Perseus Book Group
1700 Fourth Street
Berkeley, CA 94710, USA
www.moon.com

Editor: Tiffany Watson
Series Manager: Elizabeth Hansen
Copy Editor: Christopher Church
Graphics and Production Coordinator:
    Lucie Ericksen
Cover Designer: Lucie Ericksen
Map Editor: Brice Ticen
Cartographers: Kat Bennett, Allison Rawley
Indexer: Deana Shields

ISBN: 978-1-59880-640-3
ISSN: 2156-650X

Printing History
1st Edition — 2010
5 4 3 2 1

Some photos and illustrations are used by permission and are the property of the original copyright owners.

Front cover photo: Flowers, Northern Thailand © Neil Emmerson/Robert Harding World Imagery/Corbis
Title page photo: Side view of Buddha overlooking the setting sun © Steven Heap/123 RF

Interior photos: pages 4-7, 8 top right: © Suzanne Nam; page 8 top left and bottom: © Monika Murphy
Back cover photo: Ayutthaya Historical Park © Suzanne Nam

Printed in Canada by Friesens

KEEPING CURRENT

Although we strive to produce the most up-to-date guidebook that we possibly can, change is unavoidable. Between the time this book goes to print and the time you read it, the cost of goods and services may have increased, and a handful of the businesses noted in these pages will undoubtedly move, alter their prices, or close their doors forever. Exchange rates fluctuate — sometimes dramatically — on a daily basis. Federal and local legal requirements and restrictions are also subject to change, so be sure to check with the appropriate authorities before making the move. If you see anything in this book that needs updating, clarification, or correction, please drop us a line. Send your comments via email to feedback@moon.com, or use the address above.